GOVERNING (THROUGH) RIGHTS

Taking a critical attitude of dissatisfaction towards rights, the central premise of this book is that rights are technologies of governmentality. They are a regulating discourse that is itself managed through governing tactics and techniques—hence governing (through) rights. Part I examines the 'problem of government (through) rights'. The opening chapter describes governmentality as a methodology that is then used to interrogate the relationship between rights and governance in three contexts: the international, regional and local. How rights regulate certain identities and conceptions of what is good governance is examined through the case study of non-state actors, specifically the INGO, in the international setting; through a case study of rights agencies, and the role of experts, indicators and the rights-based approach in the European Union or regional setting; and, in terms of the local, the challenge that the blossoming language of responsibility and community poses to rights in the name of less government (Big Society) is problematised. In Part II, on 'resisting government (through) rights', the book asks what counter-conducts are possible using rights language (questioning rioting as resistance), and whether counter-conduct can be read as an ethos of the political, rights-bearing subject and as a new ethical right. Thus, the book bridges a divide between critical theory (ie Foucauldian understandings of power as governmentality) and human rights law.

Volume 21: Human Rights Law in Perspective

Human Rights Law in Perspective

General Editor: Colin Harvey
Professor of Human Rights Law
School of Law
Queen's University Belfast

The language of human rights figures prominently in legal and political debates at the national, regional and international levels. In the UK the Human Rights Act 1998 has generated considerable interest in the law of human rights. It will continue to provoke much debate in the legal community and the search for original insights and new materials will intensify.

The aim of this series is to provide a forum for scholarly reflection on all aspects of the law of human rights. The series will encourage work which engages with the theoretical, comparative and international dimensions of human rights law. The primary aim is to publish over time books which offer an insight into human rights law in its contextual setting. The objective is to promote an understanding of the nature and impact of human rights law. The series is inclusive, in the sense that all perspectives in legal scholarship are welcome. It will incorporate the work of new and established scholars.

Human Rights Law in Perspective is not confined to consideration of the UK. It will strive to reflect comparative, regional and international perspectives. Work which focuses on human rights law in other states will therefore be included in this series. The intention is to offer an inclusive intellectual home for significant scholarly contributions to human rights law.

Recent titles in this series

Children's Socio-Economic Rights, Democracy and the Courts
Aoife Nolan

Rights in Divided Societies
Edited by Colin Harvey and Alexander Schwartz

Health and Human Rights
Thérèse Murphy

Discrimination, Equality and the Law
Aileen McColgan

Property and Human Rights in a Global Context
Edited by Ting Xu and Jean Allain

For the complete list of titles in this series, see 'Human Rights Law in Perspective' link at www.hartpub.co.uk/books/series.asp

Governing (Through) Rights

Bal Sokhi-Bulley

·HART·

OXFORD · LONDON · NEW YORK · NEW DELHI · SYDNEY

HART PUBLISHING

Bloomsbury Publishing Plc

Kemp House, Chawley Park, Cumnor Hill, Oxford, OX2 9PH, UK

HART PUBLISHING, the Hart/Stag logo, BLOOMSBURY and the Diana logo are
trademarks of Bloomsbury Publishing Plc

First published in Great Britain 2016

First published in hardback, 2016
Paperback edition, 2019

A catalogue record for this book is available from the British Library.

Library of Congress Cataloging-in-Publication Data

Names: Sokhi-Bulley, Bal, author.

Title: Governing (through) rights / Bal Sokhi-Bulley.

Description: Oxford ; Portland, Oregon : Hart Publishing, an imprint of
Bloomsbury Publishing Plc, 2016. | Series: Human rights law in perspective ;
volume 21 | Includes bibliographical references and index.

Identifiers: LCCN 2016015042 (print) | LCCN 2016015641 (ebook) |
ISBN 9781849467391 (hardback : alk. paper) | ISBN 9781509903832 (Epub)

Subjects: LCSH: Human rights.

Classification: LCC K3240 .S65 2016 (print) |
LCC K3240 (ebook) | DDC 323—dc23

LC record available at https://lccn.loc.gov/2016015042

ISBN: HB: 978-1-84946-739-1
PB: 978-1-50992-682-4
ePDF: 978-1-50990-384-9
ePub: 978-1-50990-383-2

Typeset by Compuscript Ltd, Shannon

To find out more about our authors and books visit www.hartpublishing.co.uk. Here you will find
extracts, author information, details of forthcoming events and the option to sign up for our
newsletters.

to Dan

Acknowledgements

This book was written during my time at Queen's University Belfast and I am grateful for the space and environment I had to write it there, and to the friends and colleagues who helped make it possible. In particular, to Colin Harvey, who prompted the whole thing and believed that I had something to offer his series on *critical perspectives*. I hope he still feels the same now that it is complete. My sincere thanks go to my once supervisor and now mentor Thérèse Murphy (particularly for being sparing with the red pen). To my stellar and 'monographing' colleagues Dug Cubie (especially for his, as always, generous comments on Chapter 3) and Natasa Mavronicola, and to my PhD students, Ivanka Antova and Edward Cooke (for sharing with me their ideas on parrhesia and resistance) I owe a thanks. To my TPOT project partners who instigated the work on migration—Mike Bourne, Dan Bulley, Heather Johnson, Debbie Lisle and Tom Walker—I'm glad that you asked me to be a part of it. I am also glad to know the wider network of people who have encouraged the way of thinking behind the book, invited me to speak at events, and offered considered and helpful comments on papers that feature here in some form, in particular: Mark Bevir, Ben Golder, Louiza Odysseos, Sara Ramshaw and Dagmar Schiek. And to those friends who have challenged me, believed that the 'permanent struggle' of this project would one day end, or just bought me numerous cocktails to drown out the pain, you have been invaluable to me—so thank you, Tarik Kochi, Andrew Pepper, Mirjami Schuppert and, of course and always, Yvette Russell.

Those affected by 'writing the book' and who showed incredible patience and belief include also Mum, my brothers Rajinder and Arjun; together we got through the challenges of the last year and I thank you. And Carol Shergold, whose practical wisdom and kindness really is unparalleled.

As I was writing, I fantasised that this book would be premised as 'to *me*' ... after all, wasn't I the one who toiled, grieved and moaned over it? But I cannot in all honesty write that. This book has to be and is *for Dan*—because, quite simply, without him—his love, faith, intelligence and of course ruthless reading/editing of it in its entirety—it would not have been possible. Nor, of course, without Bella and Bruno. You are my *jaan*—this is for you too.

Contents

Part II: Resisting Government (Through) Rights

Part I

Government (Through) Rights

1

Introduction

Human rights are the fate of postmodernity, the energy of our societies, the fulfillment of the Enlightenment promise of emancipation and self-realisation.

Costas Douzinas[1]

My point is not that everything is bad, but that *everything is dangerous*, which is not exactly the same as bad. If everything is dangerous, then we always have something to do. So my position leads not to apathy but to hyper- and pessimistic activism.

Michel Foucault[2]

I. THE PROBLEM OF GOVERNMENT (THROUGH) RIGHTS

WHY DO WE write? A colleague recently started a postgraduate training workshop with that question. It was just meant as an icebreaker but it has stayed with me. Why *do I* write? For the most part it is an arduous, even painful, process that involves doubt, anxiety and a constant questioning of whether what is being said is significant or original or worth saying at all. I have concluded that I write out of dissatisfaction and a position of refusal. That it is a way to challenge the conventional methods in which we are taught to think problems and events, and a way to say 'I do not want to be told to think like that'. The problem I tackle here in this book is 'the problem of government' (through) rights.

This book is about a dissatisfaction with and a refusal of rights discourse. It is not interested in whether rights are 'good' or 'bad'—that, I think, is not worth saying given they are the 'fate of postmodernity'—but in how the discourse of rights and what it produces in terms of good governance tactics and subject identities, might be dangerous. It was fashionable to study human rights when I began my postgraduate studies and I did so thinking I wanted to work for an international human rights organisation, or be a human

---

[1] C Douzinas, *The End of Human Rights* (Oxford, Hart, 2002) 1.
[2] M Foucault, 'On the Genealogy of Ethics: An Overview of Work in Progress' in P Rabinow (ed), *The Foucault Reader* (Pantheon Books, New York, 1984) 340, 343.

rights practitioner, because, well, like so many law students who had chosen human rights law I wanted to 'do good' in the world. Rights are now less fashionable, I think it fair to say. In the face of a security/rights dichotomy in which heightened military response in the name of security prompted by fear, terror and crisis subordinates rights concerns,[3] and confronted with discourses of responsibility and community in place of individual rights, rights have at least at the national level lost some of their energy and promise. But 'rights' are still 'the magic wand of visibility and invisibility, of inclusion and exclusion, of power and no power';[4] in the mouths of those who are oppressed and singled out as victims or in need of special protection, rights are 'deliciously empowering',[5] and they are markers of how we measure good governance, good practice and progress in state behaviour. Rights still of course 'do good' in the world. But what *else* do they do? As well as being an emancipatory and promising discourse, do rights also have the potential to be regulatory and limiting? Are they 'magic', or are they the privileges that are afforded only to those who are visible within our societies because they are responsible, working, non-threatening citizens, and do they define good governance and progress at the expense of concealing the assumptions as to what these markers mean and how they are produced?

I argue that rights are technologies of governmentality. When Foucault coined this 'ugly' term,[6] he meant 'governmentality' to refer to the 'problem of government', that is, 'how to govern oneself, how to be governed, by whom should we accept to be governed, how to be the best possible governor?'[7] He was thus interested in the *how* of government—both how governing happens and how it is thought. Governing happens through rights, I argue in this book; and so I am interested in interrogating *how* the relationship between rights and governance works. Rights are increasingly spoken about in a language of governance; this is true at the local level where rights and their being conditional on responsibility is echoed

---

[3] The *Guardian* uses the heading 'Terror in Europe' to speak about terror alerts in Brussels, the 'heart of the EU', following the Paris terrorist attacks in November 2015: J Burke and I Traynor, 'Brussels "very dangerous" as several terrorist suspects remain at large', *Guardian*, 2 November 2015, available at www.theguardian.com/world/2015/nov/22/brussels-lockdown-terror-threat-paris-attacks (see also E Vulliamy, 'Paris attacks: security and surveillance cast a dark shadow over France's love of "liberté" and "fraternité"', *Guardian*, 22 November 2015, available at www.theguardian.com/world/2015/nov/22/paris-attacks-security-liberte-fraternite. The term 'crisis' has been used to speak about the recent influx of migrants into the European Union, see eg D Trilling, 'Europe could solve the migrant crisis—if it wanted', *Guardian*, 31 July 2015, available at www.theguardian.com/commentisfree/2015/jul/31/europe-migrant-crisis-political-choice-toxic-waste-sanctuary.

[4] P Williams, *The Alchemy of Race and Rights* (Cambridge, MA, Harvard University Press, 1991) 164.

[5] Ibid.

[6] M Foucault, *Security, Territory, Population, Lectures at the Collège de France 1977–1978* (M Senellart (ed), G Burchell (trans), Basingstoke, Palgrave Macmillan, 2007) 115.

[7] Ibid 88.

through the UK government's Big Society ethos. It is true at the regional level, where, in the EU, new governance agencies are set up with the specific objective of providing assistance and expertise on rights. And it is true also at the international level where human rights non-governmental organisations (NGOs) must fulfil certain good governance criteria to be considered good participants in the rights project. How is this language of governance, which is used to speak about rights, actually a language of government, or more accurately still, of governmentality? I uncover the *how* by looking at the processes of governing (through rights) with reference to particular initiatives or agencies, namely, the Fundamental Rights Agency of the EU (FRA, Chapter 2), the international NGO Human Rights Watch (Chapter 3) and the Big Society agenda in the United Kingdom (Chapter 4). Within these national, regional and international sites at which rights and governance intersect, rights operate as mechanisms of regulation and control that manage the production of certain political identities (such as the EU as a virtuous human rights actor). Rights also produce a governmentable subject of rights, the individual that can be permanently observed and is politically useful (eg the 'irregular migrant'). Moreover, rights language is itself regulated to the extent that experts and how they measure rights tells us what the 'truth' about rights is (and should be) within a particular region or area, and how to properly 'do' rights using the right kind of (rights-based) approach. We are thus experiencing government *through* rights and government *of* rights—hence 'governing (through) rights'. Should we accept this form of being governed? Can we do otherwise? The other side of the problem of government is how to *counter* it. And so the second part of this book is concerned with how government (through) rights is countered. The *ethos* of the Big Society is one situated in an ethic of responsibility that poses a direct threat to rights since it replaces individual rights with a *right to* community. What are the dangers of this counter-narrative of responsibility? And what possibilities are there for recognizing unruly counter-conduct on the part of the rights-bearing citizen? Do rights experts have a duty to counter government through rights? The governmentality framework can, I suggest here, be stretched to examine resistance to a governmentality (through) rights.

As such, the book has two central aims: first, to interrogate and 'encounter'[8] the relationship between rights and governance at the three sites I have mentioned (national, regional and international) and, second, to explore the possibilities and dangers of resistance to governing (through) rights. In this way, the book hopes to contribute, on the one hand, to a better understanding of human rights by examining the *how* of rights—the actors, tactics and processes involved in their realization. On the other

---

[8] W Walters, *Governmentality: Critical Encounters* (Abingdon, Routledge, 2012) 143. Walters suggests 'encountering' rather than 'mapping' governmentality as a novel way of using this theoretical tool and overcoming its limits.

hand, it hopes to intervene in Foucauldian studies and make the tool of governmentality 'protest and groan'[9] through applying it to a study of rights—an endeavour that Foucault left somewhat neglected despite his 'curious' turn towards rights in the late 1970s.[10]

II. GOVERNMENTALITY AS A METHODOLOGY

A. Methodology: A (Critical) Attitude

The refusal of the governmentality of rights that this book attempts is an outlook that can perhaps best be described as a 'critical attitude';[11] that is, 'a certain *way of thinking, speaking and acting,* a certain relationship to what exists, to what one knows, to what one does, a relationship to society, to culture and also a relationship to others'.[12] This attitude has, I suggest, three important features. It is, first, encouraged by a curiosity, a characteristic that:

> evokes 'care'; it evokes the care one takes of what exists and what might exist; a sharpened sense of reality, but one that is never immobilised before it; a readiness to find what surrounds us strange and odd; a certain determination to *throw off familiar ways of thought and to look at the same things in a different way*; a passion for seizing what is happening now and what is disappearing; a lack of respect for the traditional hierarchies of what is important and fundamental.[13]

This lack of respect for what appears fundamental and important is the second feature: the critical attitude is 'a way of thinking ... which I would very simply call the art of not being governed or better, the art of not being governed like that and at that cost ... the art of not being governed quite so much'.[14] And third, the critical attitude provides an alternative way of

---

[9] I take inspiration here from Foucault, who responded to a question about his use of Nietzsche with the following: 'The only valid tribute to thought such as Nietzsche's is precisely to use it, to deform it, to make it groan and protest. And if commentators then say that I am being faithful or unfaithful to Nietzsche, that is of absolutely no interest': M Foucault, 'Prison Talk' in *Power/Knowledge: Selected Interviews and Other Writings 1972–1977* (C Gordon (ed), C Gordon *et al* (trans), Longman, London, 1980) 37, 53–54.

[10] See B Golder, *Foucault and the Politics of Rights* (Stanford, CA, Stanford University Press, 2015) on 'Foucault's curious deployment of rights', 13–20.

[11] M Foucault, 'What is Critique?' in M Foucault, *The Politics of Truth* (S Lotringer and L Hochroth (eds), Los Angeles, CA, Semiotext(e), 1997) 24. See also P Minkkinen, 'Critical Legal "Method" as Attitude' in D Watkins and M Burton (eds), *Research Methods in Law* (Abingdon, Routledge, 2013) 119 and B Sokhi-Bulley, 'Alternative Methodologies' (2013) 2 *Law and Method [Rechte en Methode]* 6.

[12] Foucault, 'What is Critique?', ibid.

[13] M Foucault, 'The Masked Philosopher' in M Foucault, *Ethics*, vol 1, *Subjectivity and Truth: Essential Works of Foucault 1954–1984* (P Rabinow (ed), R Hurley (trans) (London, Penguin, 2000) 321, 325 (emphasis added).

[14] Foucault, 'What is Critique?', above n 11, 29.

thinking familiar things; it provides alternative truths. The critical attitude of this book allows us to think the language of rights differently; to be curious about the claims that rights make to being the 'enlightenment promise of emancipation' and ask what *else* do rights do?

The *critical* attitude, furthermore, refers to a type of criti*que*, rather than criti*cism*. It is thus not negative in its outlook (as the words 'refusal' or 'critical' might connote). Criticism suggests disapproval that is based on a perceived fault—it may imply a dismissal of the thing being criticized. Criticism may also be constructive; it may be intended to improve the thing being criticized. It is usually a stance or a position that one takes. For instance, a criticism of human rights might be that they do not achieve in practice what they set out in theory. This book does not disapprove of, dismiss or seek to improve rights discourse.[15] Rather, it presents a way of thinking rights that exposes features about this discourse (namely, the tactics and technologies of governmentality) that might not otherwise be apparent. It asks questions of rights discourse that are based in *how* they operate. This way of thinking is critique. Critique re-reads and re-considers the claims of a discourse, searching for what is authentic in it. Before uncovering the power relations within the discourses that regulate and govern us, critique re-asserts the importance of the said discourses. Critique is, therefore, far from negating. It does not dismiss, reject or refute its object. It cannot, since by re-reading it must affirm the object. Critique is thus an act of reclamation, which takes over the object, or the discourse, for a purpose other than that for which it is currently employed.[16] The claim has often been made that critique is 'disinterested, distanced, negating or academic'[17] and that it does not provide insights into progressive change.[18] However, critique is neither disinterested nor distant; rather, it engages the discourse which it contests. Nor is critique 'just theorizing'[19] that bears no relation to 'practice'. The case studies in this book—on the European Union's rights agency, on human rights international NGOs, on the Big Society and its (dis/ab)use of rights rhetoric and on riots as counter-conduct—illustrate the 'practical' application of critique. Critique is an attitude; it provides a way of thinking, perhaps even a better way of understanding because it focuses on what is ordinarily hidden; in terms of a governmentality critique this would be the

---

[15] So I do not engage historiographies of human rights that go to questioning the soul of human rights; see notably S Moyn, *The Last Utopia: Human Rights in History* (Cambridge, MA, Belknap Press of Harvard University Press, 2010); P Alston, 'Does the Past Matter?: On the Origins of Human Rights' (2013) 126(7) *Harvard Law Review* 2043.

[16] W Brown, *Edgework: Critical Essays on Knowledge and Politics* (Princeton, NJ, Princeton University Press, 2005).

[17] Ibid 7.

[18] W Brown and J Halley, 'Introduction' in W Brown and J Halley (eds), *Left Legalism/Left Critique* (Durham, NC, Duke University Press, 2002) 1, 25.

[19] Ibid 2.

intricate, minor and heterarchical forms in which power operates, and the resultant identities and *ethos* that is produced.

A 'governmentality critique' is therefore a way of thinking (rights), an *attitude* (towards rights)—it is in other words a methodology. A methodology is, as I understand it, about 'how to think' a project. This is different to how to think *about* a project (which is the method).[20] As a way of thinking, that is, as an attitude, methodology is therefore about an approach, a perspective, or a lens through which to see a project. The typical legal education does not give much consideration to questions of methodology; most of us are trained in law schools that follow the doctrinal tradition and experience the law in a largely or even purely positivist sense.[21] So, for instance, human rights *law* courses are taught with a focus on concepts and institutions for the protection and promotion of rights; the philosophy of rights, critical approaches to rights and a general curiosity about the discourse is not encouraged.[22] There is perhaps an aversion to methodology because it is associated with *theory*—and so it is left to singular courses such as legal theory or jurisprudence to tackle different ways of thinking law. Positivism is the dominant methodology within law schools; it is 'the "properly" legal perspective' and presents law from the perspective that it is 'created and laid down ('posit-ed') by a law-making authority, that the validity of a rule of law lies in its formal legal status (not its relation to morality or other external validating factors, ie law is self-referential); that there is a concern with social standards that are recognised as authoritative: judicial decisions, legislation, custom'.[23] There are, however, a variety of other approaches, of 'alternative methodologies'[24] that may be used in the study of law and in legal research. These are 'alternative' to legal positivism and

---

[20] A method has empirical and sociological connotations, so, is the method a qualitative or quantitative analysis? What methods of data collection are used: documentary analysis, case studies, observation, interviews, for example? It is essentially about *what you do* in a project, as opposed to *how you think it*. For more on 'method' versus methodology see R Cryer, T Hervey and B Sokhi-Bulley, *Research Methodologies in EU and International Law* (Oxford, Hart, 2011) 8.

[21] Sokhi-Bulley, 'Alternative Methodologies', above n 11.

[22] For work that adopts a critical attitude towards rights, see eg, C Douzinas, *Human Rights and Empire: The Political Philosophy of Cosmopolitanism* (Abingdon, Routledge-Cavendish, 2007) and C Douzinas, *The End of Human Rights* (Oxford, Hart, 2000); W Brown, *States of Injury: Power and Freedom in Late Modernity* (Princeton, NJ, Princeton University Press, 1995) and W Brown, *Regulating Aversion: Tolerance in the Age of Identity and Empire* (Princeton, NJ, Princeton University Press, 2006); W Brown and J Halley (eds), *Left Legalism/ Left Critique* (Durham, NC, Duke University Press, 2002); B Golder (ed), *Re-Reading Foucault: On Law, Power and Rights* (B Golder (ed), Abingdon, Routledge, 2013) and Golder, *Foucault and the Politics of Rights*, above n 10.

[23] Sokhi-Bulley, 'Alternative Methodologies', above n 11, 9 and 10. See also B Sokhi-Bulley, 'Learning Law Differently: The Importance of Theory and Methodology' in B van Klink and B de Vries (eds), *Academic Learning in Law: Theoretical Positions, Teaching Experiments and Learning Experiences* (Edward Elgar Publishing, forthcoming 2016).

[24] Ibid.

demand an engagement with other disciplines such as political theory, international relations, philosophy and sociology. What are these 'alternative methodologies' and how many are there?

Cryer *et al* have attempted to put together a list of legal research methodologies that begins with the 'main jurisprudential approaches' (which include legal positivism and natural law) and then goes on to examine 'extensions and negations' to these, which are split into 'modern and critical approaches' and the 'law and' approaches. The former includes, for example, Marxism, critical theory (which covers a range of poststructural approaches), feminist perspectives and postcolonial theory. The latter includes law and geography, law and international relations and leaves room open for other areas such as law and literature. These approaches are all different ways of looking at law. The first important point is that methodology reflects research questions and so influences what you say in a project. Different attitudes prompt different questions; so for instance, as the Feminist Judgments Project shows, a feminist consciousness or philosophy engages questions about the ways in which law constructs gender.[25] Re-reading judgments through a feminist lens opens up possibilities for alternative truths, in the form of different judgment altogether or a different reasoning/rationale. So, '[i]t makes such a difference how the story is told'.[26]

This book attempts to provide an alternative truth about rights by telling a different story about them; employing a poststructural critique or attitude that uses Foucault's concept of governmentality, it shows how rights operate as technologies of government. My critical attitude is one that is interested in *how* questions, in power and in the social structures that have the effect of governing us in the name of values that we are told we ought to aspire to, such as rights, or responsibility and opportunity. So, the book examines how rights act as techniques of government within specific sites (the EU, the international NGO and the United Kingdom's Big Society) and shows how such an observation is made possible by using a governmentality lens. It thus uses governmentality as a tool by which to better understand rights as strategies of power.

B. Governmentality as a Critical Attitude

'Governmentality' as the 'problem of government' refers then to both the processes of governing and to a *way or system of thinking* about the nature of the practice of government (who can govern; what governing is; what or

---

[25] R Hunter, C McGlynn and E Rackley, *Feminist Judgments: From Theory to Practice* (Oxford, Hart, 2010) 5–6.
[26] Baroness Hale, 'Foreword' to Hunter, McGlynn and Rackley, ibid.

who is governed)'.[27] It is thus both the art (process) and rationality (way of thinking) of government. The art of government refers not to government in the 'old' sense of the term but to a regulatory or conducting power, that is:

> This word [government] must be allowed the very broad meaning it had in the sixteenth century. 'Government' did not refer only to political structures or to the management of states; rather, it designated the way in which the *conduct* of individuals or of groups might be directed—the government of children, of souls, of communities, of the sick ... *To govern, in this sense, is to control the possible field of action of others.*[28]

The art of government(ality) thus refers to the 'conduct of conducts';[29] or, in other words, the regulation (conduct) of behaviour (conduct). The rationality of government sees it as 'govern/mentality';[30] a mental attitude, outlook or methodology for understanding the techniques of government.

In a lecture given at the Collège de France in 1978, posthumously given the title 'Governmentality', Foucault presents his most concise definition of the term. He explains that 'governmentality' means three things:[31] first, 'the ensemble formed by the institutions, procedures, analyses, reflections, calculations and tactics that allow the exercise of this very specific albeit complex form of power, which has as its target population ...'. Second, governmentality refers to 'the tendency that, over a long period and throughout the West, has steadily led to the pre-eminence over all other forms (sovereignty, discipline and so on) of this type of power, which may be termed "government"'. Third, governmentality is the (result of the) process by which the state gradually 'becomes governmentalised'. It is this idea of shifting the focus from *an* authority that needs to be legitimated or tamed to social practices of governing that touch all and each (*omnes et singulatum*)[32] that forms the basis of a now well-established field of governmentality studies, which is typically appropriated by the social sciences and geographers. For instance, Garland and Rose use a governmentality perspective to understand technologies of crime control;[33] Rose develops the concept of 'ethopolitics'

---

[27] C Gordon, 'Governmental Rationality: An Introduction' in G Burchell *et al*, *The Foucault Effect: Studies in Governmentality* (Chicago, IL, University of Chicago Press, 1991) 1, 3 (emphasis added).

[28] M Foucault, 'The Subject and Power' in M Foucault, *Power*, vol 3, *Essential Works of Foucault 1954–1984* (J Faubion (ed), R Hurley (trans), London, Penguin, 2002) 326, 341 (emphasis added).

[29] Ibid 341.

[30] A Barron, 'Foucault and Law' in J Penner *et al* (eds), *Jurisprudence and Legal Theory: Commentary and Materials* (Oxford, Oxford University Press, 2005) 955, 984.

[31] M Foucault, 'Governmentality' in *Power*, vol 3, *Essential Works of Foucault 1954–1984* (J Faubion (ed), R Hurley (trans), London, Penguin 2002) 201, 219–20.

[32] See further M Foucault, '"*Omnes et Singulatem*": Toward a Critique of Political Reason' in M Foucault, *Power*, vol. 3, *Essential Works of Foucault 1954–1984* (J Faubion (ed), R Hurley (trans), London, Penguin, 2002) 298.

[33] D Garland, 'Governmentality and the Problem of Crime' (1997) 1 *Theoretical Criminology* 172; N Rose, 'Government and Control' (2000) 40 *British Journal of Criminology* 321.

to describe the government and politics of healthcare and a general 'death of the social' to allow for the birth and growth of 'community';[34] Bigo, Darling, Inda and Walters discuss the regulatory function of immigration and asylum laws, and question control at border sites, whilst Elden examines the notion of 'territory' as a political technology.[35]

The shift in focus is a different understanding of power that is concerned with the *how* of power relations. The shift means looking at rights as a process rather than as an outcome, such that we examine the tactics and technologies that enable a wider strategy of government (through) rights. Hence, the actors involved in rights discourse and the mundane and minor processes by which they operate become significant. Expertise forms a significant tactic of government, as experts within non-state rights bodies (agencies, international NGOs), as policy-makers, bureaucrats, humanitarians, activists, the media engage in processes and procedures that narrate what rights are, and what the right way to do rights is. Within the mundane and minor instruments of policy documents, White Papers, reports and indicator criteria we find the technologies that govern through information. Data and indicators are thus hugely significant since they are the great numerical technologies that enable government (through) rights. Government by experts and/through numerical and mundane tactics involves elements of direction, guidance and manipulation that reveal 'technologies of pastoralism'.[36] Experts are concerned with narrating (the right kind of) stories, with compiling how to measure rights and how to indicate well-being, good governance and progress. Pastoral power as a technology of governmentality, as the manifestation of processes within the modern state and within the modern human rights architecture that regulate the behaviour of (non-) citizens, states and rights experts themselves, is thus another important methodological tool which we can use to uncover government (through) rights. Of course, governmentality, whilst it cannot be escaped (for power, as a 'complex strategical situation', 'is everywhere')[37] features a disruption in its rhythm, cracks in the governmental design and so leaves room for rupture or struggle. As well as observing the conduct of conducts,

[34] N Rose, 'The Politics of Life Itself' (2001) 18 *Theory, Culture and Society* 1; P Miller and N Rose, *Governing the Present* (Cambridge, Polity Press, 2008) 89.

[35] D Bigo, 'Security and Immigration: Toward a Critique of the Governmentality of Unease' (2002) 27 *Alternatives* 63; J Darling, 'Domopolitics, Governmentality and the Regulation of Asylum Accommodation' (2011) 30 *Political Geography* 263; JX Inda, *Targeting Immigrants: Government, Technology, and Ethics* (Oxford, Blackwell, 2006); W Walters, 'Secure Borders, Safe Haven, Domopolitics' (2004) 8(3) *Citizenship Studies* 237; JW Crampton and S Elden, *Space, Knowledge and Power: Foucault and Geography* (Aldershot, Ashgate, 2007) and S Elden, *The Birth of Territory* (Chicago, IL, Chicago University Press, 2013).

[36] B Golder, 'Foucault and the Genealogy of Pastoral Power' (2007) 10(2) *Radical Philosophy Review* 157, 167–68. See also Foucault, *Security, Territory, Population*, above n 6, 165.

[37] M Foucault, *The History of Sexuality: Volume 1: The Will To Knowledge* (R Hurley, trs) (Penguin, London 1998) 93.

we can then also observe *counter-conducts* in rights:[38] how the rights-bearing actor (as a citizen with rights) finds ways to counter government and enact the impulse to no longer obey. The counter-conduct perspective allows us to ask what political and ethical possibilities can be imagined for the unruly, struggling subject (of rights): is she a courageous truth-teller, or parrhesiast?[39] And can her struggle be recognized within the discourse of rights, or do we need something else, a new technology, by which to understand and *see* it?

III. THE CHAPTERS

The book then essentially uses the methodological tool of governmentality to show government of and through rights language, and related and contesting discourses (such as the ethic of responsibility and spontaneous unrest). So, the book attempts to challenge our understanding of new rights agencies that spring up in the name of good and better governance; to interrogate humanitarian and human rights actors and their role in governance; to highlight the challenge that the responsibilisation of individuals through Community and Society initiatives poses to rights; and whether the rights-bearing citizen can refuse to be governed and what space there is for counter-conduct in rights.

In the next chapter, I explore the 'problem of government' (through) rights at the EUropean level to interrogate the case study of the EU and its FRA. I identify the features of the FRA that show it to be a vehicle of governmentality (and not simply governance) which both governs rights and governs through rights, as being experts, the rights-based approach and indicators. Thus, the chapter will argue that through the presence of vast networks of experts, through the adoption of a rights-based approach (to the example of migration policy) and through the measurement of progress in rights using newly developed indicators (eg on the rights of the child), rights are made technical and thus governmental. Rights become a complex, authentic and self-reinforcing discourse of conducting power that creates an empowered and right-eous identity for (rights) experts and the EU at the same time as it disempowers other subject identities (eg the 'irregular' migrant).

Chapter 3 looks at another level of non-state actor, the international non-governmental human rights organisation (INGO), in order to observe the potential of rights to govern and to be governed within this wider international human rights architecture. This architectural design is made up of a vast palette of actors and I observe the 'rulership' role of the experts of

---

[38] Foucault, *Security, Territory, Population*, above n 6, lecture eight, 191–226.
[39] M Foucault, *The Courage of Truth: The Government of the Self and Others II* (F Gros (ed), G Burchell (trans), Basingstoke, Palgrave Macmillan, 2011) 1–23.

the archetypal human rights INGO that is Human Rights Watch (HRW).[40] Relying on the tactic of expertise, HRW demonstrates how this kind of non-state, human rights actor comes to play a key role in the government of rights, which intersects with and utilises a humanitarian ethic. It thus demonstrates humanitarian government (through) rights. The activities of HRW are, furthermore, regulated by rights and by the requirement that it, like other human rights NGOs that are part of the same global architecture, be active, responsible and suitable participants in the discourse. So I examine HRW's structure and functioning methods to question the extent to which the actors/experts involved govern (through) rights by virtue of their expertise, which allows for the ability to narrate rights stories and to scrutinise state behaviour (through) rights.

Chapter 4 moves to the local level and will consider the link between rights and a new improved version of responsibility in the context of the UK government's Community and Society initiatives (formerly the Big Society). I focus on the nationwide National Citizen Service (NCS) and the construction of desirable and useful youth who will become desirable and useful active citizens in place of rights-bearing citizens. The active citizen is the ideal citizen and is a new type of governmentable subject created in the face of a reaction against rights language, in favour of responsibility and opportunity. The ethic of responsibility is thus a direct reaction against rights, a counter-narrative which exposes a failure in the governmentality of rights and poses a dangerous threat to rights discourse. For instance, the focus on individual responsibility over individual right stifles the kind of spontaneous struggle, or counter-conduct, that I discuss in Chapter 5 as being essential to the political and ethical agency of the rights-bearing citizen—that is, riotous behaviour. Chapter 5 therefore questions whether and how it is possible to counter rights language; how might the 'revolting subject',[41] who refuses the regional and international human rights architecture, and the ethic of responsibility and its emphasis on community rights, enact a *new ethical* right to struggle? I focus on the unsavoury figure of the rioting subject by examining recent unruly events that challenge our perception of the right way to resist within democratic, neoliberal society that have taken place in London and in Ferguson in the United States, and indeed challenge the limits of rights discourse in allowing for a 'right to resistance'. I thus question the possibility of reading these events as counter-conduct, which necessities that I describe what counter-conduct means and how it recognises political agency. I also ask whether counter-conduct can be an ethical position of *parrhēsia*.

---

[40] The specific nature of HRW as 'archetypal' and as only one of a range of INGO-types involved in the protection and promotion of rights, as well as the intersection of rights talk and the language of humanitarianism, are considered further in Chapter 3.

[41] Taken from I Tyler, *Revolting Subjects* (London, Zed Books, 2013).

And so, what is the point? The point is to permanently critique—and not to point out the ways in which rights are *bad* but the ways in which they are *dangerous*. That is, to contest the assumption that rights are '*the* fulfilment of the Enlightenment promise of emancipation', to discover and highlight the minor tactics of measurement and the specificities of expert involvement and how they produce normalised identities and forms of behaviour—the governmentable subject of rights and the governing non-state actor. Perhaps then, there is 'hope' of an 'other world' in which there might be a right to contest rights, a scope for 'transformation' through critique;[42] this is the challenge I leave open in Chapter 6. This continual struggle within rights and refusal of the different ways in which activities of government happen and have been made possible (through) rights will, I hope, always give us something to do.

---

[42] Foucault, *The Courage of Truth*, above n 39, 315; M Foucault, 'Practicing Criticism' in LD Kritzman (ed), *Michel Foucault, Politics Philosophy and Culture: Interviews and Other Writings 1977–1984* (A Sheridan (trans), New York and London, Routledge, 1988) 154–55; and see Chapter 6.

2

Governing (Through) Agencies: The EU and Rights in EUrope[*]

> The European Union Agency for Fundamental Rights (the Agency) is
> hereby established ... The objective of the Agency shall be to provide
> the relevant institutions, bodies, offices and agencies of the Community
> and its Member States when implementing Community law with assistance
> and expertise relating to fundamental rights in order to support them when
> they take measures or formulate courses of action within their respective
> spheres of competence to fully respect fundamental rights ... the Agency
> shall collect, record, analyse and disseminate relevant, objective, reliable and
> comparable information and data.
>
> Regulation Establishing the FRA[1]

> What numbers do, then, is basically make up governmental object domains ...
> they single out a certain segment of existence, identify its properties
> and processes, and give it categorical visibility.
>
> Jonathan X Inda[2]

OR ALL THE association that human rights have with noble and
romantic notions such as dignity, humanity and justice, human
rights practice is often about something far more mundane, tedious
and unremarkable: measurement. The implementation and enjoyment of
human rights depends on being able to identify how good governance, good
practice and progress in rights can be calculated. The 'problem of government' (through) rights, introduced in the previous chapter, is thus nowhere
more starkly revealed than in 'all the mundane tools—surveys, reports,
statistical methodologies, pamphlets, manuals, architectural plans, written
reports, drawings, pictures, numbers, bureaucratic rules and guidelines,
charts, graphs, statistics, and so forth—that represent events and phenomena as information, data and knowledge'.[3] And this information, data and

---

[*] As to my use of the term 'EUrope', see below n 6.
[1] Council Regulation 168/2007/EC establishing a European Union Agency for Fundamental
Rights, 15 February 2007 [2007] OJ L53/1, arts 2 and 4(1)(a) ('FRA Regulation').
[2] JX Inda, *Targeting Immigrants: Government, Technology, and Ethics* (Oxford, Blackwell,
2006) 65.
[3] Ibid 7.

knowledge is collected, recorded, analysed and disseminated by experts. The problem of government (through) rights is thus the problem of calculation in which there is a technical role for experts and the methods they design to measure and to mainstream rights. Rights become governmental by *becoming technical*[4]—they must be able to be measured and implemented into good governance strategies through a rights-based approach because this is how to *do* good governance. The making technical of rights is interesting and important because rights are now not only tools of good gover*nance* but techniques of good govern*ment*; rights have become coopted, through numerical tactics and expert networks, into being a discourse of conducting power. And it is important to critique how this power operates and how far it extends: in other words, who governs (through) rights? How does the government happen? And ought we to question whether this is what the promise of rights is intended to fulfil?

Both this chapter and the next are concerned with the human rights 'architecture'[5] and the role of non-state actors within the complex design of who *does* human rights. In the spirit of dissatisfaction in which this book is written and refusal of how we, as rights experts and as rights holders, are told to think rights and how they work, my objective in this chapter is to explore how rights become *technical* instruments of government enacted through new governance structures that are in place to measure, disseminate and thus define what rights are and what the right way to do rights is.

I begin here with the EUropean context since the deliberate connections between rights and good/new governance are drawn so clearly here.[6] Rights in EUrope are protected and promoted by a vast array of expert actors that go beyond the sovereign and judicial channels; governments and regional and national courts have been supplemented by rights experts and agencies that ensure greater flexibility, effectiveness and participation in the protection and promotion of rights. Part of the fundamental rights toolbox of

---

[4] See, on the governmentalisation of 'community' through technical means, N Rose and P Miller, *Governing the Present* (Cambridge, Polity Press, 2008) ch 4.

[5] See Chapter 3.

[6] I use the term 'EUrope' to recognize 'that the spatial and legal limits of the "EU" are related to but not coterminous with that or "Europe"', as per N Vaughan-Williams, 'We are Not Animals!' Humanitarian Border Security and Zoopolitical Spaces in EUrope' (2015) 45 *Political Geography* 1, endnote 2 and L Bialasiewicz (ed), *Europe and the World: EU Geopolitics and the Transformation of European Space* (Aldershot, Ashgate, 2011). My focus, when I speak of 'Europe' is on the EU and excludes direct attention to the Council of Europe (COE); I am interested in particular sites of governance, the (new) rights agency (here, the FRA), the supranational organisation that claims to be a rights actor (the EU), and not in (a) the established rights structure of the COE and the Strasbourg Court and its procedures per se, on which much work had already been done, and (b) the geographical space of 'Europe' but the space of circulation and mobility within the EU's borders.

EUrope is new agencies,[7] most notably the Fundamental Rights Agency (FRA) of the EU.[8] This chapter interrogates the 'assistance and expertise' functions of the FRA and the framework of good governance within which it fits.

When Foucault wrote in 1975 on the nature of power, he described it as:

> a strategy, that its effects of domination are attributed not to 'appropriation', but to dispositions, manoeuvres, *tactics, techniques, functionings*; that one should decipher in a *network of relations*, constantly in tension, in activity rather than a privilege that one might possess...[9]

In 2005, when the European Union (EU) was establishing a Fundamental Rights Agency, its intended Director described it as more than a network of relations, it was to be a 'network of networks'.[10] Not part of the institutional structure of the Union, the FRA is a new governance initiative that aims to fulfil an advisory and data collection and dissemination role that is open, participatory, accountable, effective and coherent.[11] Since its inauguration in March 2007, the Agency has, I argue, been exercising a governmentality (through) rights under this governance banner through reliance on its network of networks structure and data gathering role. These processes form the 'tactics, techniques and functionings' of a general strategy of power (or government (through) rights). I aim to show that the Agency both governs rights and governs through rights so that it is able to determine what subject identities merit rights, it is able to secure a *right-eous* identity for the Union. In this way, rights are continually transformed from being primarily a discourse of resistance against power and are now coopted into a discourse through which that power operates. This is hugely problematic since the subjects who can claim rights are able to be selectively identified by technical means, and the experts who are in place to secure rights ensure good govern*ment* (and not only govern*ance*) in the name of rights. It is the rights expert, and not the rights holder, who is thus empowered by rights. Moreover, the trust in numbers means that indicators on how to measure

---

[7] The interest in developing new tools for the toolbox that ensure and enhance human rights protection in the EU is growing; see eg the FRAME Project (Fostering Human Rights Among European (External and Internal) Policies), available at www.fp7-frame.eu/# and FRAME Policy Brief (November 2015), available at www.fp7-frame.eu/category/publications/.

[8] Note also the European Gender Institute for Equality (http://eige.europa.eu). The FRA replaces the former EUMC (European Monitoring Centre for Racism and Xenophobia).

[9] M Foucault, *Discipline and Punish: The Birth of the Prison* (A Sheridan (trans), London, Penguin, 1991) 26 (emphasis added).

[10] Morten Kjærum, European Policy Evaluation Consortium (EPEC), *Preparatory Study for Impact Assessment and Ex-Ante Evaluation of the Fundamental Rights Agency: Public Hearing Report* (February 2005) 26–27.

[11] European Commission, *European Governance: A White Paper*, COM(2001) 428 final (25 July 2001).

good governance, good practice and progress in rights are burgeoning at such a rapid pace that we do not stop to interrogate *what else* they are doing besides measurement.

I identify three tactics of governmentality that show the FRA to be governing (through) rights. The first is expertise. The labyrinth of experts within the FRA form a technical design, or assemblage, within which a technology of power we can call 'pastoralism' operates. Under the guide of education, advice and learning experts govern rights and rights actors. The assemblage is increasingly complex and this complexity has added to the technicality of expertise, making it almost impenetrable to any sort of challenge or resistance. Furthermore, experts must gather data through quantitative and objective methods to ensure it is reliable and comparable, hence the trust in indicators.[12] Rights-based indicators form the second tactic of a governmentality (through) rights. Following the lead of the United Nations, the EU's FRA is fast developing indicators on how to calculate rights (and thus good practice, good governance and progress in rights). Using the example of the rights of the child indicators, the first area developed by the FRA, I explain how indicators make targets such as (child) justice calculable and achievable. There is no apparent limit to what can be measured in the name of calculating good governance in rights—and so no limit to how far we can be governed through rights. Calculating how to ensure good practice, good governance and progress in rights is made visible requires a rights-based approach, and this forms the third tactic of control by and through rights. Reform and progress increasingly necessitate a turn to rights and so the rights-based approach infiltrates EUropean policy areas. Taking the example of migration policy and the EU's attempts to instill a 'rights-based EU migration policy'[13] in response to the EUropean 'migrant crisis' of the past decade, I look at the governmental effects of taking a rights-based approach to migration. The rights-based approach creates a category of 'the empowered' who is *not* the (irregular) migrant (she is, rather an illegitimate rights claimant) but the experts who *do* rights.[14] Hence the FRA, Frontex (European Agency for the Management of Operational Cooperation at the External Borders of the Member States of the European Union) and the EU are the empowered; the (irregular) migrant is unable to rely on rights as a discourse of resistance at the same time as the EU is able to sustain a

---

[12] A Rosga and ML Satterthwaite, 'The Trust in Indicators: Measuring Human Rights' (2009) 27(2) *Berkeley Journal of International Law* 253.

[13] FRA (European Union Agency for Fundamental Rights), 'FRA re-iterates call for rights-based EU migration policy following latest deaths in Mediterranean', 24 April 2015, available at http://fra.europa.eu/en/news/2015/fra-reiterates-call-rights-based-eu-migration-policy-following-latest-deaths-mediterranean.

[14] ML Satterthwaite, 'Indicators in Crisis: Rights-based Humanitarian Indicators in Post-Earthquake Haiti' (2011) 43 *International Law and Politics* 865, 964.

righteous image in an area of action that has caused significant controversy internationally.

I. TACTIC ONE: EXPERTISE

Agencies, in the EUropean context, are good governance structures. The FRA, though not explicitly named, is one of the regulatory agencies referred to in the White Paper on European Governance that has been entrusted with a reformation role in how 'governing' happens in the EU.[15] This reform is concerned with 'a new process of governing; or a changed condition of ordered rule; or the new method by which society is governed'.[16] The task of regulatory agencies is the 'better application of rules' in fulfilment of a new form of rule that advocates *less government*; it is 'governance without government'.[17] How then does the governing happen? Who, or what, enacts it? The answer is in the expert assemblage of the FRA.

A. The Complexity of the Assemblage

The structure of the FRA is important; the network of networks conceals a technicality and a complexity. Taken from the French, 'assemblage' refers to a collection, or an assembly, that is, the result of a joining together. I use 'assemblage' in place of 'structure' since the latter implies a 'fixity and boundedness'[18] that does not accurately describe the designs of good governance entities such as the FRA; these are a joining together of expert actors to form a collective, but they are not fixed. There is an experimental and effervescent element to good governance designs that the concept of assemblage captures; they are evolving, must develop their own concepts, forms of behaviour and regulation, and may disappear or be replaced.[19] They also thus do not have the rigidity of an *apparatus*. The apparatus is by contrast 'relatively stable'; an assemblage might then grow into an apparatus, or it might disperse and cease to exist.[20] I would see the structure of the Union in terms of its institutions and the Member States as an apparatus in the

---

[15] *White Paper*, above n 11.

[16] R Rhodes, 'The New Governance: Governing Without Government' (1996) 44 *Political Studies* 652, 653.

[17] Per EU-sponsored 'New Modes of Governance Project', an integrated project coordinated by the European University Institute and funded by the EU under its Sixth Framework Programme, 2004–2008, available at www.eu-newgov.org/index.asp.

[18] W Walters, *Governmentality: Critical Encounters* (Abingdon, Routledge, 2012) 77.

[19] For instance, the FRA replaced the old European Monitoring Centre for Racism and Xenophobia (EUMC).

[20] Walters, *Governmentality*, above n 18.

context of this chapter; the new governance structures that bubble up and come to the boil within it are assemblages. The idea of assemblage therefore conveys complexity but it is also significant because it is impenetrable. This means that how rights govern through the everyday practices of vast numbers of experts is hidden within the assemblage. The experts within the FRA's assemblage are multifarious, unknowable and by consequence unaccountable. We know them as 'experts' without any specifics. The heightened significance of this is that government by experts is concealed.

If you looked it up, you would learn that the FRA has 90 staff members that include legal *experts*, political and social scientists, statisticians, and communication and networking *experts*.[21] The FRA gives a list of experts under a separate 'experts' tab under the 'who we are' section of its website;[22] it mentions and provides biographies for, for instance, the heads of the five departments of the Directorate (eg Head of Equality and Citizens' Rights Department), the Head of the Executive Office (Directorate) and programme heads (eg Programme Manager, Social Research, Freedoms and Justice Department). The specialisations, qualifications and any publications (where relevant, many of the experts are academics) are listed.[23] However, the complexity of the assemblage is much more expansive and intricate than this, and these are not the *only* 'experts' that make up the assemblage. Three other levels of expert are clearly visible: first, the four bodies of the Agency itself; second, the less visible and more intricately dispersed national level actors; and finally, the external bodies with which the FRA cooperates at the national, regional and international levels.

First, the more visible 'nodes' of the FRA's structure are the four bodies of the Agency itself. According to the FRA's founding Regulation, the Agency is to consist of a Management Board, an Executive Board, a Scientific Committee and a Director.[24] As the FRA has grown, so too has its core structure. The Director is now supported by a Directorate, that 'guides and manages' the FRA, and is supplemented by five further departments: freedoms and justice; equality and citizens' rights; communications and outreach; administration; and human resources and planning.[25] Second, a national level of actors fit in to the FRA structure by virtue of article 6 of the 2007 Regulation which, in describing the Agency's 'working methods', specifies that the Agency is to draw on the expertise of a variety of organisations and bodies in each Member State and to involve national authorities in the collection of data. Thus, the FRA is to set up new information networks, use existing networks and organise meetings of external experts at

---

[21] See fra.europa.eu/en/about-fra/who-we-are.
[22] See fra.europa.eu/en/about-fra/structure/experts.
[23] Ibid.
[24] FRA Regulation, art 11.
[25] See http://fra.europa.eu/en/about-fra/structure.

the national level. There are two further nodes of networks at the national level. The first is the primary point of contact for the Agency in a Member State, known as the National Liaison Officer, a government official nominated by the Member State.[26] Extending out from this point of contact is FRANET, the agency's multidisciplinary research network.[27] It is made up of contractors in each Member States, who are called upon to provide reliable and comparative data to the FRA.[28] Third, aside from the bodies of the Agency and the national level networks, the FRA is to work with a variety of 'other' bodies that form part of the Agency's structure. They are bodies with which the FRA is to 'cooperate' and exist at the EU, regional, national and international levels. At the EU level, these 'other' bodies are the Union institutions, and offices and agencies of the Community.[29] At the regional level, the Regulation makes special mention of cooperation with the Council of Europe (COE).[30] The national level bodies include the Member States, non-governmental organisations (NGOs) dealing with human rights and universities.[31] At the international level, the Regulation refers to the Organisation for Security and Cooperation in Europe (OSCE), the United Nations (UN) and 'other international organisations'.[32] Some of these 'other' bodies come together in a structure called the 'Fundamental Rights Platform' (FRP). This is described in the Regulation as a 'cooperation network' that consists of almost 400 civil society organisations,[33] including NGOs dealing

[26] FRA Regulation, art 8(1). The National Liaison Officer for the United Kingdom is Helen Reid from the Ministry of Justice, see http://fra.europa.eu/en/cooperation/eu-member-states/national-liaison-officers.
[27] FRANET has been operational since 2011 and was previously the RAXEN and FRALEX networks. RAXEN had been operational since 2000 and referred to the groups of National Focal Points (NFPs) that reported on racism, xenophobia and related intolerances. FRALEX referred to the FRA's 'group of legal experts' reporting on legal aspects of fundamental rights issues in all Member States within the thematic areas of the FRA's competence; eg, the first thematic study undertaken by the FRALEX experts was a report on homophobia that forms part of EU-MIDIS (European Union Minorities and Discrimination Survey), part of a now wider thematic area of 'LGBT' (see FRA (European Union Agency for Fundamental Rights), *Homophobia and Discrimination on the Grounds of Sexual Orientation in the EU Member States: Part I: Legal Analysis* (30 June 2008) and FRA (European Union Agency for Fundamental Rights), *Homophobia and Discrimination on the Grounds of Sexual Orientation in the EU Member States: Part II: The Social Situation* (31 March 2009), available at fra.europa.eu/sites/default/files/fra_uploads/192-FRA_hdgso_report_Part%201_en.pdf and fra.europa.eu/sites/default/files/fra_uploads/397-FRA_hdgso_report_part2_en.pdf.
[28] See fra.europa.eu/en/research/franet.
[29] FRA Regulation, art 4.
[30] Ibid arts 4 and 9.
[31] Ibid arts 4, 8 and 10. The full list refers to: the Member States; research centres; NGOs (dealing with human rights); National Liaison Officers; National Human Rights Institutions; trade unions and employers' organisations; relevant social and professional organisations; churches, religious, philosophical and non-confessional organisations; and universities.
[32] Ibid arts 8 and 10.
[33] FRA (European Union Agency for Fundamental Rights), 'Introducing FRA: The EU Agency for Fundamental Rights', 2, available at fra.europa.eu/sites/default/files/2014-fra-factsheet_en.pdf.

with human rights.[34] The FRA would also have a relationship of cooperation with other EU agencies in the interests of securing a rights-based
approach to policy; a pertinent example for this chapter is Frontex. I examine how cooperation is a relation of government of Frontex through rights in
section III.

Together, these many and various nodal points form the assemblage of
good governance through rights protection in the EU. They represent the
collective of actors who share two characteristics that join them together:
independence and *expertise*. The independence criterion signifies an independence from the Union's institutions and is self-explanatory.[35] It is the
expertise criterion that interests me more.

B. Expertise as Pastoral Power

The complex of multi-level actors referred to share the characteristic of being
experts on fundamental rights issues. Experts are distinguishable by virtue
of the fact that they share 'expertise'—a distinct field of knowledge known
only to experts (that is, 'expert knowledge').[36] This knowledge resembles a
mutual disciplinary sensibility; experts share a set of assumptions, an intellectual history, a vocabulary of arguments, issues about which they disagree
and a style or consciousness.[37] Experts, I argue, also share the sensibility of
'pastoralism'.[38] Given the concern of this chapter and indeed this book with
the 'problem of government', how experts exercise a rationality and operational dynamic that resembles a type of policing and guidance concerned
with well-being in the name of rights is a theme echoed throughout the
chapters. Here I equate the FRA experts with a modern day pastorate that
enacts government (through) rights.

In his *Security, Territory, Population* lectures, Foucault showed a particular interest in the interplay between the (Christian) pastorate of the sixteenth
and seventeenth centuries and *government*.[39] His concern was to show that

---

[34] FRA Regulation, art 10. NGOs dealing with human rights include, eg, Human Rights
Watch, the subject of my next chapter. Other civil society actors referred to in the FRA Regulation are: trade unions and employer's organisations; relevant social and professional organisations; churches, religious, philosophical and non-confessional organisations; universities; and
other qualified experts of European and international bodies and organisations.

[35] See FRA Regulation, art 16 which specifies that '[t]he Agency shall fulfill its tasks in
complete independence'.

[36] D Kennedy, 'Challenging the Expert Rule: The Politics of Global Governance' (2005)
27 *Sydney Law Review* 5.

[37] Ibid.

[38] N Rose, 'The Politics of Life Itself' (2001) 18 *Theory, Culture and Society* 1, 9. I re-visit
the features of pastoral power in relation to a different kinds of expert(s) in Chapter 4.

[39] M Foucault, *Security, Territory, Population, Lectures at the Collège de France 1977–1978*
(M Senellart (ed), G Burchell (trans), Basingstoke, Palgrave Macmillan, 2007) 191.

the pastorate contained its own set of 'techniques and procedures', otherwise called an 'economy of souls'.[40] 'Economy' here can be translated into management, or government, or *conduct*. Hence, within the pastorate we can see a technology of governmentality, whereby the behaviour of individuals, families and communities is regulated through techniques such as the confession, enabling an education, reformation, guidance and ultimately control of all and of each.[41] The pastorate translates into modern forms of governmentality where, through a 'power of care',[42] experts, acting like the modern-day pastor govern through 'education, control, influence, regulation, administration, management, therapy, reformation, guidance'.[43] Pastoral power thus necessitates a relationship of obedience; this much is retained from its early Christian origins. The great new technology of government in this regard I suggest is rights. Rights discourse necessitates obedience (rights are seen as moral standards and require submission) and obedience is secured via more and more disparate mechanisms of *policing* and *guidance*.

In place of policing 'men and things', the FRA's experts primarily police Member States into ensuring compliance with a good governance standard measured through rights. They also police how the Member States should do rights, what the right way to do rights is, how to narrate rights and what rights stories are narrated. It does this by instituting codes of practice, statistical data and empirical findings. The FRA places a great stress on its large-scale surveys, drawing attention, for instance, to EU-MIDIS (European Union Minorities and Discrimination Survey), the first EU-wide survey on the discrimination and vicitimisation of immigrants and ethnic minorities which surveyed 23,500 people from immigrant and ethnic minority groups; the largest ever survey on gender-based violence against women in all EU Member States, surveying 42,000 women; and the largest ever EU-wide survey of lesbian, gay, bisexual and transgender hate crime and discrimination, surveying 93,000 LGBT people.[44] The experts, by providing data and information through conducting surveys are able to define the rights situation in the EU, pointing to examples of good, bad and promising practice in rights and so regulating the correct way in which the Member States and its citizens ought to behave by example.[45] Moreover, expert status allows the

[40] Ibid 192.
[41] Ibid 127. See also M Foucault, '"*Omnes et Singulatem*": Toward A Critique of Political Reason' in M Foucault, *Power*, vol 3, *Essential Works of Foucault 1954–1984* (J Faubion (ed), R Hurley (trans), London, Penguin, 2002) 298.
[42] Foucault, *Security, Territory, Population*, above n 39, 127.
[43] N Rose, *Powers of Freedom: Reframing Political Thought* (Cambridge, Cambridge University Press, 1999) 4.
[44] See fra.europa.eu/en/survey/2012/eu-midis-european-union-minorities-and-discrimination-survey. See FRA (European Union Agency for Fundamental Rights), *EU-MIDIS Main Results Report* (December 2009), available at fra.europa.eu/sites/default/files/fra_uploads/663-FRA-2011_EU_MIDIS_EN.pdf.
[45] See further B Sokhi-Bulley, 'Government(ality) by Experts: Human Rights as Governance' (2011) 22(3) *Law and Critique* 251.

FRA to identify victims in need of protection, for example, ethnic minorities. Of course, this is a recognisably vulnerable group, though, as we shall see, there are problematic implications of casting individuals in this vulnerable light. The policing of the FRA is affirmed by the fact that it is *requested* by virtue of its expertise to conduct this research into vulnerable groups, to formulate opinions on the specific thematic topics within its competence, or to deliver a legal analysis of legislation or of a legislative proposal from a fundamental rights perspective.[46]

In terms of its guidance role, the FRA identifies 'promising practices' in Member States, which are then meant to inform and instruct others on how to behave. The Agency specifies that this 'gives Member States the opportunity to learn about successful models and solutions to common problems from each other'.[47] The FRA's job is thus to facilitate a process of collective learning. So, the Agency for instance produces training materials and organizes training programmes for professionals; for example, the *Handbook on European Non-discrimination Law* (2011) was produced together with the COE and acts as a guide for legal practitioners. Furthermore, 'communicating and raising rights awareness' is described as one of its three tasks (along with collecting and analysing information and data, and providing assistance and expertise) in the FRA Booklet.[48] The assemblage of experts in the FRA thus offers direct guidance for teachers through its Handbook for teachers (2011), which supports teachers providing Holocaust and Human Rights education.[49] Databases (such as the FRA Caselaw Database), social media presence (Facebook, Twitter, LinkedIn, YouTube) and even a mobile app (Fundamental Rights Charter app) are all techniques used by the Agency to increase awareness in rights and to educate professionals and young people in particular. The professionals targeted are those that 'play an important role in delivering or have an impact on our rights, such as teachers, media professionals, the police and legal practitioners'.[50] This educational role demonstrates an exercise of pastoral power, in which *experts* determine the information deemed important to be conveyed (correct rights practice), how it will be conveyed (reports, social media, etc) and to whom (eg select professionals). In this way the FRA is governing by guidance through education in terms of setting the standard for human rights protection and promotion.

---

[46] For example, the European Parliament requested an opinion from the FRA on the proposed Directive on the use of Passenger Name Record (PNR) data in 2011, see FRA (European Union Agency for Fundamental Rights), *FRA Booklet: Who We Are, What We Do, How We Do It* (February 2012) 15, available at fra.europa.eu/sites/default/files/fra-2014-booklet_en_0.pdf.

[47] Ibid 15.

[48] Ibid 7. This role builds on the FRA Regulation (above n 1) and the functions of the FRA outlined therein, see arts 2 and 4.

[49] *FRA Booklet*, above n 46, 17.

[50] Ibid.

Policing and guidance is facilitated by the very way in which FRA does rights, that is, its methodology. The FRA fits into the dominant mode of doing social science research; it produces *socio-legal* research,[51] that is, research that is objective, detached, predominantly quantitative and *technical*.[52] The interest is not so much in personal 'stories'[53] and doing rights according to an 'ethic of caring and accountability'[54] but in producing 'objective, reliable and comparable information and *data*'.[55] This data is collected, recorded, analysed and disseminated through the technical instruments of measurement indicators and through an umbrella approach (or methodology) that seeks to apply the fundamental rights lens to all EU policies, ie a rights-based approach. Indicators and an overarching rights-based approach thus form objective, detached and reliable forms of rule, enabling the FRA to govern through numbers and a fundamental rights lens.

II. TACTIC TWO: INDICATORS

An 'indicator' as 'a thing, especially a trend or fact that indicates the state or level of something'; or, a 'measure, gauge, barometer, index, mark, sign, signal, guide to, standard, touchstone, yardstick, benchmark, criterion, point of reference'.[56] Quite simply, '[i]ndicators are statistical measures that are used to consolidate complex data into a simple number or rank that is meaningful to policy makers and the public'.[57] There are indicators of sustainable development, Millennium Development Goal indicators, governance indicators, and so the list goes on. The stimulus for *human rights* indicators came from the UN Office of the High Commissioner for Human Rights (OHCHR) in 2005 as a popular method for assessing the criteria by which to hold human rights actors to account.[58] The European Commission had previously been involved with the United Nations Development Programme (UNDP) in generating 'governance indicators' to measure

---

[51] Ibid 15.

[52] See H Mander, '"Words from the Heart": Researching People's Stories' (2010) 2(2) *Journal of Human Rights Practice* 252 on the distinction between 'objective' (quantitative) and 'engaged' (qualitative) research.

[53] P Gready, 'Introduction: "Responsibility to the Story"' (2010) 2(2) *Journal of Human Rights Practice* 177, 184.

[54] Mander, '"Words from the Heart"', above n 52, 254.

[55] FRA Regulation, art 4(1)(a) (emphasis added).

[56] United Nations Development Programme (UNDP), *Governance Indicators: A User's Guide* (New York, UNDP Oslo Governance Centre, 2004) 1.

[57] SE Merry, 'Measuring the World: Indicators, Human Rights and Global Governance' (2011) 52(3) *Current Anthropology* 83.

[58] Indicators were originally used in development: note the Human Development Index (HDI), Human Poverty Index (HPI), Gender-related Development Index (GDI) and Gender Empowerment Measure (GEM), indicators listed in the Human Development Reports in 1990.

progress in democracy, human rights and governance.[59] A human rights indicator *measures* compliance with and fulfilment of human rights commitments, progress of human development in human rights terms, and measures the impact/success of particular rights-based development programming.[60]

In 2007, the Commission's 'Strategy on the Rights of the Child' involved asking the FRA to invent indicators to assess how child rights are implemented, protected, respected and promoted across the EU.[61] Since then, FRA experts have worked to construct indicators in the areas of poverty and social inclusion, education, pensions and healthcare, and disability rights.[62] What the FRA adds is a 'rights-friendly' approach to these indicators, that includes considerations of enforceability (eg monitoring complaint mechanisms), substance (criteria pertaining to the indicator area) and equality (disaggregation of data on grounds including gender, age, disability, religion and sexual orientation).[63] The rights of the child indicators provide the most elaborated area of FRA work and involvement and so I look at them here to analyse how indicators not only *measure* 'things' but are a technical and contemporary form of rule.[64] Rights indicators, as compiled by experts like the FRA, represent complex, distant and scientific tactics of governmentality (through) rights.

A. Rights of the Child Indicators

The rights of the child indicators developed by FRA experts follow the OHCHR model of three broad types of indicator: structural (reflecting existing legal institutions and instruments); procedural (reflecting national efforts to implement the structural provisions); and outcome (reflecting individual and collective achievements in the realisation of the rights of children). These are to comply with four general principles outlined in the UN Convention on the Rights of the Child (CRC): participation (listening to children's views); non-discrimination (accommodate diversity to capture the variety of childhood experience); best interests (to ensure that the interests of the child are the paramount concern of all stages of regulation, policy and

---

[59] UNDP, *Governance Indicators*, above n 56.

[60] Rosga and Satterthwaite, 'The Trust in Indicators', above n 12, 257.

[61] Communication from the Commission, *Towards a Strategy on the Rights of the Child*, COM(2006) 367 final (4 July 2006).

[62] M Kjærum (Director of the European Union Agency for Fundamental Rights), Speech at FRA Symposium, Vienna, 12–13 May 2011, available at fra.europa.eu/sites/default/files/fra_uploads/1598-MK-speech-fra-symposium2011.pdf.

[63] Ibid.

[64] Satterthwaite, 'Indicators in Crisis', above n 14, 875. Some of the arguments in this section also appear in B Sokhi-Bulley, 'The EU as a "Virtuous International Actor": Human Rights Indicators and Global Governmentality' in D Schiek (ed), *The EU Economic and Social Model after the Global Crisis: Interdisciplinary Perspectives* (Aldershot, Ashgate, 2013) 187.

decision-making); and, finally, life, survival and development rights (guaranteeing the child the best possible conditions for personal development).[65] The indicators are developed in four areas identified as 'core': family environment and alternative care, protection from exploitation and violence, adequate standard of living and education, citizenship and cultural activities. Each area is further divided into 'indicator groups'. So, for instance, the indicator area 'protection from exploitation and violence' is split into indicator groups (a) child trafficking; (b) sexual and economic exploitation; and (c) violence against children. Each indicator group details 'why the indicator is important to measure'; its basis in the CRC and other international legal instruments; its relevance to EU law; and finally to the indicator list. There are further sub-groups within the groups (eg 'identification of victims' is a sub-group within the group 'child trafficking').[66]

In 2012, following the adoption by the COE's Committee of Ministers of Guidelines on Child-friendly Justice, and of the FRA's project on Children and Justice by the FRA's Management Board, the FRA began developing its indicators in the field of 'civil justice', with a primary focus on family justice: cross-national divorce and parental separation.[67] This focus would be supplemented by two other contexts: children separated from parents as a result of migration, and children and the family reunification process.[68] The FRA is to examine practices and procedures of child participation in justice proceedings, or 'child-friendly justice'. Cross-national divorce and parental separation was deemed to fit into indicator area 'Family environment and alternative care'.[69] 'Family' was thus deemed to be a key area for achieving 'child-friendly justice'. 'A wealth of research literature explores and highlights the role of the family in shaping children's sense of personal and cultural identity, assuring their safety and well-being, and nurturing the life-skills needed to aid their social integration and attainment.'[70] They refer to something called 'the sanctity of the family' (with reference to the CRC and European Convention on Human Rights (ECHR)),[71] which is to

---

[65] See United Nations Convention on the Rights of the Child (CRC), arts 12, 2, 13 and 6; and FRA (European Union Agency for Fundamental Rights), *Developing Indicators for the Protection, Respect and Promotion of Rights of the Child in the European Union, Summary Report* (2009), available at fra.europa.eu/sites/default/files/fra_uploads/358-RightsofChild_summary-report_en.pdf.

[66] FRA (European Union Agency for Fundamental Rights), *Developing Indicators for the Protection, Respect and Promotion of the Rights of the Child in the European Union* (Conference edn, November 2010), available at fra.europa.eu/sites/default/files/fra_uploads/1308-FRA-report-rights-child-conference2010_EN.pdf.

[67] FRA (European Union Agency for Fundamental Rights), 'Child rights indicators in the field of family justice', available at fra.europa.eu/sites/default/files/child-friendly-justice-indicators-v1-0.pdf.

[68] Ibid 3.

[69] Ibid 2.

[70] Ibid 3.

[71] Note CRC, arts 2, 3, 6 and 12 and ECHR, arts 2, 3 and 8.

be interpreted 'beyond the nuclear, traditional heterosexual model'.[72] The result is that two sets of indicators are presented by the FRA, one based on guidelines from the COE and another based on guidelines from two sets of EU Regulations, Brussels II*bis* Regulation (on parental responsibility) and the Maintenance Regulation (relating to maintenance obligations).[73]

The indicators will be, and are being, used to measure limitations and gaps in the current provisions and data. Thus, the indicators drafted according to COE guidelines focus on 'non-discrimination'; the 'right to information'; 'personal data protection'; the 'right to be heard'; 'legal capacity and legal assistance'; 'interdisciplinary approaches'; 'access to child-friendly proceedings'; 'treatment by police/judges/officials/carers'; and 'alternative procedures'.[74] So, for instance, under 'access to child-friendly proceedings', the structural indicator 'existence of legislation which facilitates the access to justice for children to remedy possible violations of their rights, and the use of remedies to protect them, through judicial or non-judicial proceedings' is listed; the corresponding procedural indicators include, 'percentage of court cases that adapted the proceedings to child's pace and attention span, allowing for regular breaks and shorter hearings' and 'percentage of courts having child-friendly facilities for the conduct of proceedings'; and the relevant outcome indicators include 'length of time lapsing between the issuing and the enforcement of a decision concerning children calculated by number of cases per pre-defined time intervals', and 'percentage of children participating in judicial and non-judicial proceedings who evaluate the procedures as appropriate'.[75]

The Brussels II*bis* Regulation indicators are not categorised, nor are they so numerous as the Maintenance Regulation indicators, but replicate and supplement these. They include for instance measurements such as 'international treaties related to child abduction and parental responsibility ratified by the Member State including any possible reservations' (structural indicator); 'percentage of judges, prosecutors, lawyers, law enforcement officers and Central Authorities staff involved in return and access cases trained on international and regional instruments on child abduction/parental responsibilities' (process indicator); and 'percentage of children who declared to have been properly assisted by the social services, court staff, legal counsels,

---

[72] See the jurisprudence on ECHR, art 8 and the FRA, *EU-MIDIS Main Results Report*, above n 44.

[73] Council Regulation (EC) 2201/2003 of 27 November 2003 on jurisdiction and the recognition and enforcement of judgments in matrimonial matters and in matters of parental responsibility [2003] OJ L338 and Council Regulation (EC) 4/2009 of 18 December 2009 on jurisdiction, applicable law and enforcement of decisions and cooperation in matters relating to maintenance obligations [2009] OJ L7.

[74] FRA, 'Child rights indicators', above n 67.

[75] Ibid 9–10.

police services during the access/return proceedings' (outcome indicator).[76] These indicators are intended to be a 'springboard' for future legal policy and research development.[77] This language indicates that they are to provide *impetus* for progress, development in child rights and in achieving child justice. It is through this measurement of 'justice' that indicators *govern*.

B. Measuring Child 'Justice'

The indicators on child justice evidence a tactic of governmentality of and through rights by, on the one hand, determining *what* to measure and, on the other, determining *how* it is measured. This in turn has implications for how we understand rights (and justice), what becomes prioritised, how we understand victim identities (such as the child) and the identity of the EU as a right-eous actor.

In terms of *what* is being measured, the FRA's network of experts will collect data and statistics in certain *priority* areas.[78] The experts and statistics collected through surveys, questionnaires and reports will determine what those priority areas are, that is, how to move forward in protecting and promoting rights of the 'most vulnerable' individuals. Hence the FRA's strategy in the area of child rights focuses currently on *family* justice, on separation from the *family* as a result of migration, and on the *family* reunification process. It thus determines that the *family* is an area of priority. Moreover, it determines what 'justice' in terms of the child's best interests means, and quantifies the factors (the three contexts of family justice: cross-national divorce, separation as a result of migration, reunification with the family) that will provide a measure of justice having been achieved.

The FRA's strategy thus operates via tactics of governmentality, those factors that govern conduct in the name of rights and that govern rights; that determine 'at a distance'[79] how Member States, NGOs, national human rights institutions should act and react to what the FRA's experts and statistics have determined to be the correct way to measure rights. So, for example, to record relevant measures and actions that indicate specific efforts made (process indicators), the FRA will record according to the Commission's criteria the 'percentage of judges, prosecutors, lawyers, law enforcement officers and Central Authorities staff involved in return and access

---

[76] Ibid 12.
[77] Ibid 1.
[78] On a separate critique of statistics as tactics of governmentality, see further B Sokhi-Bulley, 'Governing (Through) Rights: Statistics as Technologies of Governmentality' (2011) 20(2) *Social and Legal Studies* 139.
[79] D Garland, 'Governmentality and the Problem of Crime' (1997) 1 *Theoretical Criminology* 172.

cases trained on international and regional instruments on child abduction/parental responsibilities'.[80] Yet, will measuring, for instance, the 'percentage of children who have received publications in child-friendly format adapted to their needs on the existing norms and proceedings'[81] *achieve* justice? This is not actually the question that is important and this is interesting in itself. What is important is how 'justice' is calculated, that it is assumed to be something that can be calculated and calibrated using rights, that this measurement is considered accurate and objective.

In terms of *how* to measure justice (ie progress in rights, towards achieving child-friendly justice), indicators govern rights by determining how to *do* rights and identifying who is *doing them well*. We saw in the above section how one of the features of governmentality by experts is determining the methodology to be used in rights research. Measurement via indicators represents a methodology whereby structural, process and outcome indicators tell us the situation of rights within a given Member State, which in turn tells us the situation of rights in the EU. The measurement criterion comes to be part of an objective, apolitical and unproblematic equation. Questioning the achievement of *effective* participation of the governed (in this case, children) is an important critique that Rosga and Satterthwaite have made about the effectiveness indicators.[82] The Brussels II*bis* Regulation gives prominence to child participation in family proceedings, and this is reflected in the indicator 'Court system in place to facilitate the *participation* of the applicant in return proceedings (video-conference, telephone)' (structural) and 'Percentage of cases where the court facilitated the *participation* of the applicant in the return proceedings (through video-conference, telephone)' (procedural).[83] Participation is to be facilitated through adherence to the principle of 'competence' whereby Member States are obliged to ascertain the wishes of 'competent' children.[84] There are no indicators on how to measure or quantify competence. How then to equate this to effective participation?

Indicators thus measure those elements (of rights) that can be statistically quantified, so, for instance, the availability of video-conferencing, or telephone as numerical assessments of participation in court proceedings. Defining those elements regulates what becomes good practice, good rights practice and good practice in the name of justice. Much is missing from

---

[80] Indicator based on Brussels II*bis* Regulation, FRA, 'Child rights indicators', above n 67, 12.

[81] An 'outcome indicator', per FRA, 'Child rights indicators', above n 67, 7.

[82] Rosga and Satterthwaite, 'The Trust in Indicators', above n 12. On 'reciprocal research', a methodology that uses a rights framework together with participatory research action, see E Pittaway, L Bartolomei and R Hugman, '"Stop Stealing our Stories": The Ethics of Research with Vulnerable Groups' (2010) 2(2) *Journal of Human Rights Practice* 229.

[83] FRA, 'Child rights indicators', above n 67, 12–13 (emphasis).

[84] Brussells II*bis* Regulation, art 11(2).

this objective, quantitative and detached methodology, such as qualitatively examining (and perhaps not even recording, just hearing) through listening to personal 'stories' whether *effective* participation is *felt* by the child.[85] Yet, measurement becomes what the rights way to do rights is. The EU is then able to appear 'virtuous' when it points to and advocates 'good' and 'promising' practice, and when it names and shames 'bad practice'.

The implementation of the indicators on the rights of the child are to be assessed by means of a 'rights of the child scoreboard' that ranks not just good but 'best practice' in the Member States.[86] Observing the Member States in this way, to determine whether there is an equality body in place, whether there are special support measures in place to ensure child participation, whether there are mechanisms in place to ensure children understand court procedures and court rulings), is a kind of monitoring. But it is not 'monitoring' in the legal sense since 'monitoring' falls outside the agency's competence (which is to provide assistance and expertise only) and is a role reserved only for the 'guardian' body of the EU, the Commission. The FRA, via indicators, exercises a monitoring that can be described as 'auditing'; it monitors monitoring.[87] Auditing is distinguishable for being a form of self-monitoring, or self-government, where the Member State regulates its own behaviour according to a code of conduct, or 'toolkit'.[88] The governmentality relation in the audit is thus self-reinforcing or reflexive; the Member States govern themselves so as to stay high on the scoreboard, to be seen as 'good states', or the 'best states', engaging in 'good or best (rights) practice' and thereby in 'good (or better) governance'.

The implications of this governmentality by indicators are twofold. First, there are implications for the subject identities that are produced as a result of this governmental power relation. The EU is represented as 'right-eous', that is, a virtuous human rights actor;[89] it is 'virtuous' in that it is promoting good governance (less government, as the Member States govern themselves better together) and it is doing so through a set of shared, indisputable norms (human rights) that it is possible to measure and quantify (via indicators). Moreover, a victim identity is continually reproduced. Indicators allow for a determination of who is vulnerable (eg the child), who will then be prioritised, and what features of vulnerability will be prioritised

---

[85] For more on 'alternate methodologies' based on more 'engaged' research see Mander, '"Words from the Heart"', above n 52.

[86] FRA (European Union Agency for Fundamental Rights), *Using Indicators to Measure Fundamental Rights in the EU: Challenges and Solutions*, FRA Symposium Report, Second Annual FRA Symposium, Vienna, 12–13 May 2011, available at fra.europa.eu/sites/default/files/fra_uploads/1697-FRAsymp2011-outcome-report.pdf.

[87] Rosga and Satterthwaite, 'The Trust in Indicators', above n 12, 278.

[88] FRA, *Developing Indicators*, above n 66, 7.

[89] On the 'virtuous' nature of the EU, G de Búrca, 'The European Court of Justice and the International Legal Order after *Kadi*' (2010) 51(1) *Harvard International Law Journal* 1; and Sokhi-Bulley, 'The EU as a "Virtuous International Actor"', above n 64.

(eg family justice)—and then in turn how these victims will be 'saved' via simple mechanisms and solutions (for example, by making court proceedings more child-friendly). Here I looked at children but a similar critique can be applied to the more recent indicator area of persons with disabilities, where 'opportunity', 'capability' and 'creating enabling conditions for political participation' are quantified and thereby managed using rights indicators.[90]

Second, there are implications for critique: What questions should we ask about what to measure and how to do rights? Who are the experts who decide what to measure and how? Who should they be? What methodologies are used to assess vulnerability; to assess participation? Can measurement affect change? Can it achieve 'justice', 'integration'—and what do these terms mean? I am not proposing to have answers to these questions. In fact, I want to ask a bigger question: as a technical discourse of conducting power, is there a limit to what it can measure?

C. Measuring ... Everything

It has been fascinating to watch the FRA grow over the last ten years since its inception. Its assemblage has become more complex as it appropriates more and more experts (see below on Frontex) and expands its areas of expertise. The information and data that it disseminates through reports, press releases, email updates, etc is endless. And it is a task in itself keeping up with the rapid rate at which it is developing rights indicators. In short, the Agency has made rights technical. Rights language is appropriated by experts as they make the rights situation within the Member States and the EU visible and intelligible, and how well the rights situation is doing is now completely *measureable*.

For instance, under the Asylum, Migration and Borders theme, a key and ongoing challenge for the FRA in 2016 is social inclusion and migrant participation in society.[91] According to the Strategic Plan 2013–17, migrant 'integration' should be made possible using a rights-based approach, that is, it should take place within a framework that respects fundamental rights.[92] The indicators will build on the framework of the pilot study regarding common integration indicators completed by Eurostat (the statistical office of the EU),[93] and relevant work by the European Commission,

---

[90] See FRA (European Union Agency for Fundamental Rights), *The Right to Political Participation for Persons with Disabilities: Human Rights Indicators* (May 2014), available at fra. europa.eu/sites/default/files/fra-2014-right-political-participation-persons-disabilities_en.pdf.

[91] See *A Year in Review: FRA 2015*, available at fra.europa.eu/en/news/2015/year-review-fra-2015.

[92] See fra.europa.eu/en/project/2015/social-inclusion-and-migrant-participation-society-0.

[93] See further at europa.eu/eurostat.

the OECD and other actors. Under the theme People with Disabilities, FRA has developed indicators on the right to political participation of people with disabilities.[94] The things being measured are grouped under the four key themes of: lifting legal and administrative barriers; increasing rights awareness; making political participation more accessible; and expanding opportunities for participation.[95] The indicators have been developed by the FRA, in close cooperation with the European Commission and ANED (Academic Network of European Disability Experts).

This burgeoning development of indicators means that rights are made increasingly technical. Developing measurement criteria requires continually and perhaps infinitely extending the expert assemblage of the FRA (to include, for example, Eurostat and ANED) and so making more impenetrable the already complex 'network of networks' that is the FRA. It involves compiling more and more data and information, adding to an already saturated rights discourse. Of course, expert collaboration develops expert knowledge through sharing and the collaboration is in itself skilful and 'right-eous'. Rights discourse ought not to be static, and so extending and elaborating how to do rights and measuring this performance is, actually, progress. And as this happens, as the expert assemblage grows and as information on how to do rights and what rights are is elaborated, so government becomes more diffuse, more invisible, more unquestionable, less resistible—in short, *better*.

Furthermore, 'indicators', as Satterthwaite observes, 'tend to "render technical" the core tensions that led to their creation, displacing rather than solving those issues'.[96] The tensions within, for instance, what it means for the (irregular) migrant to be 'integrated' and what qualifies as 'participation' and for whom tend to dissipate. Answering questions in the affirmative (like, is the migrant in employment or seeking employment? Does the migrant have a good grasp of the language of the host Member State? Does the migrant have children who are attending school in the home Member State?) signals that integration is being achieved. Once we have an indicator we have made progress, we are implementing a rights-based approach and we can identify good practice. Satterthwaite, Rosga and Merry make this point well in relation to human rights indicators and indicators on global governance.[97] Satterthwaite also identifies the *problem*—which is not data and measurement. The problem is that once data becomes codified in an

---

[94] FRA, *The Right to Political Participation*, above n 90.The full set of indicators is also available on the FRA website, fra.europa.eu/en/publications-and-resources/data-and-maps/comparative-data/political-participation.

[95] Ibid.

[96] Satterthwaite, 'Indicators in Crisis', above n 14, 963.

[97] Ibid; Rosga and Satterthwaite, 'The Trust in Indicators', above n 12; Merry, 'Measuring the World', above n 57.

indicator, concerns regarding accountability and ensuring human rights 'tend to retreat from view' and we forget that these tools are only 'one among many possible agreements at the end of a human process'.[98] More importantly for the problem of government through rights indicators, 'indicators tend to *disproportionately empower* those with the *greatest technical expertise*' rather than the disenfranchised who are targeted by these indicators.[99]

Rights indicators are thus tactics of governmentality. The increased focus on measurement in rights, which is done by experts, makes rights technical and thereby coopts rights into being a discourse of conducting power. The extent to which the technology of rights should be resisted by the experts, who are both the *empowered* and those *in power*, who rule through rights at a distance, is then even more pertinent.

III. TACTIC THREE: A RIGHTS-BASED APPROACH

Despite there being no 'universal recipe' for what constitutes a 'rights-based approach', the OHCHR confirms that UN agencies agree on a number of 'essential attributes'.[100] These are that the main objective (of development policies and programmes) be the fulfilment of human rights; that a human-rights based approach identifies rights holders and their entitlements and duty bearers and their obligations, and works towards ameliorating the capacities of rights holders.[101] This approach to doing rights is echoed in the UN 2030 Agenda for Sustainable Development, where a key message from the OHCHR on 'Human Rights and Post-2015' is that 'people should be *empowered* to hold their governments accountable', '*leave no one behind*' and that a 'human-rights based approach to the *collection, production, analysis and dissemination of data*' should be embraced.[102] Crucially, for the purposes of my argument in this chapter, a 'human rights based approach is about ensuring that both the standards and the principles of human rights are *integrated into policymaking* as well as the *day to day running* of organisations'.[103] This is crucial because it explains how a

---

[98] Satterthwaite, 'Indicators in Crisis', above n 14, 963.

[99] Ibid 964 (emphasis added).

[100] UN OHCHR, *Frequently Asked Questions on a Human-Rights Based Approach to Development Cooperation* (New York and Geneva, 2006) 15, available at www.ohchr.org/Documents/Publications/FAQen.pdf.

[101] Ibid.

[102] UN OHCHR, 'Transforming our World: Human Rights in the 2030 Agenda for Sustainable Development', www.ohchr.org/Documents/Issues/MDGs/Post2015/HRAndPost2015.pdf (emphasis added).

[103] Scottish Human Rights Commission, 'What is a Human Rights Based Approach?', www.Scottishhumanrights.Com/Careaboutrights/Whatisahumanrightsbasedapproach (emphasis added).

rights-based approach is a tactic of governmentality; rights become coopted into policy strategies and inform the day to day behaviour of experts within organisations. In this instance, I show how the FRA governs through rights to inform the day to day behaviour of other actors and create problematic identity constructions and entitlements.

The FRA's previous Director confirms the EU's commitment to main-streaming human rights in efforts to avoid a loss of faith in rights and their 'end times'.[104] Perhaps this loss of faith in rights is an accurate symptom of an ever-growing problem the EU now faces: the 'migrant crisis'. This is a 'good crisis' in the sense that it allows for increased intervention from expert actors in the name of human rights violations.[105] Intervention in the name of rights means that the FRA manages the behaviour of other experts, and here I discuss Frontex; this management produces Frontex and in turn the EU as right-eous actors, at the same time as it subjugates the migrant identity and its claim to rights.

A. A Rights-based Approach to Migration

In April 2015, a shipwreck in the Mediterranean off the southern coast of Italy resulted in a death toll of at least 950 men, women and children and what was previously a chronic problem of migration became an acute 'migrant crisis'.[106] The event sparked increased calls for a 'rights-based EU migration policy'.[107] The 2011 Frontex Regulation further confirms that 'development of a forward-looking and comprehensive European migration policy, *based on human rights*, solidarity and responsibility, especially for those Member States facing specific and disproportionate pressures, remains

[104] M Kjærum, 'Human Rights: Early Days or End of Times?', Lecture, 3 November 2015, available at www.ucl.ac.uk/global-governance/ggi-events/humanrightsearlydays. Mainstreaming embodies the idea of a rights-based approach; the UN Entity for Gender Equality and the Empowerment of Women defines 'gender mainstreaming' as a 'strategy, an approach, a means to achieve the goal of gender equality', see www.un.org/womenwatch/osagi/gendermainstreaming.htm.
[105] H Charlesworth, 'International Law: A Discipline of Crisis' (2002) 65(3) *Modern Law Review* 377, 379. For more on an 'ethic of crisis' as a code of conduct for human rights experts, see Chapter 3.
[106] P Kingsley, S Kitchgaessner and A Bonomolo, 'EU ministers meet for crisis talks after hundreds of migrants drown in the Mediterranean', *Guardian*, 25 April 2015, available at www.theguardian.com/world/2015/apr/19/italian-prime-minister-matteo-renzi-emergency-summit-700-drown-mediterranean?CMP=EMCNEWEML6619I2. This figure added to a total of 3,224 deaths in the Mediterranean in 2014, see International Organization for Migration, quoted in FRA (European Union Agency for Fundamental Rights), *Legal Entry Channels to the EU for Persons in Need of International Protection: A Toolbox* (February 2015), available at fra.europa.eu/sites/default/files/fra-focus_02-2015_legal-entry-to-the-eu.pdf.
[107] FRA, 'FRA re-iterates call', above n 13.

a key policy objective for the Union'.[108] The UN Special Rapporteur on the Human Rights of Migrants, François Crépeau, highlighted the absence of such in comment on the Lampedusa tragedy of 3 October 2013 by stating that human rights guarantees for migrants have not been adequately developed.[109] He made the general recommendation that the EU should 'further implement a *human rights-based approach* to migration and border management, ensuring that the rights of migrants, including irregular migrants, are always the first consideration'.[110]

In response to the 2013 Lampedusa tragedy, the EU in conjunction with the Italian state, launched Mare Nostrum, a patrolling, rescue and surveillance operation set up 'to enhance the humanitarian rescue activities in the Mediterranean'.[111] It was considered a manifestation of solidarity and shared responsibility, a principle set out in Article 80 of the Treaty on the Functioning of the European Union (TFEU), yet remained short of funds, with the United Kingdom, for instance, refusing to contribute. Two years later in April 2015, 'A renewed focus on patrolling EU waters' and '[o]ther "fortress Europe" measures' was seen with the revival of operation Triton. This somewhat unsuccessful Triton mission, coordinated by Frontex and set up in November 2014, was also underfunded and less ambitious than the previous Italian Mare Nostrum mission. The EU's focus is thus on patrolling the border rather than on the push factors that drive migrants out of Libya, Syria and Eritrea, for instance, or on the pull factors that attract migrants to the promised land in the first place.[112] This point was underlined by the UN Special Rapporteur and the EU was admonished for it, when Mr Crépeau

---

[108] Council Regulation (EU) 1168/2011 of 25 October 2011 amending Council Regulation (EC) 2007/2004 establishing a European Agency for the Management of Operational Cooperation at the External Borders of the Member States of the European Union [2011] OJ L304/1, recital 1 ('Frontex Regulation').

[109] A shipwreck off the Italian coast resulted in the death of 'at least 360' migrants from Libya. See F Crépeau, *Report of the Special Rapporteur on the Human Rights of Migrants, Regional Study: Management of the External Borders of the European Union and Its Impact on the Human Rights of Migrants* (24 April 2013) 20, para 89, available at www.ohchr.org/Documents/HRBodies/HRCouncil/RegularSession/Session23/A.HRC.23.46_en.pdf; his comments are based on a study of Italy, Greece, Tunisia and Turkey. See the institutional response here: European Parliament Resolution, 'Migratory flows in the Mediterranean, with particular attention to the tragic events off Lampedusa', 2013/2827 (23 October 2013); European Parliament Resolution, 'The situation in the Mediterranean and the need for a holistic EU approach to migration', 2014/2907 (11 December 2014).

[110] Crépeau, *Report of the Special Rapporteur*, above n 109, 20, para 82 (emphasis added). See also UNHCR, 'Saving migrant lives is imperative but what next? UN human rights experts ask EU leaders', Press Release, 24 April 2015, available at www.ohchr.org/EN/NewsEvents/Pages/DisplayNews.aspx?NewsID=15889&LangID=E.

[111] European Parliament Resolution 2013/2827, above n 109, 3, para I.

[112] Human Rights Watch, *The Mediterranean Migration Crisis: Why People Flee, What the EU Should Do* (19 June 2015), available at www.hrw.org/report/2015/06/19/mediterranean-migration-crisis/why-people-flee-what-eu-should-do.

stated in 2013 that the 'repression of irregular migration cannot be the only solution to the recurrent problem of masses of people drowning at sea'.[113] His point, which he repeated in 2014 at the further development of the 'migrant crisis', was that EU leaders' decisions continued to prioritise 'securitisation of borders' without adequate human rights guarantees and this would continue to repeat and exacerbate the abuse of migrants.[114] The EU must, the Special Rapporteur urged, acknowledge the needs of its low-wage labour market and rapidly open up many more legal migration avenues into the 'home'.[115] What was needed more than patrols was the development of a massive resettlement policy and more harm reduction policies that took the *human rights of migrants* as a central concern, incentivising migrants so as to avoid having recourse to smugglers.[116]

The FRA's work under the thematic area of Asylum, Migration and Borders can be seen as a response to this call. It has focused on fundamental rights at borders, the rights of migrants in an irregular situation, and asylum. It has highlighted concerns in access to healthcare, severe forms of labour exploitation and social integration.[117] More recently and in response to the 'crisis' that has seen an influx of refugees, asylum seekers and migrants entering the promised land of the EU, the FRA has been collating weekly updates on the fundamental rights situation of people arriving in those Member States most affected by increasing numbers.[118] It also works in cooperation with Frontex.[119]

B. The Empowered: FRA, Frontex and the EU

Frontex was established to improve the integrated management of the external borders of the EU's Member States, which will be achieved in part by providing the Commission and Member States with 'the necessary technical support and expertise in the management of the external borders

---

[113] F Crépeau, 'EU must develop innovative mobility solutions now to stop deaths at sea', *UN OHCHR News*, 20 April 2015, available at www.ohchr.org/EN/NewsEvents/Pages/DisplayNews.aspx?NewsID=15865&LangID=E.

[114] F Crépeau, *Report of the Special Rapporteur on the Human Rights of Migrants: Labour Exploitation of Migrants* (3 April 2014), available at www.ohchr.org/Documents/Issues/SRMigrants/A.HRC.26.35.pdf.

[115] Ibid.

[116] Crépeau, *Report of the Special Rapporteur*, above n 109.

[117] See the Asylum, Migration and Borders theme of the FRA, available at fra.europa.eu/en/theme/asylum-migration-borders.

[118] These countries are Austria, Bulgaria, Croatia, Germany, Greece, Hungary, Italy and Slovenia, see fra.europa.eu/en/theme/asylum-migration-borders/overviews.

[119] See Frontex Regulation 2011, new art 13, which outlines that Frontex 'may cooperate with ... the European Union Agency for Fundamental Rights'.

and promote solidarity between Member States'.[120] The EU institutions have been mandating agencies to regulate migratory flows; to establish global approaches to mobility; to foster a holistic approach (whilst stressing a focus on the Mediterranean countries such as Italy, Greece and Malta); and enforcing a shared responsibility to tackle securitisation of borders.[121] This includes Frontex and its European Border Guard Teams. The full commitment of Frontex should now be to the 'development of a forward-looking and comprehensive European migration policy, based on *human rights, solidarity and responsibility*, especially for those Member States facing specific and disproportionate pressures'.[122] Interestingly, the Frontex Regulation of 2004 has been amended to include increased references to fundamental rights.[123] The new 2011 Regulation confirms that the 'mandate of the Agency ... be revised in order to strengthen in particular its operational capabilities while ensuring that all measures taken are proportionate to the objectives pursued, are effective and fully respect *fundamental rights*'.[124] The 2011 Regulation specifically identifies a code of conduct based on the principles of the rule of law and respect for fundamental rights;[125] European Border Guard Teams are instructed to 'fully respect fundamental rights' in 'the performance of their tasks and in the exercise of their powers',[126] an instruction that extends to 'other personnel of the Member States' and 'guest officers'.[127] Frontex now has a 'Fundamental Rights Strategy', which requires review from the European Commission and the Council, and Frontex is instructed to 'put in place an effective mechanism to monitor the respect for fundamental rights in all the activities of the Agency'.[128] Not only are rights more often mentioned in the operational framework of the Agency but they are now the *code of conduct* and a *strategy*. Rights are governmental technologies that direct the behaviour of the border guards, the guest officers and other personnel. As a code and strategy of *correct*

---

[120] Council Regulation (EC) 2007/2004 of 26 October 2004 establishing a European Agency for the Management of Operational Cooperation at the External Borders of the Member States of the European Union, arts 1(1) and (3) [2004] OJ L349/1. Note the newer European Border Surveillance System with which Frontex cooperates (Eurosur), see Council Regulation (EU) 1052/2013 of 22 October 2013 establishing the European Border Surveillance System (Eurosur) [2013] OJ L 295/11.

[121] For instance, see European Parliament response, above n 109.

[122] Frontex Regulation 2011, recital 1 (emphasis added).

[123] Ibid. Note the minimal reference to rights in the previous Frontex Regulation 2004, recital 22.

[124] Frontex Regulation 2011, recital 9. Relevant Union law (eg the Charter of Fundamental Rights of the EU) and relevant international law (eg the Convention on the Status of Refugees) is referenced at art 1(1)(2).

[125] Ibid new art 2(a).

[126] Ibid new art 3b(4).

[127] Ibid new art 5(a) and new art 10(2).

[128] Ibid new art 25(2) and 26a.

behaviour, Frontex thus manages itself through rights. Government through rights is thus self-reinforcing and 'reflexive'.[129]

While Frontex is self-governing through rights, it is also governed by the FRA which manages the observance of the fundamental rights strategy. It acknowledges the fundamental rights strategy as an ethical code of conduct, affirming the right-eous identity of Frontex: 'All people involved in Frontex operational activities maintain the highest standards of ethical conduct, professionalism and respect for fundamental rights'.[130] And it engages in both a disciplinary a pastoral role, at once observing and monitoring Frontex and its adherence to rights,[131] whilst providing expertise and guidance on how it ought to behave. The guidance is 'an art of conducting, directing, leading, guiding ... and manipulating'[132] that represents a type of pastoral power through 'care' and a 'directing of conscience'.[133] It targets the experts, polices the activities of Frontex through calculated, technical practices. For instance, the FRA will read Frontex evaluation reports through a 'fundamental rights lens' (these reports are required for each operation and presented to FRA's Management Board).[134] The FRA thus magnifies how (and whether) Frontex operations maintain and fulfil a code of conduct based in rights. This surveillance of Frontex allows the FRA to draw conclusions that point to shortcomings in observance of the code. For instance, one report notes that fundamental rights are not part of the indicators used to measure achievements in the area of borders and visas; in fact, rights language does not feature significantly enough in the instruments on borders and visas.[135] The FRA is thus able to pronounce that in the interests of EU solidarity (in terms of coherence in measures established to support those countries most affected by irregular arrivals by sea), a rights-based approach is the right code of conduct for Frontex. FRA thus governs this additional layer of experts (ie Frontex) through rights. And the wider implication is that rights become a technical form of government; they become the right way for experts who are part of a right-ous EU to behave.

In educating, surveilling and guiding, the FRA is also managing this right-eous identity of the EU more broadly, allowing it to present its migration policy as rights-based in the face of massive criticism from European civil

---

[129] M Dean, *Governmentality: Power and Rule in Modern Society* (London, Sage, 1999) 2.

[130] FRONTEX Operational Plan, Poseiden Sea 2011, cited in FRA (European Union Agency for Fundamental Rights), *EU Solidarity and FRONTEX: Fundamental Rights Challenges* (14 September 2013) 12, available at fra.europa.eu/sites/default/files/tk3113808enc.pdf.

[131] For more on observation as disciplinary power in the context of FRA, see B Sokhi-Bulley, 'The Fundamental Rights Agency of the EU: A New Panopticism' (2011) 11(4) *Human Rights Law Review* 683.

[132] Foucault, *Security, Territory, Population*, above n 39, 165.

[133] B Golder, 'Foucault and the Genealogy of Pastoral Power' (2007) 10(2) *Radical Philosophy Review* 157, 167.

[134] FRA, *Solidarity with Frontex Report*, above n 130, 13.

[135] Ibid 16.

society, NGOs and charities.[136] The Commission's 'European Agenda on Migration' of May 2015 thus emphasises the role that rights have come to play.[137] The Agenda is about 'reinforcing protection of the *fundamental rights* of asylum-seekers, paying particular attention to the needs of vulnerable groups, such as children' and promises to issue 'guidance to facilitate systematic fingerprinting, in full respect of fundamental rights'.[138] The FRA, under request from the Commission, will continue to provide the updates on migration-related fundamental rights concerns that I mentioned earlier.[139] The FRA experts (here, its cooperative research network, FRANET) through the collection of data and information on these updates, as well as through the data and information compiled within the many and various reports prepared under the Asylum, Migration and Borders theme, narrate a story about the EU as a virtuous human rights actor.[140] The Union, the story says, is a place where rights holders are identified and empowered. FRA thus governs the identity of the Union through rights. Rights, as a coopted discourse of conducting power which tells us that the rights way to *do* migration is to be 'coherent' and that this means respecting fundamental rights, thus govern the identity of the Union.

Hence, a rights-based approach to migration policy allows the FRA experts to govern Frontex in the way it acts in relation to migrants. It also allows FRA to govern the identity of the EU as a right-eous actor in the face of a crisis supported by a policy that has been one of the most damaging with respect to EUrope's international image.[141] And, it also allows for the better management of migrants such that they are regulated more effectively, more efficiently and in a manner that is more caring. The rights-based approach thus empowers expertise: the FRA, Frontex and the EU are the empowered; they are the right-eous actors who seek to empower *others*, to leave no one behind and to collect, produce, analyse and disseminate data right-eously by integrating rights into policy-making and their day to day running.

---

[136] Deutsche Welle, 'Amnesty International Slams EU Migrant Policy in Fortress Europe Report', 9 July 2014, available at www.dw.com/en/amnesty-international-slams-eu-migrant-policy-in-fortress-europe-report/a-17769353.

[137] Communication from the Commission, *A European Agenda on Migration*, COM(2015)240 final (13 May 2015); see further Communication from the Commission, *Managing the Refugee Crisis: State of Play of the Implementation of the Priority Actions under the European Agenda on Migration*, COM(2015)510 final (14 October 2015).

[138] Communication from the Commission of 13 May 2015, above n 137, 12 and 13.

[139] See fra.europa.eu/en/theme/asylum-migration-borders/overviews; and FRA (European Union Agency for Fundamental Rights), *Weekly Data Collection on the Situation of Persons in Need of International Protection*, Update #1 (28 September–2 October 2015), available at fra.europa.eu/sites/default/files/fra_uploads/fra-2015-weekly-compilation-1_en.pdf.

[140] See Sokhi-Bulley, 'Governing (Through) Rights', above n 78 for more on how numerical technologies create this virtuous international actor identity.

[141] See eg, D Johnson, 'This migration crisis could test the European project to destruction', *Daily Telegraph*, 26 August 2015, available at www.telegraph.co.uk/news/worldnews/europe/germany/11826675/This-migration-crisis-could-test-the-European-project-to-destruction.html.

Yet in all this, the migrant as a rights-holding identity is 'left behind'. In the face of the 'supra-citizens' that make up the FRA, Frontex and the wider EU expert network (for it is expertise that brings the 'supra' quality), migrants are produced as 'sub-citizens'[142] or 'illegitimate rights claimants'.[143]

C. The 'Left Behind': The Migrant

Following urging from the UN Special Rapporteur to '[a]void criminalization of irregular migrants in language, policies and practice, and refrain from using incorrect terminology such as "illegal migrant"',[144] the Commission and the FRA have actively abandoned the use of the term. 'Irregular migrant' is now used to refer to third country nationals who do not have valid authorisation to stay or reside, having entered the EU by improper means or become irregular as they overstay the period to which they are entitled.[145] The FRA recognises a difference between legal migrants and illegal ('irregular') migrants; the latter are still human beings and so should not be deprived of certain basic rights shared by all human beings due to non-compliance with the conditions for entry, stay or residence in the EU.[146] The FRA is concerned with the fundamental rights implications for irregular migrants of the imposition of criminal measures by Member States to deter irregular migrants from entering or staying in their territory, in particular, the right to liberty and security of person, human dignity, the right to life, right to an effective remedy and access to social rights such as housing.[147]

---

[142] On supra-citizens (as, for example, human rights workers) and sub-citizens within the international refugee regime, see KB Sandvik, 'Review Essay: Unpacking World Refugee Day: Humanitarian Governance and Human Rights Practice' (2010) 2(2) *Journal of Human Rights Practice* 287, 290.

[143] KB Sandvik, 'Rights-based Humanitarianism as Emancipation or Stratification? Rumours and Procedures of Verification in Urban Refugee Management in Kampala, Uganda' in B Derman, A Hellum and KB Sandvik, *Worlds of Human Rights: The Ambiguities of Rights-Claiming in Africa* (Leiden, Koninklijke Brill NV, 2013) 257.

[144] Crépeau, *Report of the Special Rapporteur*, above n 109, 20, para 89.

[145] FRA (European Union Agency for Fundamental Rights), *Fundamental Rights of Migrants in an Irregular Situation, Comparative Report* (2011), available at fra.europa.eu/sites/default/files/fra_uploads/1827-FRA_2011_Migrants_in_an_irregular_situation_EN.pdf. There are two broad sub-groups of irregular migrant: undetected persons (migrants who live in hiding and have no residence status), and non-removed persons (migrants known to the immigration authorities, issued with an expulsion or return decision, but not yet removed usually for humanitarian reasons). Note that the FRA specifies that persons *not* considered to be in an irregular situation are: 'asylum seekers and persons granted refugee status or subsidiary protection; persons working in breach of their visa or residence permit (these persons are not included, as they (still) have a right to stay in an EU Member State)', 16.

[146] Ibid 7.

[147] FRA (European Union Agency for Fundamental Rights), *Criminalisation of Migrants in an Irregular Situation and of Persons Engaging with Them* (March 2014) 1, available at fra.europa.eu/en/publication/2014/criminalisation-migrants-irregular-situation-and-persons-engaging-them. These rights are found in arts 6(1) (liberty and security), 1 (dignity),

Yet, I argue here that the FRA's rights-based approach to migration entrenches an existing security-based government. Government through rights only adds *minimal* rights to swift return, proportionate detention or imprisonment and an unenforceable right to compassion. Far from ensuring that no one is 'left behind', the irregular migrant is actually left behind, disempowered and unable to claim the rights she wants. Moreover, rights cannot be used as a language of resistance to the EU or to its Member States since it has been appropriated as a language, a mode, by which the government of her left behind status is happening.

The status of the irregular migrant must be 'regularised' or she will be issued with a return decision, and perhaps detained during the removal process or even imprisoned.[148] It is not entirely clear what being 'regularised' means: does it mean she will be treated as a 'regular' human being, with rights? That regularisation implies leave, that is the right, to stay or remain is implied. Detention can be from six up to 18 months.[149] Imprisonment, and fines, for both irregular entry and stay are enforced by almost all Member States.[150] Some Member States also punish facilitation of entry or stay with fines or imprisonment or both,[151] although where the crime is committed for reasons of 'strong human compassion' this can constitute mitigating circumstances.[152] The FRA's position is that punishment for irregular entry or stay must not take precedence over applying the Return Directive and consequently adhering to its fundamental rights safeguards.[153] The state of limbo that many non-removed irregular migrants, who have been in a Member State for a sustained period of time,[154] find themselves in (also termed a 'tolerated' state in which they do not (yet) have residence) should be avoided and basic rights should be guaranteed during

---

2 (life), 47 (effective remedy) of the European Convention on Human Rights and in art 1 of Council Directive 2008/115/EC of 16 December 2008 on common standards and procedures in Member States for returning illegally staying third-country nationals ('Return Directive') [2008] OJ L348 (a general human rights obligations provision).

[148] FRA, *Criminalisation of Migrants*, above n 147, 3; and Return Directive, art 6.

[149] Return Directive, art 15. See also C-357/09 *Kadzoev* [2009] ECR I-11189 (30 November 2009) para 72(1), where the Court of Justice of the European Union confirmed that the maximum period of 18 months cannot be exceeded in any circumstances.

[150] See FRA, *Criminalisation of Migrants*, above n 147, 4–5 for details; for example, the maximum length of imprisonment for irregular entry is five years (Bulgaria); for irregular stay, the maximum imprisonment is three years (Cyrpus); and fines for irregular entry and stay can be up to 10,000 euros (Italy).

[151] FRA, *Criminalisation of Migrants*, above n 147, 9. See Council Directive 2002/90/EC of 28 November 2002 defining the facilitation of unauthorised entry, transit and residence ('Facilitation Directive') [2002] OJ L328/17, enacted to combat smuggling in human beings.

[152] This is a criterion used in assessing the punishment for facilitation of entry or stay in Sweden, for example, see FRA, *Criminalisation of Migrants*, above n 147, 9.

[153] Ibid 15.

[154] See Return Directive, recital 12, on the status of this category of non-removed persons.

this time.[155] At present, these migrants risk violations of their fundamental rights;[156] the safeguards in the Return Directive, which cover a right to family unity with family members, emergency healthcare and access to education for minors, should be respected, and the FRA also points out that these safeguards do not cover all rights.[157]

It is important to mention that Member States of course have a right to control immigration. The FRA is not disputing this but pointing out that irregular migrants face (risk of) exploitation and their rights are precarious and unevenly protected.[158] For instance, the negative effect and disproportionate impact on the effective exercise of fundamental rights of migrants is visible in measures such as workplace inspections that are checks on immigration, arrest in front of schools and routine searches of accommodation.[159] Evidence of negative sentiment that adds to the precariousness of the irregular migrant status is rife. For instance, in the wake of attacks in Cologne, Germany on New Year's Eve 2015, that were said to be perpetrated by 'about 1,000 men, described as coming from "the Arab or North African region"',[160] the German Chancellor has spoken of making it easier to deport migrants who commit crimes, posing a direct threat to Germany's *Willkommenskultur* (welcome culture) and the ability of the always and already criminalised migrant to effectively claim rights.[161]

But my focus is not on what the Member States are doing, rather on what the FRA is doing by virtue of its expertise. The FRA is doing good governance through rights, as it is mandated to do. On the Cologne events, the FRA's Director comments: 'There is no hierarchy of rights holders: respect must be shown to everyone ... The events of last month must not be used as an excuse to incite prejudice against migrants or any other groups'.[162]

---

[155] FRA, *Fundamental Rights of Migrants*, above n 145, 13. 'Toleration', which can be both informal (migrant is in limbo) and formal (migrant has a toleration permit but not a residence permit), is an in-between stage in situations where temporary residence can be granted.

[156] Ibid 36.

[157] Ibid 38 and Return Directive, art 14(1). Moreover, the rights only apply where removal has been formally postponed.

[158] FRA, *Fundamental Rights of Migrants*, above n 145, 17. The FRA specifically mentioned a concern regarding enforcement measures, the labour market, housing situations, healthcare and access to education, 19–21.

[159] Ibid 17 and 39.

[160] SA Harris, 'Angela Merkel says she'll consider making it easier to deport migrants who commit crimes in the wake of Cologne attacks', *Huffington Post*, 9 January 2016, available at www.huffingtonpost.co.uk/2016/01/09/angela-merkel-deport-migrants-crimes-cologne-attacks_n_8943508.html.

[161] D Akrap, 'Germany's welcome for refugees has to survive the Cologne attacks', *Guardian*, 10 January 2016, available at www.theguardian.com/commentisfree/2016/jan/10/ensure-germany-welcome-refugees-cologne-attacks.

[162] Michael O'Flaherty, FRA Director since 16 December 2015, 'FRA calls for action to end widespread violence against women throughout the EU', *FRA News*, 13 January 2016, available at fra.europa.eu/en/news/2016/fra-calls-action-end-widespread-violence-against-women-throughout-eu.

The FRA is also, in doing good governance, implementing a rights-based approach to migration. The rights-based approach of the FRA, as it reads the treatment of (irregular) migrants through a fundamental rights lens, *governs* their status. It advocates swift return and non-imprisonment; it allows for compassion that exempts punishment (but this may exclude the humanitarian, and not the migrant herself, from punishment). The migrant does not have the rights *she wants*, that is to enter, stay and remain; the right to work and exist as *not* a threat to security. Thus the fundamental rights implications that the FRA is concerned with, that the rights-based approach is meant to empower the migrant towards obtaining (that is, protection of liberty and security of person, dignity, life, effective remedy and social rights such as housing) become illegitimate claims. The migrant is constructed as an 'illegitimate rights claimant';[163] whilst at the same time the FRA and the EU are managed into being right-eous actors. The language of needing to be 'regularised', of being *not* tolerated (since the focus of the rights-based approach is effectively on a right-eous *return*), of being 'undesired',[164] perpetuates the illegitimate nature of the migrant identity and its claim to rights. It is thus not the migrant that the rights-based approach empowers but the experts—not the sub-citizen but the supra-citizens, the ones *doing* rights.

IV. CONCLUSION

> Would any of you ever consider driving at night in the countryside without turning your headlights on? ... If [none] would be so careless as to drive in the dark, how can we be comfortable with this situation when it comes to fundamental rights? ... If we want to move fundamental rights from globally agreed, abstract, rhetorical standards, to the level of local, practical implementation, then policy makers need headlights; they require a solid base of evidence ... [L]et us turn on the headlights, so that we can drive progress forward without losing our way.[165]

It would seem that the FRA is steering its way towards 'progress' using experts, a rights-based approach to its thematic areas, and indicators as its headlights. The road is mapped out in terms of good governance and paved in a language of rights. Of course, 'the desire to measure progress is compelling',[166] particularly in the context of 'crisis' and the current

---

[163] Sandvik, 'Rights-based Humanitarianism as Emancipation or Stratification', above n 143, 257.

[164] The Dutch Aliens Act 2014 actually uses this terminology, punishing the stay of an alien declared 'undesired': see FRA, *Criminalisation of Migrants*, above n 147, 5.

[165] Kjærum, Speech at FRA Symposium, above n 62.

[166] Satterthwaite, 'Indicators in Crisis', above n 14, 870.

migration problem with which the EU is faced, as well as the perpetual crisis of the threatened 'end times' of human rights.[167] I am not criticising the work of the FRA (and) rights experts in this chapter. I have not conducted face-to-face interviews with them, asked them what they understand a rights-based approach to mean, or what they see as the value of measuring rights; this is perhaps a legitimate criticism of the way I have done my own research on rights. I have met some of them and talked with them and, though I have questions they might not have and a critical attitude they do not share, I of course respect their work. The way in which (FRA) experts converse, share knowledge and develop links with other networks is masterly, even necessary, as is their work towards establishing and maintaining a rights-based approach to problems, and to make these problems knowable and solvable by making them measurable through rights indicators. What I am calling for is an interrogation of who these experts are, how they measure progress, how a rights-based approach is defined and measured, and how indicators are formed and applied. I am engaging in *critique* and, as such, my role is to interrogate 'progress' and to remain *dissatisfied* with the expert assemblage, with how we do rights through a rights-based approach and how we measure rights through indicators. I have been interested in asking *what else* experts and their rights-based approach does besides make progress, enact good governance and promote good practice in rights.

So I agree, as noted above, with Satterthwaite and her critique that indicators 'render technical' core tensions. I agree with Merry that indicators 'are fundamental to modern forms of governmentality'.[168] To them, I would add the notion of *complexity* and the specificity of the EUropean context, in which new modes of governance create new agencies to *do rights better*. And what *else* happens is that the complexity of the expert assemblage, which adheres to a rights-based approach that it then applies to measure and calculate good governance through rights in more and more thematic areas, becomes *good government* through rights. Experts and their methodology thus *govern rights better.* The FRA, as a governance agency responsible for providing 'assistance and expertise' to the EU and its Member States, *governs* through its experts 'by information, advice, persuasion and learning'.[169] It has a pastoral function that governs the behaviour of other EU experts that it instructs to apply a rights-based approach (ie Frontex), categorising them and in turn the EU as empowered, right-eous actors. Meanwhile, certain subject identities are 'left behind', with minimal claims to rights and no effective recourse to rights as a language of resistance because it has been coopted as a language of government.

---

[167] Kjærum, 'Human Rights: Early Days or End of Times?', above n 104.
[168] Merry, 'Measuring the World', above n 57, 83.
[169] G de Búrca, 'New Modes of Governance and the Protection of Human Rights' in P Alston and O de Schutter (eds), *Monitoring Fundamental Rights in the EU: The Contribution of the Fundamental Rights Agency* (Oxford, Hart, 2005) 36.

The tactics of governmentality I have explored in this chapter (expertise, indicators and a rights-based approach) represent a new form of rule. It is not 'ruling' in the sense of sovereign authority but a far more discrete, ingrained, participatory form of government where the combination of an assemblage of experts, rights indicators and the rights-based approach to (controversial) policies manage behaviour and construct identities based on slogans of good governance spoken in a language of rights. Rights become a technical form of government: authentic (numbers do not lie); concealed (the expert structure is complex); and self-reinforcing (the rights-based approach is the right way to do good governance). In the human rights agency context, we can now recognise this organ as a 'great new instrument of government'.[170]

This 'great new instrument of government' can be applied to more than the EU context; it is a model for rights protection in the international sphere—and rights can therefore be construed as a great technology of *global* governmentality, pushing the concept of governmentality beyond nation-state boundaries and into the sphere of the supranational (EU) and international. The latter becomes the focus of my next chapter, as I expand the definition of global governmentality and look at the operation of governmentality in the context of another, wider assemblage: the international non-governmental organisation (INGO). What tactics does the INGO use to govern (through) rights? Are they similar, or are they in competition with those of a regional agency such as the FRA? What form of 'rule' does the INGO exercise and what ethical questions does this raise?

Finally, a key question in this discussion becomes: Can the form of rule be resisted? Can the FRA resist government through rights? Experts are not rulers. And I am sure that my FRA contacts would be horrified at such an observation. They are, rather, 'the good guys, the ones trying to make things better'.[171] Perhaps this means, or can mean, something else besides what we conventionally understand as 'progress' in rights. Perhaps these unwitting governors have a duty to take part in a 'new interventionist politics of rights'[172] which involves a *duty* to expose where rights fail. This would be a duty to interrogate how rights shape a problematic understanding of progress, good practice and good governance. And I explore it a little further in Chapter 6.

---

[170] Foucault, *Discipline and Punish*, above n 9, 206.

[171] D Kennedy, *The Dark Sides of Virtue: Reassessing International Humanitarianism* (Princeton, NJ, Princeton University Press, 2004) xix.

[172] J Whyte, 'Is Revolution Desirable? Michel Foucault on Revolution, Neoliberalism and Rights' in B Golder (ed), *Re-Reading Foucault: On Law, Power and Rights* (Abingdon, Routledge, 2012) 207, 210.

3

Governing (Through) Non-Governmental Actors: The Global Human Rights Architecture and the International NGO

> We have a hard time focusing on costs in part because we do not think of ourselves as rulers. *Other* people govern, and it is our job to hold *them* responsible. It seems perverse to blame the humanitarians—the good guys, the ones trying to make things better.
>
> David Kennedy[1]

> I will therefore use the expression 'humanitarian government' to designate the deployment of moral sentiments in global politics.
>
> Didier Fassin[2]

WHAT DOES IT mean 'to rule'? Humanitarianism refers to that 'impulse to do good',[3] to 'saving lives'[4] and to 'good intentions'[5] that produces heroic results. Given this, humanitarians, surely, resist (state) power and hold it to account and so it does seem perverse to 'blame the good guys'. But apportioning blame is not the objective of a critique of humanitarianism—or, to more accurately depict what I am attempting to do here—of a critique of a humanitarianism that employs human

---

[1] D Kennedy, *The Dark Sides of Virtue: Reassessing International Humanitarianism* (Princeton, NJ, Princeton University Press, 2004) xix (emphasis in original).

[2] D Fassin, *Humanitarian Reason: A Moral History of the Present* (Berkeley and Los Angeles, CA, University of California Press, 2012) 1.

[3] Kennedy, *The Dark Sides of Virtue*, above n 1, xiv.

[4] P Redfield, *Life in Crisis: The Ethical Journey of Doctors Without Borders* (Oakland, CA, University of California Press, 2013) 1.

[5] DA Bell, 'Introduction: Reflections on Dialogues between Practitioners and Theorists of Human Rights' in DA Bell and J-M Coicaud, *Ethics in Action: The Ethical Challenges of International Human Rights Non-Governmental Organisations* (Cambridge, Cambridge University Press, 2007) 1.

rights as its main language of conversation and negotiation. How to do this critique is the classic dilemma for the academic. I am not a humanitarian. I am not a human rights activist. I am not a human rights policy-maker. I have not, then, worked 'in the field' or shared experiences of 'their (victims, witnesses) stories', or been any part of the 'kaleidoscope of form and fancy' that are the 'lawyers and activists, doctrines and institutions, dreamers and tacticians'[6] that sit locked away together for hours drafting new legislation and policies before returning to their real worlds. How could I possibly have a conception of the practical essence of the international human rights/ humanitarian non-governmental organisation (INGO) that seeks, through good intentions, to do good and save lives? How can I, to echo the sentiment of this book, take a position of dissatisfaction or refusal towards the work of 'the good guys'? I have two responses to this. The first is that I am interested, in my critique of the role of the INGO, in an academic engagement with a type of governmental rationality that is employed and that manifests itself in the working procedures and effects of these rights actors. The second is that I believe all critique is practical; whilst I may not be engaging in ethnography or first-hand research 'out there' in the field,[7] empirical critical research of the kind I attempt in this chapter is a way of thinking about the processes of international human rights *practice* that is in itself a practical exercise with practical implications. I am thus interested not in a perverse activity of blaming or in blind refusal but in asking *what else* (besides 'good') does international humanitarianism that employs a language of rights do? The 'what else' does not equate to 'bad' effects; it simply equates to making visible the other side, the 'dark sides',[8] or the *dangerous* sides of humanitarianism through rights. These are the sides where 'rulers' are created and operate without a responsibilised humanitarian ethic; where government happens in the name of less government and we do not stop to interrogate *what else* is going on.

The guise of rulership is governance. INGOs resemble the contemporary form of governing which I identify throughout the book as governmentality (through) rights. 'To govern, and not simply to rule, any legitimate sovereign needed a growing cadre of experts.'[9] These experts are the humanitarians, the rights activists, who are typically identified as the 'good guys'; they are

---

[6] Kennedy, *The Dark Sides of Virtue*, above n 1, 91.

[7] On the value of an ethnographic approach to untangle the complex of social relations within the intersection between humanitarian action and human rights, see KB Sandvik, 'Introduction to The Multiple Tracks of Human Rights and Humanitarianism' and 'Rights-Based Humanitarianism as Emancipation or Stratification? Rumours and Procedures of Verification in Urban Refugee Management in Kampala, Uganda' in B Derman, A Hellum and KB Sandvik, *Worlds of Human Rights: The Ambiguities of Rights-Claiming in Africa* (Leiden, Koninklijke Brill NV, 2013) 245 and 257, respectively.

[8] Kennedy, above n 1.

[9] Redfield, *Life in Crisis*, above n 4, 18.

also the 'active partners' in governmentality, where rights is the discourse of conducting (rather than sovereign) power. I look, in this chapter, at a wider technology of government that operates within a space of power that we can call the 'international' or the 'global'. So, I am interested here in global human rights governance, or the wider global human rights architecture.

My objective in this chapter is thus to show how a global governmentality (through) rights happens through INGOs. It is to observe and break down, on the one hand, the type of governmental rationality that governs through civil society actors and to thereby show how these actors perform a governing *of rights*, and also how *through rights* these actors are constructed as a new kind of subject in rights; as active participants in govermentality. On the other hand, I aim to examine the further regulatory potential of rights discourse and how it manages INGOs into self-regulation; the INGO governs itself, engaging in an ethic of care of the self so as to become and remain a suitable participant in governance. The implications of this government by civil society human rights actors, who act in the name of saving lives, 'keeping the flame'[10] and pressuring 'those in power',[11] lead to a series of challenging questions about how INGOs ought to behave, and I address these at the very end of the chapter. I begin in section I by defining 'global human rights architecture' in terms of the importance of the 'global', of 'architecture', of the languages of rights and humanitarianism that actors use to speak to each other, and compare (section II) the humanitarian and human rights INGO. Through my example of one of the largest international non-governmental organisations, Human Rights Watch (HRW), I show in section III how the INGO as expert, as narrator and as a self-scrutiniser contributes to a global governmentality of rights.

Let me first confess and address two ways in which my critique is perhaps a little remiss. I make, first, a contestable conflation between the discourses of human rights and humanitarianism. These two discourses do obviously have different historical lineages and form distinct disciplines (human rights law and humanitarian law, for example) and so perhaps 'require careful disentangling from one another'.[12] Yet, they also share the objective of

---

[10] Taken from S Hopgood, *Keepers of the Flame: Understanding Amnesty International* (Ithica, NY, Cornell University Press, 2006).

[11] See HRW's mission statement: 'Human Rights Watch defends the rights of people worldwide. We scrupulously investigate abuses, expose the facts widely, and *pressure those with power* to respect rights and secure justice. Human Rights Watch is an independent, international organization that works as part of a vibrant movement to uphold human dignity and advance the cause of human rights for all.' (Emphasis added), see www.hrw.org/about.

[12] RA Wilson and RD Brown, 'Introduction' in RA Wilson and RD Brown (eds), *Humanitarianism and Suffering: The Mobilization of Empathy* (Cambridge, Cambridge University Press, 2009) 1, 7. See also S Moyn, 'On the Genealogy of Morals', *Nation*, 16 April 2007, 25. On the idea of an '*acquis* humanitaire', see D Cubie, 'Clarifying the Acquis Humanitaire: A Transnational Legal Perspective on the Internationalization of Humanitarian Law' in DD Caren, MJ Kelly and A Telesetsky (eds), *The International Law of Disaster Relief* (Cambridge, Cambridge University Press, 2014).

'protecting the human'[13] and the 'essential characteristics of human welfare and human dignity'.[14] I conflate them because I am describing here how a type of 'humanitarian government'[15] happens that relies on a concern with welfare and dignity; a type of government that is humanitarian in its ethos (employing methodologies and behaving in a way that ensures protecting the human—its welfare, its dignity via a 'relation of care')[16] but that is made possible through a language of rights. Further, there are similarities in how human rights and humanitarian actors *behave* in terms of the 'ethic of crisis'[17] that they use to justify how they *do* rights and how they *do* humanitarianism (hence I include deliberate reference in the chapter to Médicins sans Frontières (MSF) for a comparison of the ethic of crisis). Second, I am perhaps careless in how I use 'non-governmental actor'. My focus is on the *international* NGO (specifically HRW) and this ignores the NGO: the regional, national, local and community organisations that might govern (through) rights. Yet this is a deliberate move; I am interested in the global human rights architecture and in how a global governmentality is made possible by the 'giants' that act on this international scale. Human rights language tends to conflate experts; and yet there are specifics, in terms of deliberate expert tactics and numerical technologies, that the international NGO, specifically HRW but also Amnesty International, uses to perform a global governmentality (through) rights. A focus on the specifics—the minor, mundane and everyday processes that the INGO uses and that make it an expert, a narrator and a scrutinizer—allows for a more convincing assessment of humanitarian government (through) rights.

I. A GLOBAL HUMAN RIGHTS ARCHITECTURE

There is something 'intuitively appealing' about the term *architecture* when discussing the global human rights regime.[18] 'The language of *design* provides a reassuring sense of *structure* to often highly decentralized, loosely coupled realms of politics.'[19] As 'design' with a focus on 'structure', I understand

---

[13] 'Protect the Human' has been a global campaign of Amnesty International (see 'Amnesty International's Protect the Human campaign', *Guardian*, 21 September 2008, available at www.theguardian.com/world/gallery/2008/sep/21/amnesty.international).

[14] Wilson and Brown, 'Introduction', above n 12, 5. Note that HRW, as part of its Core Values, states: 'Our work is guided by international human rights and humanitarian law and respect for the dignity of each human being', see www.hrw.org/about.

[15] Fassin, *Humanitarian Reason*, above n 2, 1.

[16] P Redfield, 'Conclusion: A Measured Good' in S Ambramowitz and C Panter-Brick, *Medical Humanitarianism: Ehtnographies of Practice* (Philadelphia, PA, University of Philadelphia Press, 2015) 242.

[17] Redfield, *Life in Crisis*, above n 4, 33–34.

[18] T Pegram, 'Governing Relationships: The New Architecture in Global Human Rights Governance' (2015) 43(2) *Millenium: Journal of International Studies* 618, 625.

[19] Ibid (emphasis added).

architecture as a useful tool, schema or lens by which to illustrate and comprehend connections and linkages between actors in 'spaces above, beyond, between and across states'.[20] That is, the space of the 'global', which I use in a rather loose sense to mean beyond the national but involving the transnational (ie the EU context I previously talked about). *Human rights* architecture has arguably gone from being about 'human rights' to being about 'Human Rights', where the latter represents a global structure of laws, courts, norms and organisations that raise money, write reports, run international campaigns, etc.[21] But far from seeing what Hopgood calls the 'endtimes' of Human Rights, we are I think seeing in contrast a proliferation of human rights *plus* Human Rights; a humanitarian concern with dignity and intrusion into more spheres of rights protection including economic and social rights by organisations that claim expertise in and knowledge of 'the human'. Perhaps we need new terms to understand this global architecture of human rights—and, though the term is not 'new' in terms of academic engagement with it, I argue for a (re)turn to *global governmentality*.[22]

The focus of a global governmentality perspective is on recognizing the actors in the architecture of rights but also on acknowledging *how power is exercised* through the 'multi-layered and polyarchic networks'[23] that make up the global rights design. The architecture is of a *flat* design within which there is no set hierarchy; and I could have used the tool of 'network', or more specifically actor-network-theory (ANT) to describe the 'flows of translations' (or relations) within the space of civil society that I refer to here.[24] But I will not pretend to be so robust or thorough in my use of 'network'; I simply borrow from Latour the idea that this vague term can give a 'social explanation' of a state of affairs.[25] Where I use 'network', I mean a flat and intricately connected set of *actors, and* the *processes* by which they operate to deliver, promote and protect (through) rights. Hence I prefer the term 'technology' to 'network' for how it designates both individuals or actors *and* types or processes of government. The global human rights design represents a different art of government to sovereign control—a different

---

[20] W Walters and W Larner (eds), *Global Governmentality: Governing International Spaces* (Routledge, Abingdon 2006) 2.

[21] S Hopgood, *The Endtimes of Human Rights* (Ithica, NY, Cornell University Press, 2013).

[22] On 'global governmentality', see also Walters and Larner, *Global Governmentality*, above n 20, and IB Neumann and OJ Sending, *Governing the Global Polity: Practice, Mentality, Rationality* (Ann Arbor, MI, University of Michigan Press, 2010).

[23] Ibid 130.

[24] B Latour, *Reassembling the Social: An Introduction to Actor-Network-Theory* (Oxford, Oxford University Press, 2007) 131 and 132.

[25] Ibid 1. For a more robust account, see G Kendall, 'Global Networks, International Networks, Actor Networks' in Walters and Larner, *Global Governmentality*, above n 20.

way of calculating, rationalising and regulating the art of government.[26] What is different is that the art of governing is given a new reality on which to be exercised: global civil society.[27] So, what we see is a modern governmental *technology* within the global human rights architecture. Rights become technologies of global governmentality that operate via civil society actors, namely INGOs.

Two further points are important to highlight about this modern governmental technology. First, the relationships between the levels of the global human rights structure are important in themselves. How, for instance, does the INGO relate to the other layers of actors within the global human rights design? How does Human Rights Watch connect with the United Nations (UN)? What is its relationship to regional rights actors or agencies such as the EU's Fundamental Rights Agency (FRA)?[28] What is interesting here is the different type of expertise that these various organisations have whilst being part of the same global architecture (and indeed questioning whether it *is* different); and how and whether this engenders any competition between them: who, for instance, is more of an expert than whom in a particular context? Who can scrutinize whom? Second, it is important to observe how they speak to each other. The language of human rights is now widely spoken amongst civil society actors, such that '[i]nternational human rights has become by far the most common vocabulary for humanitarian activists'.[29] Thus, although human rights law and humanitarian law are distinct vocabularies, there is strong overlap and linkage between them in the global human rights architecture. They are vocabularies that distinguish humanitarian and human rights actors whilst also linking them. For instance, an actor such as MSF, which exercises a 'medical humanitarianism',[30] is concerned with the basic humanitarian impulse of saving lives by providing for the basic human needs of shelter, food, water, sanitation, medicine, and better hygiene practices.[31] MSF's humanitarian work evokes a 'deep sense of moral authenticity' and, as a response to crisis and emergency, constitutes a real-time 'humanitarian response to suffering'.[32] Advancing the cause of human rights for all, rather than sustaining and

---

[26] M Foucault, *The Birth of Biopolitics, Lectures at the Collège de France 1978–1979* (M Senellart (ed, G Burchell (trans), Basingstoke, Palgrave Macmillan, 2008) 313.

[27] Ibid 295.

[28] There are other questions I might have asked, for instance: How does HRW connect with the local? How different are the different branches of HRW, and how does HRW Headquarters affect local branches? My interest, however, in this of course limited chapter is in its operation in 'the world'; in how it operates within the 'global' to enact a global governmentality and so I have had to narrow my attention to these particular specificities.

[29] Kennedy, *The Dark Sides of Virtue*, above n 1, xvi.

[30] Redfield, *Life in Crisis*, above n 4, 11.

[31] MSF fundraising brochure, *Help us Save a Life Today* (2008), as quoted in Redfield, *Life in Crisis*, above n 4, 1 and 18.

[32] Ibid 31 and 18.

prolonging lives, is the concern of a human rights actor such as HRW. The organisation's Mission Statement clarifies that what they *do* is investigate, expose and pressure in the name of 'human dignity and to advance the cause of human rights for all'.[33] Perhaps they are 'a bit theoretical, because what they do is research'[34]—they employ a naming and shaming method-ology and write reports. What *else* does this human rights actor do? How relevant are its experts, its methodologies, the truth it portrays about rights through its reporting mechanisms to the global governance architecture and to how it *governs (through) rights*? I attempt to answer these ques-tions in this chapter with a focus on HRW as the 'archetypal' human rights INGO. I examine how its experts narrate a truth about rights and how they engage in self-scrutiny, all of which are features and processes of a global governmentality of rights.

II. THE INTERNATIONAL NON-GOVERNMENTAL ORGANISATION

INGOs are 'other actors' with which states and regional and international organisations cooperate within the global human rights architecture. They are 'other' because they are non-state or civil society actors. Rosenau has argued for 'spheres of Authority' as units by which to analyse non-state actors;[35] but this analysis maintains, as Neumann and Sending recognise, a state-centred focus based on a concern with authority and ignores the workings of power relations in global governance networks.[36] Placing instead a focus on actual governance practices that are then observed under a lens of governmentality, we see the power relations that produce civil society actors as subjects (rather than passive objects under the authority of the state) of government. Rather than 'spheres of Authority' then, we can see them as 'self-associating units with political significance' because of their capacity to communicate preferences and mobilise whole communi-ties, and their capacity to carry out regulatory functions. Non-state, civil society actors are thus powerful actors in global politics in their own right who do not just hold power to account. This 'power' they exercise—or, the governmental rationality by which civil society actors operate to enact a governmentality (through) rights—can be seen in the extent and reach of the *watchdog* role of human rights INGOs and in how they go about their

---

[33] HRW mission statement, above n 11.

[34] Comment of a veteran female researcher for Amnesty International on HRW, in Hopgood, *Keepers of the Flame*, above n 10, 3.

[35] JN Rosenau, 'Change, Complexity, and Governance in Globalizing Space' in J Pierre (ed), *Debating Governance: Authority, Steering and Democracy* (Oxford, Oxford University Press, 2000) 167 and Neumann and Sending, *Governing the Global Polity*, above n 22, 111–14.

[36] Neumann and Sending, *Governing the Global Polity*, above n 22, 111–14.

work, that is, the *methodology* they use which is shared by their humanitarian counterparts thus illustrating humanitarian government (through) rights.

In its 'About Us' video, HRW is described by the news network CNN as a 'watchdog'.[37] Against a backdrop of melancholy music and images of destruction and suffering in Syria that might be termed a 'pornography of poverty',[38] we see pictures of HRW's reports: the tools it uses to monitor the over 90 countries in which it works. One of the messages from the video is thus that HRW's surveillance has a global reach. The second of the two largest human rights INGOS, Amnesty International (AI), has responded to the globalisation of Human Rights by launching an 'AI brand', where the organisation's logo, a candle in barbed wire, has become a commercial symbol and members of the organisation can own AI visa cards.[39] This perhaps works against its depiction by Hopgood as a 'secular Free Church',[40] a meeting house containing a moral community of actors that are attempting a sort of globalisation of morality in the name of rights. International humanitarian organisations have a similar concern with the global and a similar operational ethic of 'crisis'. The very name of MSF declares health or medicine 'without borders'.[41] It facilitates the global mobility of medicine, or global medicine.[42] INGOs thus operate as watchdogs on a global scale, exercising a global governmentality, or humanitarian government (through) rights.

The methodology by which INGOs define their work is key to this global governmentality, or humanitarian government (through) rights. The role of international organisations in global governance is increasingly informed by how 'to respond to and administer a permanent condition of *crisis*'.[43] 'Crisis' is a useful 'umbrella term for a range of phenomena' that involve human rights violations for it allows for intervention on the part of human rights actors that is assumed to have a humanitarian nature.[44] We saw

---

[37] See www.hrw.org/about.

[38] B Plewes and R Stuart, 'The Pornography of Poverty: A Cautionary Fundraising Tale' in DA Bell and J-M Coicaud, *Ethics in Action: The Ethical Challenges of International Human Rights Non-Governmental Organisations* (Cambridge, Cambridge University Press, 2007) 23.

[39] Hopgood reports that AI Platinum Visa cards are available to staff in the International Secretariat and in the AI UK offices, Hopgood, *Keepers of the Flame*, above n 10, 11.

[40] Ibid 8.

[41] T Murphy refers to 'healthcare "without borders"' in 'Public Health *sans frontières*: Human Rights NGOs and "Stewardship on a Global Scale"' (2011) 62(5) *Northern Ireland Legal Quarterly* 659.

[42] Redfield, *Life in Crisis*, above n 4, 13.

[43] KB Sandvik, 'Review Essay, Unpacking World Refugee Day: Humanitarian Governance and Human Rights Practice' (2010) 2(2) *Journal of Human Rights Practice* 287, 288 (emphasis added).

[44] H Charlesworth, 'International Law: A Discipline of Crisis' (2002) 65(3) *Modern Law Review* 377. See also D Chandler, 'The Road to Military Humanitarianism: How the Human Rights NGOs Shaped a New Humanitarian Agenda' (2001) 23(3) *Human Rights Quarterly* 678.

this in the previous chapter in relation to intervention by the EU's FRA in migration policy. Crisis is then also an ethical code of conduct. Redfield identifies 'ethic of crisis' as the operational code of MSF.[45] The actual borders of where MSF intervenes to save lives is determined by where there is 'crisis'. Or rather, *it determines* who and what is in crisis; it is the watchdog, the gatekeeper, the sovereign in some respects who is able to act as an independent subject and decide to save some lives and not others.[46] Crisis is the ethical code of conduct that regulates MSF's actions; it is 'the purest environment for a technical expertise [to function], a context in which expertise can and clearly must engage with the immanence of problems'.[47] 'Crisis' determines the unlimited geographic and topical reach of MSF, since it has become an 'expansive concept', moving beyond classic emergency responses to war, natural disasters and epidemics such as HIV/AIDS.[48] HRW, I argue, defines a way of doing rights that means it also operates within the crisis model and is able to determine what 'crisis' is. Crisis thus forms its *ethos*—its way of being and behaviour. And this way of being and behaviour is performed using a very specific methodology of 'naming and shaming'.[49] Since its beginnings in 1978 when it was Helsinki Watch and drew attention to human rights violations in the Soviet Union and Eastern Europe, HRW has named and shamed abusive governments through media coverage and via direct exchanges with policymakers. HRW's Executive Director, Kenneth Roth, describes naming and shaming as the key to 'effectiveness', since it allows for identification of a clear 'violation', a 'violator' and a 'remedy'.[50] I explore the power relations within the crisis model and within HRW's enactment of a 'politics of embarrassment'[51] in the next section to determine how it is a useful tool both for the exercise of humanitarian government(ality) through rights, and for defining what the truth about rights within a given state, or region, is.

---

[45] Redfield, *Life in Crisis*, above n 4, 33–34.

[46] Ibid 21.

[47] Ibid 32.

[48] Ibid 13–14. See also Murphy, 'Public Health *sans frontières*', above n 41, for comment on how NGOs have shaped responses to the HIV/AIDS epidemic, especially at 662.

[49] For the historical context of this methodology, see www.hrw.org/history. See also K Roth, 'Defending Economic, Social and Cultural Rights: Practical Issues Faced by an International Human Rights Organisation' in DA Bell and J-M Coicaud, *Ethics in Action: The Ethical Challenges of International Human Rights Non-Governmental Organisations* (Cambridge, Cambridge University Press, 2007) 169.

[50] Ibid.

[51] J-M Coicaud, 'INGOs as Collective Mobilisation of Transnational Solidarity: Implications for Human Rights Work at the United Nations' in DA Bell and J-M Coicaud, *Ethics in Action: The Ethical Challenges of International Human Rights Non-Governmental Organisations* (Cambridge, Cambridge University Press, 2007) 279, 294.

III. EXPERTS, NARRATORS AND SCRUTINISERS:
HUMAN RIGHTS WATCH

As an international human rights NGO that operates worldwide, HRW perfectly illustrates the operation of a global governmentality of rights. Within the organisation's operational framework, we can identify processes of *governing through rights*, *governing rights* and *self-government* in the name of rights. By examining the processes by which they operate, we see how the actors within the organisation use a particular type of *expertise* to govern through rights; how, as *narrators*, they govern the discourse of rights; and how surveillance tactics turn these actors into (self-)*scrutinisers* that govern themselves and their own conduct through rights. The tactic of expertise operates to create a special kind of knowledge about rights that constructs the human rights activist and policy-maker as 'ruler', as a vital part of the architectural frame of global human rights governance. I am interested, when I look at experts, below, not so much in the structural make-up of organisations like HRW but in the linkages between these experts and the kind of regional experts we saw in the previous chapter (ie of the EU's FRA). And I am also keen to explore here how expertise might be in competition as organisations vie for participant or contributor status. I also want to consider the alternative role of the ruler as the narrator: organisations like HRW, in adopting a methodology that determines how to identify a violation, a violator and a remedy, as well as pronouncing on what these are, tell us the stories of the violation, of the experience of the violator and of the happy ending of the remedy. In doing so, they govern (through) rights since these stories are deemed to be true and dominant narratives. Do they interrogate their own methods? Do they engage in self-criticism? I also look at how the scrutiny of the INGO extends to the self; how the organisation engages in a care of the self to govern itself through rights, demonstrating an ethical concern with the self.

A. Expertise: Government Through Rights

Examining expertise as a tactic of government reveals a governmentality *through rights* whereby the behaviour of the INGO is managed by obedience to a set of values that are codifications of rights discourse. Let us first examine who *the people* are in HRW, before we look at their *working methods* and at how they *cooperate* with other actors on different levels of the global human rights architecture.

The people, or 'experts' at HRW are listed as 'country specialists, lawyers, journalists, advocates and academics of diverse backgrounds and nationalities'.[52] They are split into leadership staff (senior management

---

[52] See www.hrw.org/about/people.

staff) and remaining experts (part of the Advisory Committees, or program-matic divisions). There are ten programmatic divisions, five thematic (such as Children's Rights Division, Women's Rights Division) and five geographic (such as Europe and Central Asia Division, and a separate programme on the United States). HRW's research thus spans the globe (is 'global') and has a wide thematic reach; 15 topics are covered, including arms, health, migration and the UN. The experts must fulfil what appear to be criteria that equal expertise: experience, representation and respect. To be experts, HRW staff must have 'deep and broad *experience* in political, economic and social affairs ... as well as in human rights'; they must '*represent* the fields of law, journalism, social activism, public health, academia or other profes-sions related to human rights'; and they must 'elicit *respect* in their fields'.[53] Expertise is thus the dominant and uncompromising characteristic of HRW. It is also a tactic of governmentality. Experts govern rights discourse, as we saw in the last chapter in the context of the EU's rights agency and as we will see in the section on narration below. But they are also *governed by or through* rights to the extent that they conform to standards and codes of conducts set and determined by rights discourse. How does power operate within the HRW framework to regulate the behaviour of experts, to *govern them* through rights?

First, governmentality is visible in the working methods of HRW. The organisation carries out its naming and shaming methodology through preliminary or initial stages, interviews and non-interview techniques. The initial stages depend on whether the research is targeted at an emergency or a rapidly developing human rights violation, or a long-running or longer-term human rights issue, where the former requires researchers to be on the ground immediately:

> [The] goals of the initial stages of research are to develop a thorough, well-rounded understanding of the incident or rights violation and to gain a strong sense of the local political, social, and cultural context of the violation. The researcher must also frame the violation as it relates to international human rights and humanitarian law.[54]

The behaviour of the researcher and how she collects data, or stories, is thus determined by a code of conduct that is defined by rights. Interviews, with subjects that HRW calls 'victims and witnesses' (those directly affected by the abuse/s) happen according to 'guiding principles, such as the need to ascertain the truth, to corroborate the veracity of statements, to protect the security and dignity of witnesses, and to remain impartial'.[55] These guiding

---

[53] See www.hrw.org/about/people/advisory-committees (emphasis added).

[54] See www.hrw.org/about-our-research.

[55] Ibid. 'Victims and witnesses' would not be exhaustive categories of interviewees; for instance, other experts within the global human rights architecture (eg UN experts) might also be interviewed for the purposes of narrating a particular human rights story. I focus on them since I want to determine how HRW tells the stories *of the victims and their witnesses* from its own expert perspective.

principles form a similar code of conduct that is known only to experts; it is what binds them in terms of the knowledge and experience that they share, but also what manages their behaviour on the ground. Non-interview techniques (such as meticulous reviewing of media reports, domestic legislation, international law, policy papers, academic reports, and civil society reports), photographing bodies for evidence of injury, and using GPS coordinates and satellite images to visually unearth human rights abuses, follow an identical code: the aim is *doing rights* through collating research.

Second, HRW is governed through rights via the cooperation methods it must respect to remain part of the human rights architecture. Part of the organisation's role is to contribute to an exchange of information and pooling of knowledge that comes to constitute part of a global human rights discourse.[56] Cooperation happens at the international, regional, national and local levels, so that HRW must cooperate with the UN, for example, with the EU and its rights framework, with national governments and with individual contributors. I want to look at cooperation, and its imposed criteria, at the UN and EU levels. There has been much written on INGOs as trustees for their contributors and relations with national governments, in particular the ethical implications of how these organisations spend funds to ensure cost effectiveness and manage harm;[57] I want to consider instead how the global architecture functions at a level beyond the national. The challenges for HRW at the UN level are that it must secure participation rights through acquiring *consultative status*. The ECOSOC (Economic and Social Council of the UN) 'statute' for NGOs of 27 February 1950 codifies participation rights and grants INGOs consultative status to matters falling within ECOSOC competence as regards economic, social, cultural, educational, health matters and questions of human rights.[58] Of two newer resolutions, Resolution 1996/31 of 25 July 1996 sets up 'arrangements' for a 'consultative relationship' between the UN and NGOs.[59] These concern, for instance, principles to be applied in the establishment of consultative relations (Part I); principles governing the nature of consultative arrangements (Part II); arrangements concerning the establishment of consultative

---

[56] FRA identifies 'exchange of information and pooling of knowledge' as the key objective of its Fundamental Rights Platform, in Council Regulation 168/2007/EC of 15 February 2007 establishing a European Union Agency for Fundamental Rights [2007] OJ L53/1, art 10(2) ('FRA Regulation').

[57] See especially JH Carens, 'The Problem of Doing Good in a World that Isn't: Reflections on the Ethical Challenges Facing INGOs' in DA Bell and J-M Coicaud, *Ethics in Action: The Ethical Challenges of International Human Rights Non-Governmental Organisations* (Cambridge, Cambridge University Press, 2007) 257; T Pogge, 'Respect and Disagreement: A Response to Joseph Carens' in DA Bell and J-M Coicaud, *Ethics in Action: The Ethical Challenges of International Human Rights Non-Governmental Organisations* (Cambridge, Cambridge University Press, 2007) 273; and Coicaud, 'INGOs as Collective Mobilisation', above n 51.

[58] ECOSOC Resolution 288 X (B) of 1950.

[59] ECOSOC Resolution 1996/31 of 25 July 1996.

relationships (Part III); and suspension and withdrawal of consultative status (Part VIII). In its relationship with the UN, HRW merits 'special consultative status' by virtue of its 'special competence' defined as 'an interest in the field of human rights' and a continued pursuit of the goals of promotion and protection of human rights in accordance with the spirit of the Charter of the UN, the Universal Declaration of Human Rights and the Vienna Declaration.[60] The UN's aims and purposes must thus be in conformity with the 'spirit and principles of the UN Charter'.[61] Moreover, HRW must show 'recognized standing' within the field of its competence and be of a 'representative character'.[62] In its relationship with the UN, HRW must make 'substantive and sustained contributions' to the achievement of the objectives of the UN.[63] In this respect, it is monitored by being subject to 'periodic review' of activities on the basis of reports that it must submit to the Economic and Social Council and faces suspension of up to three years or withdrawal of its consultative status if it is found to no longer be making a 'positive or effective contribution' to the work of the UN, after which time it would need to formally re-apply for consultative status.[64] To keep hold of its consultative relationship with the UN, HRW must thus behave according to the ECOSOC Statute's prescribed forms of behaviour; it must maintain its 'special' status, it must be 'representative' and must continue to make 'substantial and sustained contributions'. It is 'periodically reviewed' to ensure that this code of conduct, or behaviour, is followed—and further threatened with suspension or withdrawal of status if it stops behaving in a 'positive and effective' way.

To be part of the cooperation network at a European level, HRW must similarly satisfy a code of conduct, selection procedures and fit within a predetermined strategic framework. The FRA cooperates with more than 300 civil society organisations via the Fundamental Rights Platform (FRP), which resembles a 'cooperation network'.[65] It is described by the Agency's former Director as a 'unique', 'engaging' and 'vibrant' platform.[66] It will 'engage at every stage' with civil society actors so as to ensure 'fruitful dialogue'.[67] But the INGO cannot engage by itself or in its own chosen areas of expertise;

---

[60] Ibid Part III, para 25. HRW is listed in Economic and Social Council (UN), *List of Non-Governmental Organizations in Consultative Status with the Economic and Social Council as of 1 September 2014*, UN Doc E/2014/INF/5 (3 December 2014).

[61] ECOSOC Resolution 1996/31, above n 59, Part 1, para 2.

[62] Ibid Part 1, para 9.

[63] Ibid Part III, para 22.

[64] Ibid Part VIII, para 57.

[65] FRA Regulation, art 10(1).

[66] Morten Kjaerum, speaking in the FRP Video, available at fra.europa.eu/en/cooperation/civil-society.

[67] Massimo Toschi, FRP Programme Manager, speaking in FRP Video, ibid. Note also that recital 19 of the FRA Regulation refers to the aim of the FRP as 'creating a structured and fruitful dialogue'.

it must be *called upon* to do so and the FRA will determine the priority areas for action.[68] The FRP abides by a 'Code of Conduct' that specifies 18 criteria that monitor participation requirements (points 1–9), the conduct of participants (points 10–13), and administrative conditions for participation (points 14–18).[69] Hence, participation is open to civil society organisations that, for example, have 'specific expertise, proven experience and capacity'; that are 'committed to engage in respectful and fruitful dialogue' and that can 'demonstrate that their programme of work is of direct relevance to the work of the FRA'.[70] Good conduct is demonstrated by, for instance, the organisation showing it will 'refrain from any kind of conduct endangering the "structured and fruitful dialogue" within the FRP'.[71] Participation in the FRA can be for a term of up to three years and renewed thereafter. Importantly, it can be terminated if the Director of the Agency finds violation of any of the points in the Code.[72] There is, furthermore, an internal selection procedure that comes into play once the call for participation (note the organisation must be 'called' or invited in) has been answered. This involves an assessment that takes place via a screening procedure carried out by the 'FRP Team' of the FRA; the screening process can result in a candidate organisation being rejected based on a consultation with FRA in-house lawyers and the Advisory Panel of the FRA.[73] Any questions raised with regard to any of the criteria entitles the FRP team to seek clarification from the applicant. To be officially 'recognised' as a FRP participant, the candidate organisation must receive notice of 'acceptance', which is done in writing. Following acceptance, a Strategic Framework document outlines principles of cooperation, which include: to increase public awareness about fundamental rights, and to connect civil society organisations so as to enable dialogue and the exchange of good practices.[74]

I want to make three points here as to what these codes of conduct, selection criteria and strategic frameworks do in terms of regulating INGOS, and in terms of how INGOs work with each other to *cooperate* within a global

---

[68] FRA Regulation, art 10.

[69] European Union Agency for Fundamental Rights (FRA), *Code of Conduct for the Participants of the Fundamental Rights Platform*, Decision of the Director, CAR/002/2012 (22 June 2012), available at fra.europa.eu/sites/default/files/fra_uploads/2270-FRP-code-of-conduct-2012.pdf.

[70] Ibid points 3–5, p 2.

[71] Ibid point 12, p 2.

[72] Ibid point 17, p 2.

[73] European Union Agency for Fundamental Rights (FRA), *FRP Selection—Internal Procedures*, Decision of the Director, CAE/001/2012 (2012), available at fra.europa.eu/sites/default/files/fra_uploads/2279-FRP-selection-internal-procedures.pdf.

[74] European Union Agency for Fundamental Rights (FRA), *Strategic Framework for the FRA—Civil Society Cooperation* (December 2014) 3, available at http://fra.europa.eu/sites/default/files/fra-cso_strategy_framework_2014.pdf; ECOSOC Resolution 1996/31, above n 59, Part III, para 22.

human rights architecture built upon many levels and forms of expertise. First, INGOs make linkages and connections based on sharing and exchanging expertise and pooling knowledge. As independent experts in their own right, INGOs such as HRW must nevertheless be invited and accepted as *suitable participants* within the UN and EU human rights frameworks. Their contributions, whilst 'fruitful' will also be 'structured', and 'substantive and sustained'.[75] HRW will thus be called upon to make suggestions to the FRA's Management Board on the Agency's Annual Work Programme, to give feedback to the Management Board on the annual reports of the FRA, and to communicate the outcomes and recommendations of conferences, seminars and meetings.[76] Second, expertise is thus managed according to codes of conduct and selection that are based in rights. The FRA's Code of Conduct is able to make participation conditional and available according to a set criteria of *suitability*; its selection procedure ensures screening and conditional acceptance of candidate organisations and its strategic framework is set according to the central question of: how can civil society organisations' knowledge better feed into the FRA's work?[77] Similarly, the ECOSOC Statute requires consultative relations with the UN to meet its criteria of 'recognized standing' and 'special competence', measured as interest in the field of human rights. Thus, third, there is an element of competition between experts that further ensures management of behaviour and (self)-scrutiny, thereby strengthening the governmental relations within the global human rights architecture. Candidate organisations must present themselves as suitable to avoid suspension of consultative status or withdrawal of status. They must further demonstrate that their work is useful for the UN and the EU/FRA, for enhancing its impact and for ensuring connections between civil society organisations.[78] Hence the ECOSOC Statute states that membership of the organization must be 'considerable', 'broadly representative of major segments of society in a large number of countries in different regions of the world' and that the organisation should be 'closely involved with the economic and social life of the peoples of the areas they represent'.[79] The various methods of selection and participation (through a code of conduct, selection procedure, strategic framework)

---

[75] See FRA Regulation, recital 19 on the objective of 'structured and fruitful dialogue'.

[76] As per FRA Regulation, art 4. For example, HRW made an individual contribution to the Fundamental Rights Platform Consultation (February 2009): Suggestions to the FRA Work Programme 2010 (the consultation was conducted to receive suggestions on the work programme), see the report on the consultation: FRA (European Union Agency for Fundamental Rights), *Fundamental Rights Platform Consultation: Suggestions for the FRA Work Programme 2010, Report on the Fundamental Rights Platform Consultation February 2009*, available at fra.europa.eu/sites/default/files/fra_uploads/425-CS-FRP-Consultation-report-WP2010.pdf.

[77] FRA, *Strategic Framework for the FRA*, above n 74, 4.

[78] Ibid 5.

[79] ECOSOC Resolution 1996/31, above n 59, Part III, para 22.

operate as tactics, technologies and functionings that determine suitability and so manage the behaviour of INGOs such as HRW. Even this giant amongst organisations must moderate its expertise, knowledge and its conduct so as to be selected for cooperation.

These are the mundane processes by which rights act as a regulatory discourse, as technologies of governmentality, that manage the behaviour of actors within the global human rights architecture. Will HRW, for instance, be pushed towards extending its remit and methodologies to economic and social rights to maintain 'special' status on continued periodic reviews? And how will this work with Roth's adamant position that 'there are certain types of ESC [economic, social and cultural] rights for which our methodology works well and others for which it does not'?[80] He goes on to say:

> I must admit to finding the typical discussion of ESC rights rather sterile. I have been to countless conferences and debates in which international human rights organizations are advised to do more to protect ESC rights. Fair enough. Usually, though, the advice reduces to little more than sloganeering.[81]

Will HRW need to change its behaviour, its *ethos*, to maintain its suitable, special and representative relationship to the UN? Another question that arises then is, is there consequently a hierarchy of experts? Are some more experienced, more knowledgeable than others? It is not, I think, a question of hierarchy but a matter of codified processes that operate according to rights-based standards that link different levels of experts. They are, furthermore, at once governed (as we have just seen) and governors. HRW acts as a governor, a ruler, in the sense that it a narrator.

B. Narration: Governing Rights

As narrators, the actors within HRW govern the discourse of rights in three ways: first, they determine how to *do* rights; second, they define what human rights *are*; and, third, they formulate 'extractive relationships'[82] where they *tell the stories* of victims and witnesses at the same time as sustaining themselves as suitable human rights actors within the global human rights architecture.

(i) How to Do Rights

In terms, first, of how to do rights, the organisation abides by a deliberate methodology that is presented as *the right way to do* rights. HRW's

---

[80] Roth, 'Defending Economic, Social and Cultural Rights', above n 49, 169.
[81] Ibid 170.
[82] Plewes and Stuart, 'The Pornography of Poverty' above n 38, 24.

experts work to 'pressure those in power'[83] through a 'naming and shaming' methodology.[84] 'We are at our most effective', comments Roth, 'when we can hold governmental conduct up to a disapproving public'.[85] The organisation's 'shaming' methodology is thus equated with maximum effectiveness. And it is so effective because it provides clarity on the 'violator' (the abusive government), the 'violation' (the rights shortfall) and the 'remedy' (reversing the abusive conduct).[86] Naming and shaming thus draws its efficacy from being able to identify and draw attention to 'arbitrary and discriminatory conduct'. There are numerous examples that Roth lists by way of illustration; take, for instance, how HRW investigated the conditions facing child farm workers in the United States to show that the national laws regulating working conditions for children in the United States were not applied to child farmers and thus were arbitrary and discriminatory.[87] They were shown to be arbitrary since laws governing child farmers were written in an era when the family farm was predominant and so misrepresented the field today (which is one of agribusiness); they were shown to be discriminatory since most child farmers belong to an easy to ignore political category—the children of immigrant parents.[88] The violator in this scenario can be easily identified as the government, through its arbitrary and discriminatory conduct and so effectively shamed.

There are obvious advantages, and disadvantages to this way of doing rights. There is clarity of focus in this approach;[89] it does not delve into mere 'sloganeering' and 'sterile' pronouncements on changing the economic and social situation through a wider scope of activity on distributive justice, which ignores questions such as 'who is responsible for the impoverished state of the population? Or, is the government taking steps to progressively realise the relevant rights on the basis of available resources?'[90] But, in terms of weaknesses, naming and shaming does not address and seek to alter the wider concerns of distributive justice and power inequalities; it arguably overlooks context, addressing symptoms rather than causes.[91] It also makes the assumption that states will respond to public pressure, that they will be embarrassed enough to change their behaviour.[92] Further, it can

---

[83] Mission Statement, available at www.hrw.org/about.

[84] As articulated on HRW's website, www.hrw.org/history.

[85] Roth, 'Defending Economic, Social and Cultural Rights', above n 49, 172.

[86] Ibid 178.

[87] Ibid.

[88] Ibid 175.

[89] P Gready and W Vandenhole, 'What are We Trying to Change? Theories of Change in Development and Human Rights' in P Gready and W Vandenhole (eds), *Human Rights and Development in the New Millenium: Towards a Theory of Change* (Abingdon, Routledge, 2013) 6.

[90] Roth, 'Defending Economic, Social and Cultural Rights', above n 49, 170.

[91] Gready and Vandenhole, 'What are We Trying to Change?', above n 89, 6.

[92] Ibid.

be 'counter-productive', alienating governments at times when cooperation would be useful.[93] Thus the 'politics of embarrassment' can backfire.[94] It is this engagement with the politics of the process, or its political implications, that interests me, rather than whether the methodology is good or bad. And by this I mean: what are the power relations at work here and what do they produce? How, in other words, can articulation of the correct way of doing rights potentially be dangerous? By deciding on the most effective methodology, HRW sets the boundaries of *priority areas* of work, and of *which rights matter based on their expertise and available resources*. An almost mathematical formula of violator + violation + remedy = *priority area* is visible in the shaming methodology. It allows for a practical and calculable assessment of where human rights work should be focused, and moral or ethical considerations to do with harm or suffering or wider structural issues of distributive justice are not relevant.[95] The formula is workable, whereas tackling structural issues that are arguably more significant (such as child poverty, structural racism, etc) is too hard to solve. Therefore, not only is this practical formula a highly useful methodological lens through which to select priority areas for human rights activism and advocacy, but HRW contributes through its methodology to the entrenchment of deeper inequality and rights violations. This is not to say that HRW does not face ethical challenges; in terms of its status as a Northern 'rescuer' of Southern 'victims' in distress, in terms of its relations with governments, its role in the defense of economic and social rights, of course it does.[96] My point here is that adopting and advocating a 'most effective' methodology and ignoring what is too hard to solve, allows the INGO, in this example, HRW, to determine the countries of focus, the priority areas on which to expend its expertise, knowledge and funds. It is almost a 'ruler' in the literal sense of the word in this respect, in that it retains an aspect of sovereignty 'in the sense of independently determining who is in crisis'.[97]

'Crisis' is a 'seductive'[98] term and we see the intervention, the agitation, the disruption of space that happens in efforts to remedy it as positive— human rights activists are the rescuers in this scenario. 'Crisis', from its Greek roots suggesting 'discrimination' or 'decision', 'implies a condition of instability or a moment of decisive change'.[99] The instability will be removed and the decision to intrude taken by the experts in HRW using a

---

[93] Ibid. Here Gready and Vandenhole cite the example of China.

[94] Coicaud, 'INGOs as Collective Mobilisation', above n 51, 293.

[95] See Pogge's formula for measuring the 'moral principle governing INGO conduct', which is based on cost effectiveness and harm prevention, in Pogge, 'Respect and Disagreement', above n 57, 234.

[96] Coicaud, 'INGOs as Collective Mobilisation', above n 51.

[97] Redfield, *Life in Crisis*, above n 4, 21, speaking here on MSF.

[98] Ibid 32.

[99] Ibid 32.

clear, effective methodology. But in doing so, it determines what qualifies as 'crisis'. The crisis model (as used, we saw earlier, by MSF) therefore creates an *ethos*, a way of being and behaviour, which enables humanitarian government (through) rights. HRW accumulates a set of knowledge practices through its methodological standpoint and thus its *ethos*, which guides intervention (in the 'crisis'). This is typical of NGOs; Lakoff presents an interesting critique of the regulation of global health regimes by NGOs and points to what he calls 'real-time, global disease surveillance' whereby international non-state actors (not governments) adopt global health initiatives to 'govern through the non-governmental'.[100] He mentions the example of the fight to combat AIDS, where global health initiatives effectively, as I read it, determine this as crisis and so determine the diagnosed state as 'the purest environment for a technical expertise' demanding expert engagement and intervention. Identifying the crisis also means identifying *what rights matter*. That is, as Roth confirms, the shaming methodology does not lend itself to violations of economic and social rights since it is more difficult to pinpoint discriminatory and arbitrary conduct. The violator + victim + remedy formula works best for civil and political rights; for example, determining torture, where the violator is the torturer, as well as the governments or institutions that allow the torture to take place without punishment; and the remedy is to issue clear directions to stop the torture, to recommend prosecution to support these and taking preventative measures such as ending *incommunicado* detention.[101] Through advocating and using this as its dominant methodology, HRW is thus contributing to sustaining the differentiation between civil and political rights (those that are first generation, or first class) and economic and social rights (thereby second generation, or second class).[102] It is also contributing to the entrenchment of structural rights violations by effectively ignoring them as too difficult to solve. By contrast, AI points to the need to respect, protect and facilitate economic, social and cultural rights, revealing contention amongst the giants over the right way to do rights.[103] The effect of the methodological position of HRW is to articulate that civil and political rights *matter more*. It is not then a matter of the organisation's reach, or a self-awareness of its power to effect change,[104] but of how the best way to do rights comes to

---

[100] A Lakoff, 'Two Regimes of Global Health' (2010) 1(1) *Humanity: An International Journal of Human Rights, Humanitarianism, and Development* 59, 66.

[101] Roth, 'Defending Economic, Social and Cultural Rights', above n 49, 173.

[102] C Goering, 'Amnesty International and Economic Social and Cultural Rights' in DA Bell and J-M Coicaud, *Ethics in Action: The Ethical Challenges of International Human Rights Non-Governmental Organisations* (Cambridge, Cambridge University Press, 2007) 204.

[103] Amnesty International, *Human Rights for Human Dignity: A Primer on Economic, Social and Cultural Rights*, 2nd edn (28 July 2014), available at https://www.amnesty.org/en/documents/POL34/001/2014/en/.

[104] Roth, 'Defending Economic, Social and Cultural Rights', above n 49, especially at 170.

define what rights (that matter) are. Moreover, 'naming and shaming', as the right way to do rights, sustains both the organisation's utility and its heroism. HRW is able to demonstrate expertise to the UN and to the FRA, to show suitability and special status, through 'quick and easy wins' over expert groups that tackle more difficult structural violations. In the competition between INGOs, the organisation thus 'wins'.

HRW does claim to be 'increasingly applying its research methodology to economic, social and cultural rights, particularly in the areas of education and housing'. Perhaps this will be one of its methodological challenges: how to put pressure on governments for rights violations that do not fit within its formula for how best to do rights.[105] It is also accepting the challenge of '[c]ombining its traditional on-the-ground fact-finding with new technologies and innovative advocacy' through employing new methodologies like 'statistical research, satellite photography, and bomb-data analysis', which will not only 'keep Human Rights Watch on the cutting edge of promoting respect for human rights worldwide' but will also keep it on the cutting edge of defining (new) ways to do rights.

(ii) What Human Rights Are

By determining the correct way to do rights, HRW is then able to tell us what human rights are, and where and when they are deemed protectable. By identifying a violator, violation and remedy, the INGO constructs a discourse on *what rights are*; that is, HRW tells us what the human rights situation *actually is*. I want to illustrate this using two examples from HRW's main 'tools' of naming and shaming: its rights reports, specifically its *Report on the Mediterranean Migrant Crisis*[106] and its *World Report 2015: Events of 2014*.[107] The report on the recent EU migration crisis reflects the fact that the 'EU' is one of HRW's focus areas and is also interesting in terms of observing the linkages across the various networks within the global human rights architecture that I spoke about earlier.[108] As a suitable participant for the FRP of the FRA, HRW contributes experts to 'human rights in the EU' (this is the page that you arrive at when you click on the HRW link available on the FRA's FRP participants list).[109] Through the use of dispatches,

---

[105] See www.hrw.org/history.

[106] HRW, *The Mediterranean Migration Crisis: Why People Flee, What the EU Should Do* (25 June 2015), available at www.hrw.org/report/2015/06/19/mediterranean-migration-crisis/why-people-flee-what-eu-should-do.

[107] HRW, *World Report 2015: Events of 2014*, available at www.hrw.org/sites/default/files/wr2015_web.pdf.

[108] 'European Union' is included in the country-specific section of HRW's *World Report 2015*, for instance.

[109] See the FRP participants list, available at fra.europa.eu/en/cooperation/civil-society/participant-organisations, and HRW's linked page, www.hrw.org/tag/human-rights-european-union

commentary, statements, letters and news releases it provides an extended and another level of expert knowledge on the rights situation in the EU. What does it add? It adds its own, correct way of doing rights. It applies its naming and shaming methodology to highlight rights abuses. In 2015, a popular topic has been the acutely problematic 'migrant crisis'. HRW thus calls on individual Member States to respond to the crisis; see, for instance, UK Director David Mepham's *Dispatches: Where is Britain's Compassion for Migrants in Crisis?*.[110] Mepham points to the existence of little evidence of compassion or generosity in the UK response to the crisis, evidenced by the government's rejection of the Commission's proposal for a new EU-wide migration policy where the United Kingdom would accept more refugees. In an overt act of naming and shaming, Mepham asserts that:

> Britain's response is simply indefensible. Less wealthy countries like Jordan, Turkey, and Lebanon are hosting millions of Syrian refugees; Lebanon alone has over a million. And while Europe as a whole should be prepared to do more, Britain's record compares unfavourably with that of other EU member states. In 2014, Germany, France, Italy and Sweden all granted asylum to more people than Britain.[111]

Moreover, Mepham's expert status prompts an assertive call to action; naming and shaming allows HRW's experts to be prescriptive about how rights should be done and how governments should respond to rights abuses—hence Mepham challenges, 'The British people are more compassionate than that, and their government *should be* too'.

The situation on the ground in the Mediterranean is clarified in the 2015 *Report on the Mediterranean Crisis*.[112] Through the use of statistics, elaborate maps and colourful pie charts, HRW constructs the truth about the rights situation in this region. So we are told that 'The Mediterranean is the world's deadliest migration route'.[113] The focus of the Report, unlike, as we saw in the last chapter, in the EU documents and press releases on the crisis, is on the migrants and not on EU migrant quotas or anti-smuggling measures. The statistics and data on migration focus on where the migrants come from (not on why they are trying to 'get in'); so, HRW reports that according to the UN refugee agency, UNHCR, over 60 per cent of the people who took the dangerous sea journey in the first five months of 2015 came from Syria, Somalia and Afghanistan, countries torn apart by war and generalised violence, or from Eritrea, 'which is ruled by one of the most repressive governments in Africa' (these are the four main 'sending countries').[114]

---

[110] D Mepham, *Dispatches: Where is Britain's Compassion for Migrants in Crisis?* (12 May 2015), available at www.hrw.org/news/2015/05/12/dispatches-where-britains-compassion-migrants-crisis.
[111] Ibid.
[112] HRW, *The Mediterranean Migration Crisis*, above n 106.
[113] Ibid 2.
[114] Ibid 2–3.

The Report also focuses on the situation and the harm in these 'sending countries', ie the push factors, which again provides the migrant's (rather than the EU's) point of view. For instance, a focus on Libya mentions the outbreak of new hostilities between two rival governments in 2014 that has resulted in violence that has contributed to a rise in migrant boats departing for the EU. A full picture of the scale of violence is painted:

> The beheading of 21 men, 20 of whom were Egyptian Copts and one was an African national working in Libya, in February 2015, and 28 Christian Ethiopians in April 2015—all claimed by extremist groups that pledged allegiance to ISIS— were horrifying illustrations of the risks to which some migrants are exposed.[115]

HRW is thus concerned with reporting *their* stories. They are intimate insights into individual experiences: we come to know their names, they are not a nameless migrant mass any more. So we hear, for example, about Mohannad (pseudonym), a 30-year old lawyer from Raqqah, Syria who arrived in Greece a day before his interview with HRW in May 2015 and why he was compelled to make the journey:

> Syria has become a country that is broken ... I left two months ago because I'm an activist and I'm afraid they would arrest me and beat me a lot ... My only dream is to go to another European country to show the world what is happening there.[116]

We learn also of Tariq's experience as a 19-year old Palestinian from Yarmouk camp close to Damascus who fled to Serbia:

> I left so I could escape from the war and out of fear of being arrested, just like happened to my family members. Also, I was afraid of the army ... Yarmouk camp is under siege. There is no food or anything.[117]

This telling of personal stories is another illustration of the correct way to do rights, in two ways: first, unlike the EU in its approach to migration policy (as we saw in the last chapter) HRW does not need to *read fundamental rights into* the discourse on migration; it does not need to look at the situation *through a fundamental rights lens*.[118] By contrast, HRW *does* fundamental rights. For instance, HRW notes that 'EU member states have the right to return those who have no claim to remain, but procedures for apprehension, detention, and return should ensure humane treatment, access to effective remedies, and respect for the non-refoulement obligation'.[119]

---

[115] Ibid 19.

[116] Ibid 6.

[117] Ibid 6.

[118] On 'narratives of suffering', see Wilson and Brown, 'Introduction', above n 12, 12, in particular and R Dudai, '"Can You Describe This?" Human Rights Reports and What They Tell Us About the Human Rights Movement' in RA Wilson and RD Brown (eds), *Humanitarianism and Suffering: The Mobilization of Empathy* (Cambridge, Cambridge University Press, 2009) 245 and TW Laqueur, 'Mourning, Pity, and the Work of Narrative in the Making of "Humanity"' in ibid 31.

[119] HRW, *The Mediterranean Migration Crisis*, above n 106, 24.

This is what HRW adds to the FRA, how it links to this network to form a wider global human rights architecture: it adds an objective expertise, an independent even superior knowledge and concern to identify the violator, the violation and the remedy.

Second, HRW's shaming methodology allows it to take on the role of telling the EU what it *should* do, having identified the violation (severe breaches of the human rights of migrants) and the violator (Member States who refuse entry and stay, and/or refugee status, and the EU at large). The list of remedies, measures for action include:

> The EU *should* also ensure that all measures to combat irregular migration are grounded in respect for human rights and dignity, including the right to leave one's own country, the right to seek asylum, and protection against returning people to countries where their lives or freedoms may be at risk (non-refoulement obligation).

> Individual member states and the EU as a whole *should* use their influence and resources to address the major drivers of migration, including systematic human rights violations that serve as the major push factors for refugee and migration flows to the EU from countries like Syria, Eritrea, Afghanistan, and Somalia, as well as from transit countries like Libya.[120]

In this way, HRW both constructs a discursive truth of rights by outlining, defining and narrating what the situation really is, and it constructs what the discourse should look like by making concrete suggestions for how Member States/the EU should behave to better protect rights.

The *World Report* illustrates this on a bigger and more elaborate scale. The 660 pages cover essays and country-specific chapters. Roth, for instance, in his essay 'Tyranny's False Comfort: Why Rights Aren't Wrong in Tough Times' speaks with authority about how, far from being outdated in the face of security threats, 'human rights are an essential compass for political action'.[121] His authority comes from his expert status, which signifies a shared (with other experts) knowledge and experience about rights.[122] And the authority comes from empirical evidence; this is not a grand, idealistic statement that he is making but a well-researched conclusion based on the conditions for the emergence of ISIS (which includes naming and shaming of the US government and its provocative activities in Iraq, including abuse of detainees in Abu Ghraib prison and other US-run detention centres);[123]

---

[120] Ibid 30–32.

[121] K Roth, 'Tyranny's False Comfort: Why Rights Aren't Wrong in Tough Times' in HRW, *World Report 2015*, above n 107, 1.

[122] See the previous chapter for more on 'expertise' as a tactic of governmentality through rights. See also D Kennedy, 'Challenging the Expert Rule: The Politics of Global Governance' (2005) 27(1) *Sydney Law Review* 5.

[123] Roth, 'Tyranny's False Comfort', above n 121, 2.

the international community's embarrassing response to the repression in Egypt; and the potential failure of international criminal justice through the United States' and the EU's failure to support Palestine's signature of the Statute of the International Criminal Court. Human rights *are 'moral guides* as well as legal obligations',[124] Roth states. They are thus moral codes of conduct for states, defining how states should behave on a moral as well as legal scale.

The code of conduct applies regardless of context. So, Worden uses rights discourse to intervene into the world of sport by commenting on human rights crises around 'mega-sporting events' such as the Olympics.[125] In doing so, Worden draws attention to how human rights should be done by naming good practice; Norway, for example, 'made respect for human rights part of its Olympic bid' to such a degree that it pulled out of the contest to win the 2022 Winter Games bid.[126] HRW's expertise thus extends to telling states how to be good hosts; governments should 'clean up their human rights acts before hosting'.[127] Worden further lists five examples of behaviour that should not happen, including forced evictions without due process and compensation to make room for massive building projects, and abuse and exploitation of migrant workers who are forced to work in hazardous conditions for long hours and with unfair pay to meet deadlines.[128]

Through the country-specific-chapters, the report 'summarizes key human rights issues'[129] on the basis of events occurring between the end of 2013 to November 2014. The summary is an expert, snapshot assessment of *what matters*. Not every country where HRW works is covered and neither, obviously, is every issue of importance discussed.[130] HRW asserts that: 'The absence of a particular country or issue often simply reflects staffing limitations and should not be taken as commentary on the significance of the problem'.[131] And yet, this is exactly what it is. If the country or issue was of significance, staff would be allocated to it and attention paid to the problem. An assessment of the situation must be made and is done according to certain factors based on expert assessment; hence:

> factors we considered in determining the focus of our work in 2014 ... include the number of people affected and the severity of abuse, access to the country and the availability of information about it, the susceptibility of abusive forces

---

[124] Ibid 13 (emphasis added).
[125] M Worden, 'Raising the Bar: Mega-Sporting Events and Human Rights' in HRW, *World Report 2015*, above n 107, 34.
[126] Ibid 35.
[127] Ibid 36.
[128] Ibid 36–39.
[129] HRW, *World Report 2015*, above n 107, viii.
[130] Ibid x.
[131] Ibid x.

to influence, and the importance of addressing certain thematic concerns and of reinforcing the work of local rights organizations.[132]

HRW thus acts and lives up to the assessment that it is a 'gatekeeper NGO' in that it 'sends a message about what is and is not a human rights matter'.[133] The numerical tactics of measuring people affected, severity of abuse, accessibility of data through statistics and indicators reveal government through rights, where *what rights are*, what rights matter and what rights situations are worth reporting come to be defined and determined by INGO experts. So, for instance, taking the first country on the list, Afghanistan, we are told the story of what human rights are in the context of this state in six pages, under the seven headings of: election violence and attacks on civilians; torture, extra-judicial executions and enforced disappearances; women's rights; transitional justice; freedom of expression and association; internally displaced persons and refugees; and key international actors. We learn of how a Taliban attack in January 2014 on a Kabul restaurant led to the deaths of 20 people, of which 13 were foreigners and seven were Afghans.[134] We learn that women 'remained under threat in 2014',[135] and of the 'hard work' and tireless activism of activist groups such as the Afghan Women's Network.[136] This is important, interesting information. Given the scale of HRW's work, it cannot but be a brief snapshot of the country's human rights situation. Yet what is left out of the reports is interesting because the reporting mechanism constructs HRW as an authority on what stories are worth telling (those countries included in the report and those issues that are looked into over the many that are not), as well as on what human rights are (eg unproblematic moral principles), and what good practice counts as (those governments and civil society actors that are explicitly named and held up as good participants or contributors to global human rights efforts, or discourse). Whose stories are they telling—and are there any other effects of the power relations within the storyteller-character narrative that we ought to consider?

(iii) *Extractive Relationships*

'To enter the terrain of emancipation through human rights is to enter a world of uncivilized deviants, baby seals, and knights errant.'[137] The human rights vocabulary forms the script for a 'theater of roles' in which there are three main actors: the deviants, or violators; the baby seals, or passive

132 Ibid x.
133 Murphy, 'Public Health *sans frontières*', above n 41, 670.
134 HRW, *World Report 2015*, above n 107, 46.
135 Ibid 48.
136 Ibid 49.
137 Kennedy, *The Dark Sides of Virtue*, above n 1, 14.

and innocent victims; and the knights, or experts. This is a familiar casting and features also in Sandvik's reconstruction of 'the humanitarian international',[138] Charlesworth's portrayal of the exhilarated 'international lawyer'[139] and Orford's depiction of the hero as internationalist.[140] The INGO forms a microcosm for this ideological framework.[141] The knights and the seals enter into an 'extractive relationship', where the knights (resembling Northern INGOs) 'extract' stories and information from the seals in order to sustain themselves, or their own status.[142] What are the political implications of this relationship? How does telling the story reinforce these stereotypical, problematic, roles and behaviour—in other words how does it *govern*? And whose story is really being told?

The human rights activist is seeking to 'confront, interrogate and *understand*' the victim, and the violation; to make the story a '*comprehensible narrative*'.[143] As Kennedy, writing as a humanitarian, a practitioner and a Critical Legal Studies scholar, expresses in describing his experience of meeting Ana, a political prisoner held in a Uruguay prison, the activist enters into a space that is perhaps too intimate and shocking to relate to.[144] The activist must thus look for connection and manufacture a 'discourse of connection'[145] that requires some intrusion on the narrative of the victim. How can an experience had over a 'Spring break' for the activist be translated into real life, into policy changes and communicated on a global scale so that people will want to act? Is the intended effect to make the audience want to become knights themselves? Or simply to identify with Ana and other victims as the seals?

The network of modern human rights advocacy and narration is characterised by a 'desire to *know*, *tame* and *redeem*'[146] victims and violations that seem unknowable, untamable and irredeemable. Governmental rationality operates within the expert network to continually reproduce this power relation, where the telling of the story is in itself an intrusion, an act of 'power' that constructs Ana as a victim that needs to be known, tamed and redeemed. Of course, she might desire this—she certainly freely told her story and wanted to be free from prison. This is not the point. The point is that by telling her story for her, Kennedy and his human rights activist counterparts become the narrators, editing and telling the whole story, the whole

[138] Sandwick, 'Review Essay', above n 43, 290, who attributes the phase to De Waal.
[139] Charlesworth, 'International Law', above n 44, 381.
[140] A Orford, 'Muscular Humanitarianism: Reading the Narratives of the New Interventionism' (1999) 10 *European Journal of International Law* 679, 699.
[141] See also Bell, 'Introduction', above n 5, 6.
[142] See Plewes and Stuart, 'The Pornography of Poverty', above n 38, 24.
[143] Kennedy, *The Dark Sides of Virtue*, above n 1, 39 and 42 (emphasis added).
[144] Ibid 54.
[145] Ibid 82.
[146] Ibid 80.

truth about her situation. Not only this but, as Kennedy states, they were more than 'just actors—we were the narrators and directors, creating our roles and casting others'.[147]

HRW aims to highlight abuses of rights by telling the stories of 'victims and witnesses'. In doing so, it maintains the theatre of roles where the professional, the expert, the activist is constructed as 'the knight' and the victims and witnesses must be known, tamed and redeemed. They must be known by measuring the levels of harm suffered using statistics and indicators to decide whether the harm they suffer merits priority status. They must be tamed so that their story is intelligible and palatable and fits into the formula of arbitrary and discriminatory conduct. And they must be redeemed, made civilised so that they too abide by and benefit from the code of conduct that is human rights and that creates them as ideal, rights-bearing citizens. The minor processes of interviewing victims and reporting their stories becomes a narrating—a political process by which the story is extracted from an always and already 'victim' actor and sustains the role of an always and already 'saviour' in the form of the human rights activist/ INGO. The narration thus manifests the 'damning metaphor' of 'savages, victims, saviours' (SVS) that Mutua identifies as pervading the human rights movement.[148] The metaphor is created and sustained by the main authors (what I call 'narrators') of human rights discourse, which includes 'the United Nations, Western states, international non-governmental organisations (INGOs), and senior Western academics'.[149] These narrators are then the fronts for the 'saviour' in the metaphor—'the redeemer, the good angel who protects, vindicates, civilizes, restrains, and safeguards'[150]—although the real saviour, Mutua points out, is rights discourse itself as embedded in liberal thought, philosophy and culture. We can identify a global governing (through) rights here; those cast as saviours (the narrators) *govern rights* by determining what rights are and how to do rights by maintaining extractive relationships with 'victims' (the victim is the 'powerless, helpless innocent', like Mohannad, Tariq and Ana) who need rescuing from the 'savage' (the 'cultural deviation from human rights' that is instrumentalised by the state).[151] In interviewing victims like Mohannad and Tariq, 'HRW's role is to arrive as close as possible to the truth'.[152] Yet *the truth* is whatever is narrated—we never hear from Ana again, unless HRW chooses to

---

[147] Ibid 47.

[148] M Mutua, *Human Rights: A Political and Cultural Critique* (Philadelphia, PA, University of Pennsylvania Press, 2002) ch 1.

[149] Ibid 10.

[150] Ibid 11.

[151] Ibid 11.

[152] Per T Porteous, Deputy Program Director, Washington DC Office, speaking on the HRW, 'About Us' Video, available at www.hrw.org/about.

include her in another report. Her crisis is over and her 'everyday' is now not relevant to achieving truth and justice.[153] The saviour is at the same time *governed through rights*, since the saviour status is dependent on submission to human rights norms and achieving results partly through the practice of extracting stories/truth.

Perhaps my account, relying here on Kennedy and Mutua, is somewhat outdated, for there is a 'new ethical frontier in human rights work' as Gready highlights that champions '"responsibility to the story" as a *process* spanning the telling and the representation and the reception of the telling'.[154] Alternative, qualitative methods are being used in a conscious effort to *do* humanitarianism through rights differently; to resist limited understanding of social realities and 'social devaluation'[155] that narrating 'their stories' 'for them' can bring. For instance, methods like 'individual testimonies' that are based in an 'ethics of caring and accountability'; these involve free-ranging, open-ended interviews and seek to prioritise the experience and personal memory of the individual. After all, 'we cannot ethically only extract our research from them, and write and publish their life stories. And then just walk away'.[156] This focus on 'stories as evidence', 'story circles' and 'storyboards' that will form a 'reciprocal research' claims to be empowering, rather than extractive.[157] There are two points to be made here. First, these overtly qualitative and engaged methodologies, that prize listening in a search for 'truth' and justice, perhaps pose a challenge to HRW and its quantitative and objective violator + victim + remedy formula. As part of its core values, HRW explicitly states though, 'we recognize a particular *responsibility* for the victims and witnesses who have shared their experiences with us'.[158] How does this responsibility manifest itself? What is it a responsibility for? Do human rights activists recognise a responsibility for narration—for constructing the *truth*? Do they acknowledge that their code of conduct (that is, human rights discourse and its ability to allow intrusion in the interests of finding the story) means that they become 'rulers' through rights? And this brings me to the second point; the qualitative methods like life stories still work within a standard human rights framework; they are still then subject to the governmental

---

[153] Note Charlesworth's point that a 'way forward' from the concern with crisis (which 'skews the discipline of international law' is to refocus international law on 'issues of structural justice that underpin everyday life', 'International Law', above n 44, 391 (emphasis added).

[154] P Gready, 'Introduction: "Responsibility to the Story"' (2010) 2(2) *Journal of Human Rights Practice* 177, 184 (emphasis added).

[155] H Mander, '"Words from the Heart": Researching People's Stories' (2010) 2(2) *Journal of Human Rights Practice* 252, 256.

[156] Ibid 269.

[157] E Pittaway, L Bartolomei and R Hugman, '"Stop Stealing our Stories": The Ethics of Research with Vulnerable Groups' (2010) 2(2) *Journal of Human Rights Practice* 229.

[158] See www.hrw.org/about (emphasis added).

power relations within rights. Even being engaged, enacting compassion in the face of suffering (re)produces roles; suffering is a 'recent invention' to the extent that it is has been made knowable and it must be heard.[159] Being 'engaged' is simply another politics; as Fassin notes, it is a 'politics of compassion' that 'is a politics of inequality ... a politics of solidarity' that maintains 'tensions between inequality and solidarity, between a relation of domination and a relation of assistance ... constitutive of all humanitarian government'.[160] Perhaps what is then needed to counter the conventional narrative of extractive relationships is not only new methodologies that search for new compassionate ways to work within rights, but to interrogate the very discourse of rights itself and the actors within it and produce a *counter*-narrative that challenges what it means to have an ethical duty to *resist* government/s. I return to the idea of the counter-narrative at the end of the chapter.

C. Scrutiny: Self-Government

INGOs do not *only* 'rule' through rights via expertise and narration. Governmentality is a reflexive process that results in the INGO *governing itself* through rights. It does so in order to maintain its necessary status as a suitable participant/contributor in the wider modern governmental technology that is the global human rights architecture. Civil society represents a new sort of governmentality, a new field for the functioning of the liberal art of government.[161] It is a *new* rationality of government to the extent that it is about *governing less* out of a concern for maximising the effectiveness of government (through rights).[162] Less government is possible through the tactics, technologies and functionings of expert actors, statistical knowledge and measurement through indicators that allow for experts to communicate with each other and with the outside world and tell stories of violations, violators and victims. It is also possible, and highly successful, because the actors involved are free and voluntarily engage in *self*-government through technologies of the self. I look at the INGO as a collective 'self', a type of actor that is integral to global human rights architecture and which ensures the smooth functioning of human rights as a regulatory discourse by engaging in checks on its own behaviour. Is it fair to see the INGO as a 'self'? Is there really a true 'essence' of the self that we can attribute to the INGO?

---

[159] Fassin, *Humanitarian Reason*, above n 2, 41.
[160] Ibid 3.
[161] Foucault, *The Birth of Biopolitics*, above n 26, 291.
[162] M Sennellart in Foucault, *The Birth of Biopolitics*, above n 26, 327. Senellart does not mention rights.

Certainly not, though this is equally true of each individual 'self'.[163] But it is not the essential meaning of the self per se that is interesting to observe; the self is abstract and constantly being redesigned according to the dictates of the policing process; it is, rather, the methods that we use to understand it, and that it uses to exist, that are more important.[164]

By 'technologies of the self', one of three other 'technologies' of power (that is, technologies of production, technologies of sign systems and technologies of domination), Foucault referred to 'how an individual acts upon himself'.[165] That is, the extent to which a subject participates in the policing process (enacted via technologies of domination) to monitor, and change, her own behaviour. We are thus looking at the degree to which technologies of self-management complement technologies of domination in furthering the imperatives of the policing process.[166] The various rituals of self-examination for Foucault, borrowing from the Stoics, include the confession, the spiritual retreat and meditation.[167] For the INGO, the policing technologies are represented by the criteria they must satisfy in order to secure their status as 'suitable' participants or contributors to rights discourse. Thus at the UN level, in order to secure attendance at ECOSOC meetings and those of its committees, to access the UN Secretariat and its public information resources, and to gain accreditation to UN conferences and other one-time events, the INGO must satisfy the code for participation rights in the ECOSOC Statute discussed above (eg it must continue to make 'positive or effective contribution' to the work of the UN). The code recognises the global reach of an INGO like HRW and it will seek to fulfil these criteria to have a seat at the table and so maintain its 'gatekeeper of NGOs' status.

Similarly at the EU level, the expertise of HRW must be called upon; it must be invited in to the FRP to share expert knowledge and engage in fruitful dialogue. Hence, the organisation must satisfy the Selection Criteria and abide by the Code of Conduct for participants to the FRP. HRW must, for instance, show 'expertise, proven experience and capacity'; 'demonstrate that their programme of work is of direct relevance to the work of the FRA'; and show that they are 'representative in the field of their competence at national, regional, European or international level'[168]—all of

---

[163] On the absence of a hidden self within human nature that is somehow discoverable, and the nature of the self as not static, see P Hutton, 'Foucault, Freud and the Technologies of the Self' in LH Martin, H Gutman and PH Hutton (eds) *Technologies of the Self: A Seminar with Michel Foucault* (Amherst, MA, University of Massachusetts Press, 1988) 120, especially 127 and 135.

[164] Ibid 139.

[165] M Foucault, 'Technologies of the Self' in Luther H Martin, Huck Gutman and Patrick H Hutton (eds), *Technologies of the Self: A Seminar with Michel Foucault* (Amherst, MA, University of Massachusetts Press, 1988) 16, 18–19.

[166] Hutton, 'Foucault, Freud and the Technologies of the Self', above n 163, 132.

[167] Ibid 132.

[168] FRA, *Code of Conduct*, above n 69.

which are determined, and so *policed*, by the FRA experts. The Code only applies once a screening selection assessment has been made,[169] at which point an organisation can be refused and must be 'recognised' as a 'FRP participant' to form part of the cooperation network that is the FRP. As a participant, it can then be 'called upon' (again, a monitored and policed process, rather than an open invitation) to make suggestions regarding the Annual Work Programme of the FRA, give feedback on the annual report, communicate opinions in the aftermath of conferences and be used in ad hoc consultations.[170] Participants may then talk to each other, 'share their or announce upcoming events, take part in FRA consultations, discuss new ideas and share experiences' via an interactive online platform, e-FRP;[171] but they can only log-in if they have participant status, that is, if they have been called, selected and approved. Participation and the sharing of expertise is thus regulated via this online technology of policing. The whole system of engagement with civil society actors by this regional agency so as to 'exchange information and pool knowledge'[172] is based on a complementary relationship between technologies of domination (the selection criteria, the codes of conduct) and technologies of the self. This policing of the self begins with HRW's application for participant status and continues through the reports, dispatches, press releases, etc that it produces so as to continually ensure, sustain and strengthen its role as a FRP participant.[173] What if HRW is *not* recognised as a suitable participant? Why would it allow itself to be policed and monitored, given its own extensive expertise, knowledge and work in international and European human rights? If not a suitable participant, it becomes the *failed* hero, the *failed* knight. It does not fit in to the ideological framework of the global human rights architecture, loses its access, status and funding. It must behave correctly in order to exist within this framework of which it is, according to its own experts, a vital part. This desire to 'exist better' within the global architecture of rights means HRW performs a care of the self that has ethical implications.

The INGO is not concerned with 'really knowing' its *self*—but then this 'really knowing' ourselves is not what Foucault meant by the care of the self. The care of the self is, rather, a *social practice* that is concerned with *acting correctly* with regard to circumstances.[174] It is an activity of 'self on

---

[169] FRA, *FRP Selection*, above n 73.
[170] See fra.europa.eu/en/cooperation/civil-society/consultations.
[171] See fra.europa.eu/en/cooperation/civil-society/e-frp.
[172] As per FRA Regulation, art 10(2).
[173] See 'HRW in Europe', www.hrw.org/tag/human-rights-european-union as linked from the FRA, FRP participants webpage, fra.europa.eu/en/cooperation/civil-society/participant-organisations.
[174] M Foucault, *The Hermeneutics of the Subject: Lectures at the Collège de France 1981–1982* (F Gros (ed), G Burchell (trans), New York, Picador, 2005) 527 and 536.

self',[175] which refers to 'the "techniques" by which a subject ... establishes a well-ordered relationship to the world and to others'.[176] These are the techniques we just looked at, of the selection criteria and codes of conduct that ensure suitability for participation in the international and European rights strategies. The INGO behaves as directed, or policed, by these techniques not only so that it can better itself (its own knowledge, expertise and opportunities for dialogue) but so that it can fit better and exist better within global civil society; so that it can better manage and improve its 'aesthetics of existence'.[177] What the INGO then is concerned with is its way of being and behaviour, with its *ethos*, which is a certain way of acting that is *visible* to others. If a person's *ethos* is visible in his 'clothing, appearance, gait, in the calm with which he responded to every event, and so on',[178] the international human rights non-governmental organisation's *ethos* is visible in its experts, its methodology, its outputs (reports, etc). It is the concern with this *ethos*, with this form of care of the self, that Foucault described as 'ethical in itself'.[179] It is concerned with being able to communicate and share expertise, knowledge and information. In doing so, it educates itself on how it ought to behave to be a suitable contributor. It manages linkages that lead to mutual learning and sharing of knowledge, and completion in levels of expertise and in resources, so as to maintain its status as a human rights expert.

Can this self-government be resisted? Is there space within the global human rights architecture for resistance to the governing processes that construct the INGO as a suitable participant? Perhaps, and I come to this now, the INGO can accept an ethical responsibility for the extent to which it governs through rights and thus constructs and sustains its own identity as an authority (and in HRW's case, gatekeeper) of rights.

IV. CONCLUSION

The researchers within Amnesty International, a gatekeeper NGO of comparable prowess to my HRW example, are described by Hopgood as 'keepers of the flame'.[180] They are 'the ones who have been responsible for

---

[175] M Foucault, *The Government of the Self and Others: Lectures at the Collège de France 1982–1983* (F Gros (ed), G Burchell (trans), Basingstoke, Palgrave Macmillan, 2010) 242.

[176] F Gros, 'Course Context' in ibid 377–78.

[177] M Foucault, 'On the Genealogy of Ethics' in P Rabinow (ed), *Michel Foucault: Ethics— Essential Works of Foucault 1954–1984* (London, Penguin, 1997) 253, 260.

[178] M Foucault, 'The Ethics of the Concern of the Self as a Practice of Freedom' in P Rabinow (ed), *Michel Foucault: Ethics—Essential Works of Foucault 1954–1984* (London, Penguin, 1997) 281, 286.

[179] Ibid 287.

[180] Hopgood, *Keepers of the Flame*, above n 10.

investigating, writing up cases, interpreting Amnesty policy, and generally creating the identity of this seemingly identityless organisation'.[181] They are 'the people with the good hearts', who preserve the 'magic of Amnesty'.[182] And yet, much like the secret behind magic, there is an illusion here—and it is not that these are *not* the good people with the good hearts, but that their intentions do not necessarily matter because the effect of INGOs like AI, like HRW, is that they govern (through) rights. The keepers of the flame, or the experts, govern through their expertise, as we see through their working methods and tactics of cooperation. They govern also through narration, defining how best to do rights (in HRW's case, through the shaming methodology), what rights are, and entering into extractive relationships where stories are taken from victims and witnesses and made into intelligible narratives—a political process that maintains a savage-victim-saviour prism where the INGO will always be the category doing the saving. They also govern themselves, and here we see the great success of governmentality through rights, by engaging in scrutiny to become and maintain their status as suitable participants and contributors to a global human rights architecture in which civil society is an ever-increasingly important modern governmental technology. The wider implications of this fit with the theme of this book, that rights are technologies of a *global* governmentality; they are not *only* 'deliciously empowering'.[183] And rights discourse produces the identities of the actors within the global human rights architecture, so that HRW remains the gatekeeper, the knight, the hero, creating its own identity as it names and shames in the name of rights.

Why should this matter? These 'dark sides' of rights, as in, the uncertainties and ambivalences (the 'human sides'),[184] highlight a danger where governance happens in the name of less government and 'doing good', where it is effectively humanitarian *government (through) rights*. That is not to say that HRW is not doing good; it is, rather, to ask what *else* are they doing? It is to make space for dissatisfaction and refusal of what we are told are the right ways to do and to narrate rights, and to identify what might be *dangerous* in their work. So there is a call to be self-critical here—to search for what Kennedy calls a 'grace in governance',[185] whereby we enact a responsible humanitarianism that is at once responsible, and not blind to its own power and accepting of the uncertainty of decisions. Kennedy says this in the same vain that he says the international humanitarians he has known

---

[181] Ibid 15.
[182] Ibid 17.
[183] P Williams, *The Alchemy of Race and Rights: Diary of a Law Professor* (Cambridge and London, Harvard University Press, 1991) 164.
[184] Kennedy, *The Dark Sides of Virtue*, above n 1, xxv–xxvi.
[185] Ibid xxvi and 343.

over the past years are 'intensely self-critical'.[186] Some bear a 'responsibility to the story' and construct innovative, caring and participatory qualitative methods to listen to the *real* narrative of individuals who want to tell their stories,[187] or interrogate the pervading ethic of 'crisis'.[188] Yet we (and when I say 'we', I mean human rights activists and experts) cannot escape the power relations that circulate through humanitarian government (through) rights; that we are cast into roles, where experts (like HRW) narrate how to do rights, what rights are and extract narratives based on 'suffering'.[189] The ethic of 'crisis' that motivates the activist motives critique also; for critique is a permanent state of crisis, which does not and should not cease to interrogate even the 'good guys'. For, as Redfield also concludes, 'humanitarianism … is at once crucial and dangerous, sometimes unsettling, often unsatisfying, and ever uncertain. It appears, in short, a *measured good*'.[190] Not only do we have a duty to interrogate but, I suggest, the inadvertent *governors* have a *duty* to interrogate how rights shape an understanding of progress, good practice and good governance through humanitarian action in ways that might be problematic. I explore the possibilities of what would be a counter-conduct on the part of the INGO in Chapter 6. Their responsibility is not only to 'the story' but to produce a counter-narrative to rights that highlights the continual crisis within humanitarian government.

---

[186] Ibid 328.

[187] Gready, 'Introduction', above n 154.

[188] Charlesworth, 'International Law', above n 44 and see also Redfield, *Life in Crisis*, above n 4.

[189] Fassin, *Humanitarian Reason*, above n 2, 41.

[190] Redfield, 'Conclusion: A Measured Good', above n 16, 250.

Part II

Resisting Government (Through) Rights

4

Resisting Rights with Responsibility

It will be great to have more people volunteering, more people being school governors, more people putting back into their community ... Britain is a *nation of volunteers* and this is going to take this further and faster.

David Cameron[1]

Nothing seems more appropriate today than thinking community.

Roberto Esposito[2]

B RITAIN, AS DAVID Cameron and leaders before him have stressed, is a society enriched by a strong tradition of voluntary and community activity.[3] It is a tradition that strengthens bonds between individuals to 'create a sense of citizenship'[4] and makes possible the 'one nation ideal',[5] wherein 'we come together, and work together, to solve problems'.[6] This chapter seeks to problematise the rhetoric of volunteerism and community as a technology of governmentality. Modern Britain, I propose, has adopted an *ethic of responsibility* which is a reaction against rights discourse. As such, in this, the first of two chapters in this book on 'resisting government by rights', I explain how this ethic of responsibility is a resistance to rights that emphasises community and opportunity over individualism and right. Thus, rather than the processes of governing (through) rights that we looked at in the previous chapters at the regional and international levels, what we see instead at the local level are processes of *governing (through) community*.

---

[1] 'Election 2015: Cameron pledges "paid voluntary leave"', *BBC News*, 10 April 2015, available at www.bbc.co.uk/news/election-2015-32243680 (emphasis added).

[2] R Esposito, *Communitas: The Origin and Destiny of Community* (Stanford, CA, Stanford University Press, 2010).

[3] White Paper, *Communities in Control: Real People, Real Power* (Communities and Local Government, July 2008) 34.

[4] J Straw, 'Human Rights and Personal Responsibility: New Citizenship for a New Millenium', speech made at St Paul's Cathedral, London, 2 October 2000, available at www.britishpensions.org.au/straw_speech.htm.

[5] D Cameron, 'Opportunity', speech made on 22 June 2015, available at www.gov.uk/government/speeches/pm-speech-on-opportunity.

[6] D Cameron, 'Let's Mend Our Broken Society', speech made on 27 April 2010, available at conservative-speeches.sayit.mysociety.org/speech/601479.

'Community' is increasingly replacing 'society' as something that is more readily calculable and able to be governmentalised through the deployment of various tactics that regulate the conduct, or behaviour, of individuals. Community represents not a collective of individual juridical subjects but has a life and density of its own; it refers to a mass, to the population and hence to the management of all and of each that take (active) part in it. Governing through community happens, I argue, via a renewed ethic of responsibility that creates an alternative subjectivity: the active citizen, *in place of* the rights-bearing citizen.[7] The active citizen, otherwise the 'modern citizen', the 'full volunteer', the 'user' or the 'champion', has no need for rights because she is responsible for herself: her behaviour, her choices and her general well-being as defined by the quality of her existence within a community. As active citizens, we ought to ask not what we are owed, entitled or have a *right* to but 'ask *what you can do for your community* and your country'.[8] Governing community is then the result of compliance with the ethic of responsibility: ethical communities govern themselves to ensure not just survival but optimal conditions of existence, where they 'solve their own problems to create *strong, attractive and thriving* neighbourhoods'.[9] The politics of community is made possible through complex relations of governmentality or 'ethopower',[10] of pastoral power and self-government, which together ensure better management and regulation of 'the community' via instilling values, providing guidance and maintaining freedom. The active citizen is managed into a state of refusal of, and dissatisfaction with, rights. Whilst I too have argued so far in this book from a position of refusal and dissatisfaction with rights, here I seek to highlight that the particular counter-narrative of an ethic of responsibility is problematic and itself poses significant dangers.

The counter-narrative of the ethic of responsibility is *dangerous* in that the tantalising promise of opportunity, choice and empowerment that it offers creates a subjectivity that is better managed, better controlled and left without recourse to challenging the system via rights. There is an insidious shift

---

[7] See B Kisby, 'The Big Society: Power to the People' (2010) 81(4) *Political Quarterly* 484 for background on the concept of 'active citizenship' as the initiative of the then Tory Home Secretary Douglas Hurd in the late 1980s (487) and his critique of 'the "big society", full of *active citizens* and empowered communities' (488, emphasis added); Kisby is concerned with the degree to which the '"big society … needs to ensure that all members of society can access adequate levels of welfare support when they need it' (488), whereas I am concerned with the extent to which active citizenship resists and threatens rights discourse and the rights-bearing citizen.

[8] *Conservative Party Manifesto 2015: Strong Leadership, A Clear Economic Plan, A Brighter, More Secure Future* (Conservative Party, 2015) 45 (emphasis added).

[9] See www.gov.uk/government/topics/community-and-society.

[10] See N Rose, 'Community, Citizenship, and the Third Way' (2000) 43(9) *American Behavioural Scientist* 1395 and N Rose, 'The Politics of Life Itself' (2001) 18(6) *Theory, Culture and Society* 1.

then away from individual rights to collective responsibility that betrays the very foundation of the liberal state. The shift is a dangerous reaction against rights by stifling a subject's resistance. The kind of counter-conduct I refer to in the next chapter, where a rights-bearing subject can 'revolt' against government, by creating an unruly community of rioters or parrhesiats, is suppressed since community is in itself the ideal that *you* chose and for which *you* are now responsible.

I begin this chapter by exploring the new politics of community in terms of first, defining and delimiting the ethic of responsibility that governs it and, second, explaining the shift from society to community and its implications for bigger and better government *through community*. I go on, in sections II and III, to look at the responsibilisation of, first, youth and, second, society through two major governmental policies or programmes: the National Citizen Service (NCS) programme and Community and Society policy. NCS began life as the flagship policy of David Cameron's Big Society agenda, and although the latter has been replaced in political rhetoric by 'Community and Society', NCS continues to be energetically pursued by the Conservative government as a means of achieving one of the old Big Society goals: mending Britain through 'social action'.[11] There are up to 24 initiatives under the government's new policy area of 'Community and Society' and I examine those of localism, community integration, and support for families. I thus focus on the development of 'community rights', which are, interestingly, phrased in terms of opportunity rather than either obligation or entitlement, and manifest as a *right to* community rather than individual juridical rights. Finally, I distill the implications of governing (through) community as witnessed through these programmes and policies into a problematic and even dangerous challenge to rights discourse.

I. A NEW POLITICS OF COMMUNITY

A. The Ethic of Responsibility as a Resistance to Rights

The ethic of responsibility relies on the establishment and maintenance of a politics of *community*. The idea of 'community' has, as Rose observes, long existed in political thought. But what makes the concept interesting and 'appropriate' today as per Esposito and, I argue, potentially dangerous is that it becomes technical.[12] By technical, Rose means that community

---

[11] Civil Exchange, *Whose Society? The Final Big Society Audit* (January 2015) 6 and 14, available at www.civilexchange.org.uk/wp-content/uploads/2015/01/Whose-Society_The-Final-Big-Society-Audit_final.pdf.

[12] P Miller and N Rose, *Governing the Present* (Cambridge, Polity Press, 2008) 89.

becomes calculable: 'Communities become zones to be investigated, mapped, classified, documented, interpreted ... individual conduct is now to be made intelligible in terms of the beliefs and values of "their community"'.[13] Community, in other words, becomes governmentalised; citizens are managed according to their emotional attachments to the community, their adherence to shared values. A community then, is more than a grouping, more than a side you take, more than a territory: it is an 'affective and *ethical* field ... a space of emotional relationships through which individual identities are constructed through their bonds to microcultures of values and meanings'.[14] Community becomes a *politics*, a means of governing, via *ethics*. And I argue that the politics of community happens primarily via an ethic of responsibility.

Responsibilised community is made possible by the functionings of a particular type of governmentality relation that Rose calls 'ethopower'—a concern with the regulation of behaviour, or the 'conduct of conducts',[15] that focuses on human beings as 'ethical creatures'.[16] It is a 'politics of behaviour' that brings a new dimension to the personal and political by focusing on behaving *ethically*. As a power relation, '[e]thopower works through the values, beliefs and sentiments thought to underpin the techniques of responsible self-government and the management of one's obligations to others ... a new game: the community-civility game'.[17] 'Civility' from 'civilis', or 'relating to citizens', means the game is one in which *citizenship* becomes conditional on ethical behaviour—it is now an ethical citizenship that is made possible by a 'double movement of autonomization and responsibilization', where individuals are 'set free to find their own destiny' (autonomised) and at the same time 'made responsible for their destiny and for that of society as a whole' (responsibilised).[18] What I then go on to suggest from this is that this ethical citizenship has increasingly been instrumentalised as a direct reaction against rights. So I find the 'ethic of responsibility' a helpful and accurate depiction of how governing through community happens since it connotes responsibility *over right/s*. The modern citizen is an *active, responsible volunteer* and not a rights-bearing citizen. Autonomous self-government, where the modern citizen takes responsibility for her own behaviour and choices, is intimately connected with the ambitions of good government through community. In this ethopolitical relation, rights lose their appeal, their value and thereby their emancipatory connotation; they

---

[13] Ibid 89.

[14] Rose, 'Community, Citizenship, and the Third Way', above n 10, 1400 (emphasis added).

[15] M Foucault, 'The Subject and Power' in *Power*, vol 3, *Essential Works of Foucault 1954–1984* (J Faubion (ed), R Hurley (trans), London, Penguin, 2002) 326, 341.

[16] Rose, 'Community, Citizenship, and the Third Way', above n 10, 1398.

[17] Ibid 1399.

[18] Ibid 1400.

are instead something to be resisted—as selfish, as indulgent and as a departure from the right kind of moral community (one based, as I show below in the NCS case study, in a rhetoric of opportunism, an ethical code of conduct and facilitated by mentors). Moreover, the construction 'ethic of responsibility' emphasises ethics in a Foucauldian sense; thus, not only adherence to a community's pre-determined moral codes but also with an aesthetics of existence where the focus is not the individual but existing better *with others* (in community). In addition to ethopower, the ethic of responsibility relies for its operation on pastoral power and a politics of expertise, and on an ethics of care of the self, as we will see in the NCS and Community and Society programmes, below. The ethic of responsibility mobilises an *ethos* (a spirit, a whole culture) of responsibilisation that creates an alternative subjectivity: the active citizen, in opposition to the rights-bearing citizen. The active citizen exists within the Big Society, now rebranded as 'Community and Society'.

B. Community and/or Society

Ever since he first coined the term in 2009,[19] Cameron between 2010 and 2011 repeatedly described the Big Society as his great 'passion'.[20] Indeed, it had formed the flagship policy of the 2010 Conservative election campaign. Against a backdrop of societal violence, which in April 2010 just days before the general election, manifested itself in the brutal gang killing of 15-year-old Sofyen Belamoudden,[21] Cameron spoke of the Big Society as *the only way* of mending Britain's broken society:

> There has always been violence. There has always been evil. But there is something about the frequency of these crimes—the depravity of these crimes, that betrays a deep and fundamental problem in Britain today … Something is broken. Society is broken … There is, I believe, only one way out of this national crisis—and that is what I have called the Big Society.[22]

---

[19] D Cameron, 'The Big Society', Hugo Young Lecture, 10 November 2009, available at www.conservatives.com/News/Speeches/2009/11/David_Cameron_The_Big_Society.aspx.

[20] D Cameron, 'Big Society', speech made on 23 May 2011, available at www.gov.uk/government/speeches/speech-on-the-big-society; D Cameron, 'Big Society', speech made at Liverpool, 19 July 2010, available at www.gov.uk/government/speeches/big-society-speech; D Cameron and N Clegg, 'PM and Deputy PM's Speeches at Big Society Launch', 18 May 2010, available at www.gov.uk/government/speeches/pm-and-deputy-pms-speeches-at-big-society-launch.

[21] J Herrmann, 'Sofyen Belamoudden murder: the inside story of a crime that horrified Britain', *Independent*, 25 April 2015, available at www.independent.co.uk/news/uk/crime/sofyen-belamouadden-murder-the-victims-mother-and-one-of-the-boys-involved-reveal-a-different-side-10197147.html.

[22] Cameron, 'Let's Mend Our Broken Society', above n 6.

The theme of a 'social fightback' against 'pure criminality' was resurrected in August 2011, when the Prime Minister spoke in the aftermath of the London Riots:[23]

> We need to talk about behavior and morality …We must fight back against the attitudes and assumptions that have brought parts of our society to this shocking state … Irresponsibility. Selfishness. Behaving as if your choices have no consequences … Crime without punishment. Rights without responsibilities. Communities without control.[24]

The Big Society's big solution is thus to change, or govern, behaviour—and to do so by instilling the core value of *responsibility* and a sense of community as an entity that is affected by the consequences of behavioural choices. Thus, the big idea is actually to *govern choice*. Responsibility, in its various communal forms, is the magic word behind the Big Society's *ethos*:

> The Big Society is a society with much higher levels of *personal, professional, civic and corporate responsibility*—a society where people come together to solve problems and improve life for themselves and their communities; a society where the leading force for progress is social responsibility, not state control.[25]

It is big society, *not big government*.[26] Or perhaps we should say it 'was'. Talk of the Big Society has subsided; the Prime Minister last mentioned the phrase in his 2013 Christmas address where, holding on to the ethic of responsibility we saw coming through in 2010 and 2011, he stated 'there are those millions who keep on strengthening our society too—being good neighbours, running clubs and voluntary associations, playing their part in countless small ways to help build what I call the "big society"'.[27] Moreover, according to the think tank Civil Exchange's *Final Big Society Audit*, the Big Society 'has *failed* to deliver' and 'we are more divided than before'.[28]

And yet, despite the virtual abandonment of the label and its documented failure, the *ethos* of the Big Society continues to be pursued by policies under its three main original goals: community empowerment, promoting social action, and opening up public services.[29] The main policies are NCS, Big Society Capital and Academy and Free Schools.[30] Moreover, the

---

[23] D Cameron, 'The Fightback After the Riots', speech made on 15 August 2011, available at www.gov.uk/government/speeches/pms-speech-on-the-fightback-after-the-riots.

[24] Ibid.

[25] Conservatives, *Big Society Not Big Government: Building a Big Society* (2010) 1, available at www.conservatives.com/~/media/Files/Downloadable%20Files/Building-a-Big-Society.ashx (emphasis added).

[26] Ibid.

[27] D Cameron, 'PM/s Christmas Message 2013', 24 December 2013, available at www.gov.uk/government/news/pms-christmas-message-2013.

[28] Civil Exchange, *Whose Society?*, above n 11, especially 4 (emphasis added).

[29] Ibid 6. See also C Slocock, 'What happened to David Cameron's "Big Society"', *Huffington Post*, 20 January 2015, available at www.huffingtonpost.co.uk/caroline-slocock/big-society_b_6505902.html.

[30] Ibid.

Conservative Party Manifesto 2015 included a section on 'Helping You Build the Big Society',[31] where it defines the latter as 'a vision of a more engaged nation, one in which we take more *responsibility* for ourselves and our neighbours; *communities* working together, not depending on remote and impersonal bureaucracies'.[32] Empowering communities remains one of three focus areas,[33] and the government has the ambition that 'we want every adult in the country to be an *active* member of an *active* neighbourhood group'.[34] Individuals will be given the *opportunity* to be empowered, to be active and to fulfil the 'one nation ideal', the Prime Minister promised in June of this year.[35] The Big Society has been replaced and is now being talked about as 'community and society', today a government policy area.[36] Yet the shift from society to community is a *return*, rather than a turn, for it echoes the rhetoric of New Labour's Third Way and is thus distinctly 'post-Thatcherite'.[37]

The Big Society represents Cameron's tweaking of Thatcher's infamous statement—'there is no such thing as society'[38]—to, 'there *is* such a thing as society, we just don't think it's the same as the state'.[39] Cameron's signifier is thus 'the Big Society' in contrast to Thatcher's signifier of 'free markets'; in this sense he has moved, in the construction of the Big Society *ethos*, from an obsession with GDP (economic interests) to GWB (general well-being).[40] The Big Society thus fits into a 'reformed brand of conservatism',[41] which exhibits a return to the *traditional* conservative ideas of public service, duty and social responsibility without an attachment to the 'Thatcherite new right concept of individuals as rational actors concerned only with utility maximization'.[42] Thus the explicit and exaggerated focus of Cameron's Big Society and his government's new policy of Community and Society places a stress on *social responsibility* that makes him less 'mother's boy' and more partial to one nation conservatism and the civic conservatism of the 1990s;

---

[31] *Conservative Party Manifesto 2015*, above n 8, ch 4.

[32] Ibid 45 (emphasis added).

[33] Ibid 1. The others are: public service reform and lasting culture change.

[34] Ibid 1 (emphasis added).

[35] Cameron, 'Opportunity', above n 5.

[36] Civil Exchange, *Whose Society?*, above n 11, 14. See also www.gov.uk/government/topics/community-and-society.

[37] P Kerr, C Byrne and E Foster, 'Theorising Cameronism' (2011) 9 *Political Studies Review* 193, 195.

[38] Prime Minister Margaret Thatcher, 'Epitaph for the Eighties? "There is No Such Thing as Society"', interview with *Women's Own Magazine*, 31 October 1987, available at briandeer.com/social/thatcher-society.htm.

[39] See comment in Kerr *et al*, 'Theorising Cameronism', above n 37 (emphasis added).

[40] Ibid 195 and 198.

[41] Ibid 195.

[42] MJ Smith, 'From Big Government to Big Society: Changing the State-Society Balance' (2010) 63(4) *Parliamentary Affairs* 818, 829 and 830. See also T Blair, *The Third Way* (London, Fabian Society, 1998).

more Blair's heir, in terms of the imitation of the modernisation rhetoric of New Labour's Third Way.[43] Built on ideas of 'new progressivism', the Third Way championed 'equal opportunity, personal responsibility and the mobilizing of citizens and communities'.[44] Society is therefore *not the state* but those people living *together* in *communities*. The emphasis on 'working together', 'with new purpose' that taps into 'untapped potential' was Blair's 'kind of Britain';[45] creating 'a society where the community works for the good of every individual, and every individual works for the good of the community' to create his version of the 'one nation' ideal.[46]

Blairism, Thatcherism and Cameronism are described by Kerr *et al* as three distinct hegemonic projects that, despite their differences, have the same overarching state project of neoliberalism.[47] This is a fair observation— but is it interesting? What Kerr *et al* do not acknowledge are the *distinctive* elements about Cameronism's signifier of the Big Society: first, and most starkly, that whilst it espouses traditionalism, in the values of common sense, responsibility and duty,[48] it has deliberately moved away from seeing the individual as a rational, autonomous being *with rights*. Whilst the New Labour era of 'one nation' was also the era of the Human Rights Act 1998 coming to fruition and of strong emphasis on 'positive rights' which needed to be balanced with responsibility to create a 'new citizenship' based in a 'logic of togetherness',[49] Cameron's one nation ideal threatens a virtual abandonment of positive rights in direct resistance to the regional and global human rights architecture I looked at in the two previous chapters. Under the guise of 'community rights', which are not positive rights but rather as I will show later a *right to* community, the balance has tipped in favour of more responsibility. Second, there is a deliberate, and even dangerous, move away from society toward community. This is dangerous because community is something different to society (contrary to Cameron's claim that there *is* such a thing as society, the rhetoric of his Big Society suggests otherwise): individuals are no longer citizens of society 'but of neighbourhoods, associations, regions, networks, subcultures, age groups, ethnicities and lifestyle sectors—in short, *communities*'.[50] The danger here is the

---

[43] S Evans, '"Mother's Boy": David Cameron and Margaret Thatcher' (2010) 12(3) *British Journal of Politics and International Relations* 325, especially at 325 and 331.

[44] A Giddens, *The Third Way and Its Critics* (Cambridge, Polity, 2000) 2.

[45] T Blair, *New Britain: My Vision of a Young Country* (London, New Statesman, 1996) v.

[46] Ibid vi.

[47] Kerr *et al*, 'Theorising Cameronism', above n 37, 198.

[48] Cameron, 'Opportunity', above n 5 and Cameron, 'The Fightback After the Riots', above n 23.

[49] Straw, 'Human Rights and Personal Responsibility', above n 4. For an alternative viewpoint, or a critique of the Third Way that argues it is deficient for its lack of attention to 'liberty', see R Dahrendorf, 'Whatever Happened to Liberty?', *New Statesman*, 6 September 1999, cited in Giddens, *The Third Way and Its Critics*, above n 44, 20.

[50] Rose, 'Community, Citizenship, and the Third Way', above n 10, 1398 (emphasis added).

absence, or even the direct resistance to rights talk in what ought to be a (neo) liberal society which has as its very foundation respect for the rational, autonomous individual, not the mass collective that is 'community'. There is a new politics of community at work that recognises a new type of governmentable subject: not the ideal rights-bearing citizen of a governmentality of rights but the *active citizen* of community who is responsible and ethical. Citizenship thus becomes conditional on responsible and ethical behaviour—and *this*, not respect for and protection of individual rights, becomes the ideal of the 'one nation'. In what follows, I aim to show how an ethic of responsibility operates to instil a new politics of community in which the citizen is manipulated into being an ethical, responsible, active individual who has no need of individual rights.

II. RESPONSIBILISING YOUTH: NATIONAL CITIZEN SERVICE

Described as a 'non-military programme that captures the spirit of National Service',[51] the National Citizen Service (NCS) is sold as a six to eight week programme, taking place outside term-time in the summer or autumn, designed for teenagers between the ages of 15–17. If they only 'say YES now', these teenagers are promised 'the most exciting and rewarding times of your life'—times where they will experience *adventure*, start a *future* and *make a difference*.[52] The *adventure* starts in Phase 1 of the programme and will allow them to 'live fearlessly to uncover a new you and work in a team that's part of something bigger than anything you've ever done'.[53] It involves living away from home, allowing freedom and the chance to make new friends and be part of a team of (10 to 15) 'amazing people', and taking part in adrenaline-fuelled activities such as rock-climbing, canoeing and archery.[54] 'Your *future* starts at YES'—and is a future in which you will use the 'huge life skills' you will be equipped with, such as growing your confidence, making your UCAS application stand out and getting a 'killer CV'.[55] This is Phase 2 of the programme, where teenagers are reunited with their team, away from home in university-style accommodation and meet organisations and important people from their local community, learning about the issues facing them but also finding their own passion (be it photography or football coaching). *Making a difference* also 'starts at YES' since the assurance is that 'your time at the NCS will give you the tools

---

[51] Cameron, 'The Fightback After the Riots', above n 23. See also D Bulley and B Sokhi-Bulley, 'Big Society as Big Government: Cameron's Governmentality Agenda' (2014) 16(3) *British Journal of Politics and International Relations* 452.

[52] See www.ncsyes.co.uk.

[53] Ibid.

[54] Ibid.

[55] Ibid.

to change the world around you through fundraising and volunteering'.[56] This next phase, Phase 3, is the call to 'Go out there and be amazing together'.[57] It involves agreeing on a Social Action Project with the team, something that 'will really make a mark on your local community'.[58] The final Phase 4 is graduation to *full volunteer status*. Now part of the 'bigger NCS family', young people are thrown a party, they are to be given support to develop their passion, kept involved through the chance to, for example, attend some of the greatest shows and events; the programme pledges 'Not only will you be a completely different person, but you will have made a huge network of amazing friends'.[59] NCS currently operates in England and Northern Ireland, having been piloted for two years in 2011 and 2012; it aims to increase places from 10,000 (in 2011) to 90,000 in 2014.[60] The provider organisations, comprising independent charities, social enterprises and businesses, local councils and sixth form colleges, more than doubled from 12 in 2011 to 29 in 2012.[61]

NCS illustrates the government's most robust technology for the government of youth. The agenda of creating a 'new you' that is a 'completely different person' who not only 'makes a difference' in the community through learning 'new skills' but is simultaneously having fun and fulfilling your 'own passion', is a manifestation of the new politics of community that prizes the 'full volunteer'. Youth have always been connected to their construction as a 'dangerous group' that presents a disproportionate and intolerable risk to the 'respectable public'.[62] Fifteen years ago in 2000, Vaughan pointed out that the Crime and Disorder Act 1998 resembled a new set of sanctions to correct the behaviour of young people.[63] He described a shift from a paternalistic model of regulation to a more active subjectivity where young people are made into active citizens who take responsibility for their own actions and attach themselves to an emotional community. The timing of the 1998 Act coincided with the horrific abduction, torture and killing of two-year old Jamie Bulger by two ten-year old boys, an event that shattered

---

[56] Ibid.
[57] Ibid.
[58] Ibid.
[59] Ibid.
[60] NatCen Social Research, *Evaluation of the National Citizen Service: Findings from the Evaluations of the 2012 Summer and Autumn NCS Programmes* (July 2013) 10, available at natcen.ac.uk/media/205475/ncs_evaluation_report_2012_combined.pdf. Note that since the time of writing there is now a newer evaluation report: Ipsos MORI, Social Research Institute, *National Citizen Service 2013 Evaluation: Main Report* (August 2014), available at www.ncsyes.co.uk/sites/all/themes/ncs/pdf/ncs_2013_evaluation_report_final.pdf.
[61] Ibid. NCS providers include, for example: The Challenge Network, Football League Trust, engage4life, cooperationireland and The NCS Network, see www.ncsyes.co.uk/about-ncs. For a list of regional providers in England see www.corganisers.org.uk/sites/default/files/ncs_providers_map_-_june_2013.pdf.
[62] B Vaughan, 'The Government of Youth: Disorder and Dependence?' (2000) 9(3) *Social and Legal Studies* 347, 360.
[63] Ibid.

the illusion of the 'respectable public' that children are innocent and pose no threat.[64] The launch of NCS also coincided with a challenge to the public conscience regarding the role and nurturing of young people: the London Riots of August 2011. This unruly event, in which 37 per cent of the rioters were youth (aged 10–17),[65] allowed for a separation between 'us' (the respectable general public) and 'them' (the rioting dangerous thugs) to be ingrained and then cultivated in the national consciousness; as Cameron declared, 'Those *thugs* we saw last week do not represent us, nor do they represent our young people—and they will not drag us down'.[66] With a complete disregard for political agency, struggle and the social situation which incited the riots, politicians, media and the judiciary described and reacted to the riots as threatening, criminal acts that were no more than 'bad behaviour':[67]

These riots were not about race ... these riots were not about government cuts ... and these riots were not about poverty ... No, this was about behaviour ... people showing indifference to right and wrong ... people with a twisted moral code ... people with a complete absence of self-restraint.[68]

So, it is not poverty or cuts that need to be talked about—no, 'we need to talk about behaviour and morality'.[69] We need to *change behaviour*. Cameron explicitly stated that in response to riots, NCS 'should become a great national effort', a 'rite of passage' that 'shows young people that doing good can feel good. The real thrill is from building things up, not tearing them down. Team-work, discipline, duty, decency; these might sound old-fashioned words but they are part of *the solution* to this very modern *problem of alienated, angry young people*. Restoring these values is what the NCS is about'.[70] Changing behaviour can thus happen by targeting 'young people' as *a mass*. This is how a culture change will be instigated and maintained.

So, how will NCS change the behaviour of the mass that is 'youth'? I identify three tactics whereby a politics of community operates to govern youth behaviour: first, the ingraining of a discourse of *opportunity* as

[64] Ibid 360.

[65] Based on the 'Reading the Riots' Study and interviews with 270 people who were directly involved in the riots in London, Birmingham, Manchester, Salford, Liverpool and Nottingham, see *Guardian* and London School of Economics, *Reading the Riots: Investigating England's Summer of Disorder* (2011), available at eprints.lse.ac.uk/46297/1/Reading%20the%20riots(published).pdf and see Chapter 5. See also B Sokhi-Bulley, 'Re-Reading the Riots: Counter-Conduct in London 2011' (2016) *Global Society* (forthcoming), DOI: 10.1080/13600826.2016.1143348. Available at: http://dx.doi.org/10.1080/13600826.2016.1143348.

[66] Cameron, 'The Fightback After the Riots', above n 23.

[67] Ibid. I further examine the riots as counter-conducting behaviour and problematise the political agency of the rioters in Chapter 5.

[68] Ibid.

[69] Ibid.

[70] Ibid (emphasis added).

opposed to individual right/s; second, establishing a *code of conduct* accord-ing to which youth will live and behave; and third, instilling and maintaining a form of *guided reflection*. These mirror NCS aims, which are threefold: to achieve a more cohesive society (where we all speak the language of opportunity); to make society more responsible (which it will be if all abide by the same ethical code of conduct); and to make society more engaged (which will happen if we are made aware of our need to pledge allegiance to community by guides or educators who instil reflection on oneself and one's impact on the community as good behaviour). The code of conduct represents an ethopolitics that governs behaviour, whilst guided reflection provided by experts represents a technology of pastoralism; together these create the responsibilised, self-governing mass of youth.

A. The Opportunity to Say Yes (to Cohesion)

'Opportunity' is the new magic word of the Conservative government and its plan to achieve the '"one nation" ideal'.[71] What does *everyone* have the opportunity to do? To 'get on and make a good life for themselves' and NCS, as a rite of passage for *all* 16–17 year olds (for this is the even-tual aim), will be key to '*changing attitudes* by bringing together young people from every community and giving them the skills they need to get on in life and work'.[72] Sitting in a wider discourse of responsibilisation, that is, a responsibility to yourself and to your community, that aims to nurture volunteers and not thugs, NCS is not an obligation or a right but an *opportunity*. There is a powerful emphasis on autonomy and choice rather than coerced participation: if you 'just say yes'[73] (an empowering affirmation in contrast to, though clearly referencing, the 'just say no' anti-drugs campaign of the 1980s)[74] you are giving yourself the opportunity to develop new skills and acquire new tools to be a different, a better person. And yet, as I aim to show in this section, that choice is governed—through (a) a code of conduct that is enshrined in the values of the Big Society, and (b) pastoral or expert guidance, whereby 'educators' ensure allegiance to these values. The autonomous choice to emancipate yourself is thus *also* a choice to be governed better. You are also giving yourself the opportunity to meet 'amazing people' who will become your friends and then you can 'be amazing together' to increase not only your personal well-being and secure a better future (through improving your CV, for example) but also the well-being of your community.

---

[71] Cameron, 'Opportunity', above n 5.
[72] Ibid.
[73] Above n 52.
[74] An anti-drugs advertising campaign, popularised in the United States during the late 1980s and early 1990s.

The concern for community well-being is nurtured through the end goal of NCS, which is the Social Action Project. The Project can be anything that will 'make a mark on your local community'.[75] The NCS Evaluation Report identifies examples of projects that demonstrate 'good practice'; so, for instance, young people have organised a tea party for older people; they have renovated a disused area of land; and organised fundraising for a hospice, a sexual health service and an elderly care home.[76] The Report notes more innovative examples, such as one NCS team who identified a concern that communities within their local area were not socialising together and then put together a project handing out pairs of teabags to passers-by on their local high street with the message 'do a favour for your neighbour'.[77] Young people's reaction to the projects is also recorded. The Report includes the following quotations from 'young people':

it made me feel proud—it's not something we normally do.

You see what a difference it makes. Like the festival we ran yesterday, then you think that, if you did it near us, you could make a big difference to the community.

It is interesting to note, on the one hand, these reactions of pride, a fulfilment of duty and making a difference for the extent to which they speak to the statistic that the NCS programme has a positive impact on young people's willingness to help out in the local community.[78] It also speaks to the possible and future impact of NCS; 88 per cent of young people surveyed for the NCS Evaluation said they would recommend NCS to a friend.[79] It is, on the other hand, also interesting to observe that the report treats young people as a *mass*. The quotations given do not refer to a person by name, but to a 'young person' or an 'NCS participant'.[80] The idea of youth as a mass is important since it signifies a collective that can be managed according to a communal ethic. The ethic is one of *responsibility*. By taking responsibility, young people will increase their own well-being and the well-being of others to whom they become emotionally attached 'in community' by being socially active, identifying needs and responding to them in creative ways. The NCS Evaluation actually measured well-being, using the indicators of life satisfaction, feeling in control of your life and high satisfaction with life; 37 per cent of summer NCS participants agreed with the statement that, 'If someone is not a success in life it's their own fault'; and 3 per cent confirmed a 'high satisfaction with life'.[81] These questions are

---

[75] Above n 52.
[76] NatCen Social Research, *National Citizen Service 2013 Evaluation*, above n 60, 73.
[77] Ibid 73.
[78] Ibid 1.
[79] Ibid 1. The 88 per cent applies to the Summer Programme; 86 per cent of the Autumn participants responded positively.
[80] Ibid 73–76.
[81] Ibid 24.

not only in themselves intended to prompt reflection on responsibility and so instil an ethic of duty and care, but they also reveal high life satisfaction is (being) tied to taking responsibility. I come on to prompted reflection in section C. I want now to move on to how the ethic of responsibility requires a behavioural code.

B. A Code of Conduct (For a More Responsible Society)

There is quite a mathematical formula in place to ensure the three aims of responsibilisation, cohesion and increased engagement within society through NCS. Outcomes in four key areas are singled out for improvement: teamwork, communication and leadership; the transition to adulthood; social mixing; and, community involvement.[82] In a neatly presented diagram, the NCS Evaluation Report illustrates a 'logic model' that describes a 'theory of change'; that is, how the planned programme will lead to improved outcomes for youth and have wider social impacts.[83] Hence the following formula applies, where each of the elements being added together are causal pathways to a 'more responsible society':[84] staff *expertise* and residential venues + *working together* on residentials and *guided reflection* during these phases + completion of the residential phases + improved *awareness of others* and inter-personal *skills* = a more responsible society. The code of conduct that youth operate during NCS will thus produce a more responsible society. The code functions via principles of working together, receiving guided reflection from experts, being aware of others and learning skills. It is a code based in a wider ethic of responsibility: responsibility towards others (working together, being aware of others) and towards oneself (learning skills, self-reflection).

The impact of this code can be measured and the results show a commitment to the *ethos* of community and a respect for values, aspirations and desires that are altering the behaviour and identity of young people. In other words, we see the ethopolitics of the NCS in action. Let us look at the effect the code has had so far according to statistics gathered for the NCS Evaluation Report 2012 through qualitative interviews. The most significant impacts were seen in terms of teamwork (including communication and leadership), where the proportion of young people who felt confident being the leader of a team increased by 17 per cent among

---

[82] Ibid 2.

[83] Ibid 12–13. The model is taken from HT Chen, *Theory Driven Evaluations* (Thousand Oaks, CA, Sage, 1990).

[84] See the diagram in ibid 13.

NCS participants compared to the 2011 control group.[85] Over 90 per cent of participants agreed that NCS had made them *proud* of what they had achieved and over 80 per cent of participants felt they were *capable* of more than they thought after taking part in NCS.[86] The NCS has thus far been successful in instilling the positive emotions of pride, capability and resilience in young people who work together—the working together becoming a *value* of NCS and of the community which young people are being trained to work together in once they leave the programme. Working together is thus effectively communicated as a right way to behave in a responsible society, creating proud, capable, resilient and *ethical* young people. They are made *better* people.

Second, the transition to adulthood is measured by youth attitudes towards anti-social behaviour, which were recorded as having improved more among NCS participants than the control group. Young people were presented with the following:[87]

Statement: 'Young people want to stay out of trouble'

Response: 'Just like me'

The proportion who gave this correct response increased by 4 percentage points more among NCS participants than in the control group and so the programme was evaluated as having a positive impact.[88] Anti-social behaviour is thus contrary to the NCS code of conduct, which is based, as Cameron has said, in the old-fashioned values of '[t]eam-work, discipline, duty, decency'.[89] These young people are responsible—they are not 'just like' the thugs we saw rioting on the streets of London; they are, rather, 'just like' responsible volunteers. As one 16-year-old participant, Anthony Bloomfield, is quoted as saying to the *Independent*, 'This experience has actually changed my life for the best. If I wasn't on this course, I would be on the streets causing trouble, ruining my life'.[90] Instead, Anthony, along with 15 others in his group, helped to lay the path of a community garden and painted a mural. Now part of an emotional community, Anthony engages in positive social interaction, not disruptive, unruly and criminal behaviour. This is the way to turn him and others like him from being part of a potentially dangerous mass into responsibilised, active citizens who behave according to an (etho)politics that takes into account the needs of their community.

[85] Ibid 4.
[86] Ibid 4.
[87] Ibid 5 and 38–39.
[88] Ibid.
[89] Cameron, 'The Fightback After the Riots', above n 23.
[90] J Merrick, 'Teenage volunteers show true grit at the National Citizen Service', *Independent*, 1 September 2013, available at www.independent.co.uk/news/uk/politics/teenage-volunteers-show-true-grit-at-the-national-citizen-service-8793020.html.

Third, the measure of community involvement shows a positive impact with respect to helping out in the future, as well as a positive impact with respect to local influence.[91] Thus, the proportion of NCS participants agreeing that 'when local people campaign together they can solve problems' stayed stable, as compared to a fall in the control group.[92] Seven in 10 responded that they were more likely to help out in the local area and six in 10 replied that they felt more responsible in their local community.[93] Importantly, the programme participants were more aware of the opportunities available to them (eight out of 10).[94] This kind of awareness can, for instance, help keep the spirit of London 2012 volunteers alive.[95] So we see evidence for the values of working together and awareness being taken on board and promising a mass behaviour change towards *more responsible* action.

C. Guided Reflection (Towards Being More Engaged)

Central to all five phases of NCS is a process called 'guided reflection' that 'supports participants' personal and social development during NCS'.[96] Furthermore, the process:

> encourages and supports participants to reflect on their decisions and their interactions with the aim of learning and improving their skills, talents and self-awareness. Guided reflection aims to underpin the communication, teamwork and leadership abilities developed through NCS and to facilitate *long-lasting personal resilience* which will help participants prosper during and after NCS.[97]

The NCS thus creates a further desirable category of youth: the resilient young person who will grow into a resilient citizen. Through support, mentorship and guidance, resilience is built into the values ascribed to by the programme.

Guided reflection, in its objective to secure this long-lasting effect and change to individual characteristics and behaviour, is a technology

---

[91] NatCen Social Research, *Evaluation of the National Citizen Service*, above n 60, 6.

[92] NCS statistics showed a negligible move from 55 to 54 per cent, whereas the control groups showed a fall from 56 to 47 per cent, ibid 6.

[93] Ibid 9.

[94] Ibid; note that these statistics related to the Autumn participants.

[95] The Big Society Audit identifies related projects to NCS to encourage young people to get involved in communities and charities, including 'Join In', Civil Exchange, *Whose Society?*, above n 11, 46. For more on the construction of the volunteer and the Olympics, see D Bulley and D Lisle, 'Rethinking Hospitality: How London Welcomed the World at the 2012 Olympic and Paralympic Games' in V Girginov (ed), *Handbook of the London 2012 Olympic and Paralympic Games*, vol 2, *Celebrating the Games* (Abingdon, Routledge, 2014).

[96] NatCen Social Research, *Evaluation of the National Citizen Service*, above n 60, 11.

[97] Ibid 11 (emphasis added).

of pastoralism. The relevance of pastoral power to the governance of community can be aligned to its role in the management of population.[98] The practices of governmentality within the state can be found in the model and organisation of a pastoral type of power that acts on population, where population refers not to a collective of individual juridical subjects within a determinate territory but to an entity with a life and density of its own.[99] In the modern liberal state that is Britain, population has been disaggregated and renamed 'community': each is a mass that has its own life, its own values and is not concerned with individual rights but community well-being. Pastoral power operates to ensure this well-being—and therein lies the paradox also. For pastoral power, as a 'power of care',[100] is at once a power exercised over a flock of people (on the move, which, in the NCS example, we can count as the transition into adulthood) and an individualising power, whereby the pastor must care for each separate member of the flock as a single entity; in this sense, it is also a beneficent power, where the duty of the pastor or the carer is to secure the salvation of the flock.[101] Community well-being operates through this paradox of pastoral care—both the individual young person and the mass of 'youth' must be managed at once. Of course, the form of pastoral power has altered since the origins identified by Foucault, which were to be found in the Christian pastorate of the sixteenth and seventeenth centuries. Yet, the basic principle and its defining features remain. There is, within the modern (British) state and the NCS programme a continuance, albeit in different forms to ecclesiastical authority, of an 'art of conducting, directing, leading, guiding, taking in hand, and manipulating [youth] ... collectively and individually throughout their life and at each moment of their existence'.[102] The 'problem of conduction'[103] thus remains: how to manage children, adults and families to ensure well-being. It is the rationality of that conduction that has changed, from a Christian ethic that leads to salvation, to a rationality of *raison d'etat* which operates via a doctrine of *police*.[104] The police becomes the internal mechanism of *raison d'etat* but it still operates by the same ethic, which is based in 'salvation, obedience and truth' and 'spiritual direction',

---

[98] M Foucault, *Security, Territory, Population, Lectures at the Collège de France 1977–1978* (M Senellart (ed), G Burchell (trans), Basingstoke, Palgrave Macmillan, 2007). See also B Golder's analysis of pastoral power in 'Foucault and the Genealogy of Pastoral Power' (2007) 10(2) *Radical Philosophy Review* 157.

[99] Golder, 'Foucault and the Genealogy of Pastoral Power', above n 98, 164.

[100] M Foucault, *Discipline and Punish: The Birth of the Prison* (A Sheridan (trans), London, Penguin, 1991) 127.

[101] Golder, 'Foucault and the Genealogy of Pastoral Power', above n 98, 165. See also Foucault, *Discipline and Punish*, above n 100, 125–30.

[102] Golder, 'Foucault and the Genealogy of Pastoral Power', above n 98, 167. See also Foucault, *Discipline and Punish*, above n 100, 165.

[103] Foucault, *Security, Territory, Population*, above n 98, 230.

[104] Golder, 'Foucault and the Genealogy of Pastoral Power', above n 98, 168.

that is the directing of conscience.[105] The police are today's experts—the mentors, counsellors and teachers who direct NCS. And the police targets 'everything from being to well-being, everything that may produce this well-being beyond being and in such a way that the well-being of individuals is the state's strength'.[106]

The experts, the NCS staff, are measured by the quality of their policing. Those that are considered to have 'performed well' are those that are 'energetic and enthusiastic, resilient and supportive, and also able to develop a good rapport with a whole range of young people'.[107] The experts I refer to are the NCS providers, the network of actors that work within the charities, schools, private sector partnerships etc that run the programme.[108] The practice of one provider, The Challenge Network ('Challenge'), reveals how energy, enthusiasm, resilience and support are performed through guided reflection.[109] A key part of Phase 1 for Challenge is a series of 'reflection sessions' that are supervised during the evenings of week one of the programme. These are 90-minute sessions where a mentor facilitates discussion on how to link the activities of the day to the general NCS/Big Society programme. Challenge's Chief Executive, Craig Morley, identifies three common character traits that mentors focus on throughout the programme, 'the thread' that runs through the whole eight-week programme: trust, responsibility and understanding.[110] With the right kind of committed guidance, these traits are not only a common thread but a set of values that define NCS and which inform the behaviour of young people whilst on the programme, and furthermore a thread that should be woven throughout their adult lives once they have left and gone back to life in their communities. Instilled reflection is therefore about cultivating a conscience directed towards community well-being through 'coaxing' from mentors; a superficial form of policing through counselling, training and 'guidance'.[111]

Thus guided reflection does not end when the programme ends. From now on, at each moment of their lives, young people will be encouraged to be more engaged. They are not just emotionally attached to a community now but also to the 'bigger NCS family'[112] and family is, after all, where community starts.[113] At graduation, on award of 'full volunteer status', they

---

[105] Ibid 167.

[106] Foucault, *Security, Territory, Population,* above n 98, 328.

[107] NatCen Social Research, *Evaluation of the National Citizen Service,* above n 60, 65.

[108] Above n 52.

[109] See Bulley and Sokhi-Bulley, 'Big Society as Big Government', above n 51 for a more detailed analysis of the work of The Challenge Network.

[110] Ibid 9.

[111] See Vaughan, 'The Government of Youth', above n 62, 357–58.

[112] Above n 52.

[113] Note Jack Straw's 'logic of togetherness' that 'most of us learn in families', where 'we most directly experience the values of community', 'Human Rights and Personal Responsibility', above n 4; and also Cameron's speech on 'Opportunity' where he links opportunity with 'strong families that give children the best start in life' and asserts 'families are the best welfare system there is', above n 5.

will be invited to attend 'some of the greatest shows or events' and the pastorate will 'be constantly developing new ways to keep you involved with us, your community and with all of our fantastic partners'.[114] This continued involvement will be able to be sustained because the youth is now 'a completely different person' (the full volunteer, the *active* citizen) with a 'huge network of amazing friends' who will help nourish the ethic of responsibility that NCS has cultivated. The coaxing is continued, for instance, through recognition and public celebration of people who are 'marvellous' because they are 'doing great things';[115] for example, the Prime Minister recognises 'points of light out there in our community' in the Points of Lights Awards scheme launched in April 2014.[116] Moreover, now part of the youth's conscience, the ethic of responsibility has been freely accepted such that youth govern themselves to continually reproduce volunteer status by it.

D. Responsibilised Youth

A crucial element of the governmentalisation of youth through an ethopolitical code of conduct and pastoral care, is self-government. NCS actually epitomises the slogan 'Big Society and not Big Government' since it is marked by a new rationality in the art of government that is concerned with maximising the effectiveness of government through governing less; to do so, it relies on a concern with care of the self. Government is thus maximised (it *is* in fact bigger and better government of individuals in community). That is, government becomes a reflexive relation;[117] the individual becomes responsible for her own behaviour and regulates herself through an established set of values (code of conduct) and pastoral guidance. Government thus becomes an ethical practice, wherein the individual takes care of (her)self, meaning she engages with 'the "techniques" by which a subject constructs a definite relationship to self, gives form to his or her own existence, and establishes a well-ordered relationship to the world and to others'.[118] There are therefore two elements to the care of the self: it is, first a social practice and, second, it forms an aesthetics of existence. As a social practice, the care of the self is thus not a solitary or a solipsistic exercise; it takes place, rather, in 'tightly organized institutional frameworks'[119] which I am calling 'community'.

---

[114] Above n 52.

[115] D Cameron, 'Big Society Awards Address', 6 December 2011, available at www.gov.uk/government/speeches/big-society-awards-address.

[116] The scheme borrows from the initiative developed by President George W Bush in the United States in 1990, see www.pointsoflight.gov.uk/.

[117] M Dean, *Governmentality: Power and Rule in Modern Society* (London, Sage, 1999) 2.

[118] M Foucault, *The Government of the Self and Others: Lectures at the Collège de France 1982–1983* (F Gros (ed), G Burchell (trans), Basingstoke, Palgrave Macmillan, 2010) 377–78.

[119] M Foucault, *The Hermeneutics of the Subject: Lectures at the Collège de France 1981–1982* (F Gros (ed), G Burchell (trans), New York, Picador, 2005) 536.

The institutional framework, ie community, through community-enhancing programmes such as NCS, instil practices of the self ingrained in 'the models that [the self] finds in his culture and are proposed, suggested and imposed on him by his culture, his society and his social group'.[120] These are the practices of guided reflection, of teamwork, of designing a social action project that will grow into practices of lifelong volunteering (see below). The youth performs these practices not only to better herself—to become more personally responsible, to have a killer CV and to make new friends—but to *exist better within her community*. The 'care of the self is thus ethical in itself'[121] because it is concerned with '*right conduct* and the proper practice of freedom'.[122] It is an ethos, that is, a way of being and of behaviour, that is visible, is engaged in freely and that implies a relationship with others.[123] Second, the practices of care of self represent an aesthetics of existence in that they are linked with pleasure and desire.[124] The values of teamwork, discipline, duty and decency become desirable and the proper means to exist in community. The technologies of governmentality in the modern state as exemplified by NCS become a 'technology of life' or an 'art of living', which is a 'question of knowing how to govern one's own life in order to give it the most beautiful possible form' and that might serve as an example for future generations.[125]

Perhaps my reading of NCS has failed to highlight inadequacies in the programme's implementation and to address the question of whether it will really transform the behaviour of 'cynical young people' in anything but the short term; perhaps what I have described here as a deliberate move towards a new politics of community would have 'happened anyway'.[126] In response to this, I would say two things: first, that there is strong evidence for the benefits of NCS and its continued growth to eventually target 'all teenagers', regardless of social background, religion, gender, ability and region.[127] The 'value for money' for both the recruit in terms cost of the programme (£50 in total) and the cost-benefit analysis in terms of government spending

---

[120] M Foucault, 'The Ethics of the Concern of the Self as a Practice of Freedom' in P Rabinow (ed), *Michel Foucault: Ethics—Essential Works of Foucault 1954–1984* (London, Penguin, 1997) 291.

[121] Ibid 287.

[122] Ibid 285 (emphasis added).

[123] Ibid.

[124] M Foucault, 'On the Genealogy of Ethics' in P Rabinow (ed), *Michel Foucault: Ethics—Essential Works of Foucault 1954–1984* (London, Penguin, 1997) 253, 264.

[125] M Foucault, 'The Concern for Truth' in LD Kritzman (ed), *Politics, Philosophy, Culture: Interviews and Other Writings 1977–1984* (A Sheridan (trans), London, Routledge, 1988) 255, 256–59.

[126] C Byrne, P Kerr and E Foster, 'What Kind of "Big Government" is the Big Society? A Response to Bulley and Sokhi-Bulley' (2014) 16 *British Journal of Politics and International Relations* 471.

[127] NatCen Social Research, *Evaluation of the National Citizen Service*, above n 60.

supports increased recruitment and access,[128] as does the programme's concern with 'social mixing'. Improving social mixing is one of the aims of NCS and the 2012 Evaluation reports a 'socially mixed cohort' with respect to ethnicity, religion, disability and the uptake of free school meals.[129] I have highlighted some of the positive statistics gathered in the NCS Evaluation Report, for instance on measuring impact in relation to teamwork, the transition to adulthood and community involvement. The Report further notes that NCS participants' attitudes and behaviours can be described as 'more pro-social' than the general group of 16-year-olds, such that they are more positive about volunteering and about their local community.[130] The Big Society Audit's 'social action' indicator (one of five key indicators used to measure 'community empowerment') shows that volunteering has increased amongst young people—in fact, it has more than doubled to 34 per cent in 2014 (compared to 14 per cent in 2013).[131] Young people are the largest voluntary group by age, as recorded in 2014; 38 per cent of students volunteer formally and 37 per cent of teenagers volunteer formally or informally.[132] After NCS participation, 70 per cent of recruits said that they were more likely to help out locally.[133] There is potential for widespread and long-lasting impact in the NCS. How it is being maintained through to adulthood and the rest of society is what I move on to look at in the next part of this chapter.

Second, I would respond to the point about NCS' impact by saying that I cannot and do not seek to predict its impact. My objective here is, rather, to try to understand the processes by which an alternative subjectivity is being created by targeting youth (the active citizen), to point out how this fosters an identity that is divorced from rights and in fact challenges the inherently selfish nature of liberal rights, and thereby *is already* posing a threat to rights discourse. The ethic of NCS, instilled in the Big Society's ethic of responsibility, produces young people that do not need rights to makes themselves better and to improve the conditions of their existence. They can, and ought to, be responsible and look after themselves and their communities to give their life the 'most beautiful possible form'. So, it has

---

[128] See above n 52. In terms of the cost-benefit and government spending, the *Evaluation of National Citizen Service 2012* (NatCen Social Research, above n 60) finds that a 'comparison of the initial estimate of the 2011 programme with the 2012 programme shows an increase in the range of the cost-benefit ratio', see 47 for further detail. Note that the *Evaluation of National Citizen Service* 2013 (IPSOS Mori, above n 60, 4) states that 'even under the most pessimistic scenarios, NCS is estimated to have delivered greater social benefits than the costs involved'.

[129] NatCen Social Research, *Evaluation of National Citizen Service*, above n 60, 2 and 3.

[130] Ibid 24.

[131] Civil Exchange, *Whose Society?*, above n 11, 15 and 48.

[132] Ibid 48.

[133] Ibid 48.

been important to look at in the NCS case study in terms of *how* governing through an ethic of responsibility, based in community, is increasingly
becoming the new way to manage youth through the government's rhetoric
of responsibility and opportunity; and then to recognise its potential for
governing the behaviour of all and of each, and to complete the diagnosis
of this ethic as a resistance to rights that, as I come to in the final part of the
chapter, has potentially dangerous effects.

III. RESPONSIBILISING COMMUNITY: COMMUNITY RIGHTS

A. Community and Society

The Department for Communities and Local Government (DCLG)
describes the government's role in the 'Community and Society' policy area
as, 'supporting people who care about their communities and want to get
involved in improving them. [The government] believes that people understand the needs of their area best' so as to 'solve their own problems to
create strong, *attractive* and thriving neighbourhoods'.[134] As mentioned
above, there are 24 initiatives under the 'Community and Society' policy
area, including localism (eg neighbourhood planning), community integration (eg through street parties) and support for families (eg the Troubled
Families Programme). The guiding principle behind the policy area is people power: it is up to people to be autonomous and responsible; to take the
opportunities made available to create, and to aspire to, strong, attractive
and thriving communities. 'You've got the power' is not only the slogan
that markets something called 'community rights'[135] but is also the key to
building 'community spirit'.

   What is 'community spirit'? The 'guide to community rights' document makes repeated reference to 'community spirit' as something to
aspire to, a positive thing, and a measure of success.[136] Hence, when we
achieve 'excellent results' (such as use the right to neighbourhood planning
and build more houses, a primary school and a community centre) and
'networks and relationships are formed', then 'the community spirit will
continue in abundance'.[137] This spirit reflects a 'common sense "feel" for the
community'.[138] It is akin, perhaps, to 'communion', denoting association,

---

[134] See www.gov.uk/government/topics/community-and-society (emphasis added).
[135] Department for Communities and Local Government, *You've Got the Power: A Quick and
Simple Guide to Community Rights* (September 2013), available at www.gov.uk/government/
publications/youve-got-the-power-a-quick-and-simple-guide-to-community-rights.
[136] Ibid 6, 20 and 21.
[137] Mayor of Thames, Oxfordshire, on Neighbourhood Planning, in ibid 6.
[138] Ibid 18.

fellowship and the act of sharing;[139] not exactly a tangible quality but one which is powerful in its ethos of making people strong, attractive and able to thrive together. People, should, moreover, want to integrate within their communities and even 'celebrate' their community, hence the focus on Britain's great tradition of 'coming together to celebrate national events by throwing a street party' (eg during the Queen's Diamond Jubilee in 2012, during the 70th Anniversary of VE Day in May 2015).[140] The spirit of community is in the notion that community is not properly one's own, it belongs to everyone; it is in Esposito's notion of *communitas*— community as a pledge or a tribute that implies, even necessitates, obligation.[141] There is ample guidance provided on how to celebrate community and foster community spirit; for instance, the Streets Alive website 'promotes community spirit at the street level through street parties and other neighbourly activities'.[142] The most celebrated communities can be identified and their community spirit measured; so, for example, Streets Alive identifies the Street Party Capital as Bristol, which is leading the country by holding approximately 150 street parties a year and thereby instilling 'local neighbourly culture'.[143] The visuals of images and videos, showing kids playing in the street, people who 'mix up', people who 'moved away … but wish I lived here again', portray that this is what a strong, attractive and thriving community looks like and does.[144] And *all* communities can aspire to this. The Community Rights Guide, which lists community rights as inscribed in the Localism Act 2011, assert that the 'government has given you legal powers and new opportunities … to make sure that you … have the community that you aspire to'.[145] Whether you want to stop the local shop closing, get more homes built, or improve local public services, you can 'make changes for the better' to 'protect the things that make [your] neighbourhood special and to help [your] community grow and develop in the *right way*'.[146]

---

[139] M Klusonova, 'Communion in the Czech Judicial Argumentation', paper presented at Critical Legal Conference, Poland, 3–5 September 2015, available at www.muni.cz/people/210387/publications.

[140] Department for Communities and Local Government, 'Your Guide to Organising a Street Party', www.gov.uk/government/publications/your-guide-to-organising-a-street-party. The application form, contained in the above document, to apply to your council to hold a street party is entitled 'Celebrating your Community'.

[141] Esposito, *Communitas*, above n 2, 3–5.

[142] See www.streetparty.org.uk. See also the Big Lunch website, www.thebiglunch.com.

[143] Ibid.

[144] See www.streetparty.org.uk/photos-videos.aspx.

[145] See also My Community Advice Service, http://mycommunity.org.uk; My Community Network, http://mycommunity.org.uk/my-community-network/; and Locality, www.locality.org.uk.

[146] DCLG, *You've Got the Power*, above n 135, 4 (emphasis added).

The right way is to help people take control through accepting responsibility. As Cameron asserted at the Conservative Party Conference in 2010:

> Society is not a spectator sport. This is your country. It's time to believe it. It's time to step up and own it. So mine is not just a vision of a more powerful country. It is a vision of a more powerful people ... not small people but big citizens.[147]

The size of citizenship is measured by how responsible you are and how much opportunity you take advantage of—and *not* what rights you are, as an individual, *entitled* to. Cameron and his new, re-branded Community and Society policies strongly promote active citizenship, where the modern citizen is characterised by a new style of active politics that is based in an ethic of responsibility over right/s. As such, the policies resemble Blair's Third Way and Brown's policy of civic renewal; the similarity of community and society language with the Labour Government's 2008 White Paper entitled *Communities in Control: Real People, Real Power* is stark.[148] There was a focus here on 'active citizens' and 'empowerment' as 'passing more political power to more and more people through every practical means'.[149] Moreover, agencies and bodies across England were told they had a 'duty to involve'; these bodies should take steps to involve people in decisions, policies and services that may affect them or be of interest to them.[150] The modern, active, citizen, according to the ambitions of the White Paper, will be 'willing citizens', 'not because they are forced from without, but because they are compelled from within'.[151] And as such there will be 'no limits to the capacity of the British people for self-government'. Framed in a language of power, opportunity and aspiration, the idea of willing, non-coerced self-governing citizens with responsibility for their own (community) well-being is the stimulus behind the government's community rights agenda. The discourse of rights is overshadowed by a language of opportunity where the ethic of responsibility wins out over rights to create a subject that is *active* and with no claim or concern for rights.

B. Community Rights

(i) Opportunity versus Rights

'Community rights' consist of neighbourhood planning, community right to build, community right to bid, community shares, Our Place!, community right to challenge, town and parish councils, right to manage and community

---

[147] D Cameron, Speech at Conservative Party Conference 2010, 6 October 2010, available at www.theguardian.com/politics/2010/oct/06/david-cameron-speech-tory-conference.
[148] White Paper, *Communities in Control*, above n 3.
[149] Ibid 12.
[150] Ibid 28.
[151] Comment from Community Links UK, January 2008, cited in ibid 33.

cashback and right to reclaim land.[152] The Localism Act 2011 puts in place the mechanisms to exercise these community rights, although, interestingly, the word 'rights' is used sparingly in the Act itself. The focus is, rather, on community *empowerment*, planning and housing.[153] The use of rights under the government's Community and Society agenda is thus misleading; we are not talking about the concept of 'human rights' as emancipatory ideals and justiciable legal provisions. Instead, what the Act codifies and what the government supports is a *right to* community, which is available to those who *do the right* thing, that is, empower themselves through being responsible, active citizens who take care of themselves and in turn their own communities.

Community 'rights' are thus conditional on taking responsibility and making the most of opportunity. Community, and not the individual, has become the inherent quality worth protecting; there is something almost sacred attributed to 'being in community' that deserves more protection and promotion than individual dignity. I return to the construction of community as *communitas* here; it demands a tribute to collective belonging that takes obligatory form.[154] You have a right to community *and* you have an *obligation* to community. This is not a sensationalist reading of government policy; the rise of community rights has come at a time when there has been active talk about abolition of the Human Rights Act 1998 and withdrawal from the Council of Europe. The Conservative Party Manifesto for 2015 promises to 'scrap the Human Rights Act and curtail the role of the European Court of Human Rights, so that foreign criminals can be more easily deported from Britain'.[155] It is not part of my objective here to engage with the debate over a 'British Bill of Rights' that the Manifesto also declares it wants to institute.[156] The point I want to make is that community rights, in a time when 'human rights' are being branded as criminals' rights and amidst talk of leaving the European Union and its guarantees of fundamental free movement rights,[157] are posed in overt *opposition* to rights discourse, rather than as a complement or supplement to them.[158] The 'common sense ... application of human rights in the UK' that the Conservatives guarantee to bring

---

[152] DLCG, *You've Got the Power*, above n 135.

[153] Localism Act 2011, Parts 5, 6 and 7.

[154] Esposito, *Communitas*, above n 2, 3–5.

[155] *Conservative Party Manifesto 2015*, above n 8, 60, 62 and 75. See also J Stone, 'Human Rights Act: What is it and why does Michael Gove want to scrap the policy?', *Independent*, 11 May 2015, available at www.independent.co.uk/news/uk/politics/what-is-the-human-rights-act-and-why-does-michael-gove-want-to-scrap-it-10240527.html.

[156] *Conservative Party Manifesto 2015*, above n 8, 62.

[157] 'Why, and how, Britain might leave the European Union', *Economist*, 29 April 2015, available at www.economist.com/blogs/economist-explains/2015/04/economist-explains-29.

[158] See Giddens' point that the absence of 'democratic freedoms' has been a common critique of the Third Way, from whence the notion of 'community and society' and hence 'community rights' arguably comes; *The Third Way and Its Critics*, above n 44, 20 (he refers here to R Dahrendorf, 'Whatever happened to liberty?', *New Statesman*, 6 September 1999).

about is *being implemented* in the 'common sense' ideal of 'community spirit'. There is no room in the ethic of responsibility on which community rights are based for an individual right concept: as Cameron asserts, 'all have been clear that individual freedom is only half the story ... Tradition, community, family, faith, the space between the market and the state—this is the ground where our philosophy is planted'.[159] Amongst the problematic consequences of this reaction to, and resistance to, rights is, as I discuss in the final section of this chapter (and again in Chapter 5), a suppression of resistance and the right of the rights-bearing citizen to ethically resist government. How have these community rights been used—and how do they produce the active citizen *in place of* the rights-bearing subject?

(ii) Uses of Community Rights

I briefly look at three examples of the exercise of community rights here: neighbourhood planning, the Troubled Families Programme and the Conservative Party's new voluntary work leave entitlement. These initiatives colour the broader palette of Community and Society initiatives in carrying through the original Big Society goals as seen in the NCS programme: a more cohesive, more responsible, more engaged society. They do so by 'put[ting] power back in the hands of local residents, employees and businesses, councils and civic leaders—those who know best the needs of their local areas'[160] (neighbourhood planning); by 'turning around' families who are 'troubled', a vital project since families are after all the backbone of the welfare system (Troubled Families Programme); and by rewarding doing the right thing (voluntary leave for those who work).

The neighbourhood planning 'right' has come about as a result of a £9.5 million support programme for communities that was launched in April 2013.[161] The right allows residents to decide where new homes, shops and offices will go; decide what new buildings will look like; decide what facilities, services and infrastructure is needed; grant planning permission for new buildings through a Neighbourhood Development Order.[162]

---

[159] Cameron, 'Big Society' (2011), above n 20. In terms of similarities or origins of Cameron's ideals in the Third Way, note that 'family life, crime, and the decay of community' were features of the New Democrats (US) and New Labour (UK) policies, see Giddens, *The Third Way and Its Critics*, above n 44, 4.

[160] DLCG, *You've Got the Power*, above n 135, 3.

[161] Department for Communities and Local Government, *Supporting Communities in Neighbourhood Planning 2013–15* (March 2013) 3, available at www.gov.uk/government/uploads/system/uploads/attachment_data/file/141999/Supporting_Communities_in_Neighbourhood_Planning_2013-15_FINAL.pdf.

[162] DLCG, *You've Got the Power*, above n 135, 5–6. See also the 'Neighbourhood Planning Roadmap' and related documents, and the 'Understanding Neighbourhood Planning' video at My Community Network, mycommunity.org.uk/my-community-network/.

There are five key stages to the process of planning:[163] first, defining the neighbourhood, which means local people decide how they want to work together. There is, however, ample instruction on this; so, parish or town councils are to take the lead, where there is one; where there is not such a body in place, community groups are to lead the initiative and new groups must have a minimum of 21 members and be open to new members.[164] Second, preparing the plan, for which there are ground rules, such that the plan must be in line with local and national planning policies, in line with other laws, and contribute to achieving sustainable development. The plan must present a 'vision for the future'.[165] Third, an independent check by an independent examiner to ensure the plan meets basic standards and recommendations for changes can be made. Fourth, a community referendum is required; and, fifth and finally, a 'neighbourhood plan' is made which has 'real legal weight'.[166] Thus, the 'neighbourhood' itself can only be defined by those in a role of pastoral care (parish councils or community groups), with some expertise or at least some aspiration for making their community more attractive in a way that is recognisable as such by other active citizens concerned with bettering where they live. The vision must fit within a prescribed 'vision for a future'—one that is sustainable and allows individuals in community to continue to govern themselves. Efforts, such as those to protect traditional market towns like Thame, Oxfordshire, must also promote 'community spirit'.[167] There have been over 250 projects using community rights tools under the 2015 support programme and over 2,700 since the inception of community rights under the Localism Act 2011.[168] The My Community website, which acts as a portal for rights information and grant programmes funded by the DCLG, lists 'stories' of neighbourhood planning.[169] For example, Selton Parish Council in Nottinghamshire are developing a neighbourhood plan to allow for more homes to be built in the parish, which rests on a Green Belt and so faces complex and technical development issues. Tattenhall village, a few miles South-East of Chester, proposed a complex neighbourhood plan to keep its lively village thriving, including through new walking and cycling connections and aspirations for a new railway station. Broughton-Ashley in Harborough, southwest

---

[163] Department for Communities and Local Government, *Neighbourhood Planning* (November 2012) 3–5, available at www.gov.uk/government/uploads/system/uploads/attachment_data/file/229749/Neighbourhood_planning.pdf.

[164] Ibid 4.

[165] Ibid 4.

[166] Ibid 5.

[167] Mayor of Thames, Oxfordshire, on Neighbourhood Planning, in DLCG, *You've Got the Power*, above n 135, 6.

[168] See mycommunity.org.uk/my-community-network/.

[169] See mycommunity.org.uk/programme/neighbourhood-planning/?_a=stories.

Leicestershire, are addressing the concerns of a lack of infrastructure, housing and employment in their otherwise 'thriving community' through neighbourhood planning.

Neighbourhood planning is described as a 'right not an obligation'.[170] Yet the opposite is in fact the case. Neighbourhood planning, that mobilisation of people 'who are passionate about their community'[171] under guidance provided by experts, is the *right way* to be and behave in community. We *should* feel obligated to build homes, facilitate cycling to work, etc because we *should* care deeply about where we live and aspire to better standards of well-being. Mobilisation thus represents an ethopolitical relation, whereby individuals are autonomised and responsibilised into taking the opportunity to build, into wanting to alter their behaviour to be better by existing better in a community they have built. We are encouraged, therefore, to 'connect with experts' and 'get expert advice' from organisations such as My Community Network,[172] which is delivered by Community Development Foundation in partnership with Locality (the latter describes itself as 'the national network of ambitious and enterprising community-led organisations, working together to help neighbourhoods thrive').[173] Locality aims at 'mobilising' people 'to take action on the things that matter most in their community'.[174] Mobilisation also then represents a modern form of pastoral power, a new style of subdued expertise, that directs conscience through a muted sense of obligation and instruction. Communities are pushed to aspire to better themselves by local counsellors, ministers, but most importantly 'people like you'—the ordinary resident—who can become a community 'champion' simply by *acting*.[175] The ethics behind neighbourhood planning is thus not one of individual right but of responsibility—of taking opportunity to act and being a model active citizen.

Opportunity should be available to 'every part of society', even 'troubled families'.[176] The 'logic of togetherness' that the Labour Party through Jack Straw espoused as something most of us learn in *families* and 'where we most directly experience the values of community',[177] is clearly shared by the Conservatives. Cameron's use of rhetoric on 'extending opportunity' requires '*strong* families that give children the best start in life ...

---

[170] DCLG, *Neighbourhood Planning*, above n 163.

[171] Above n 168.

[172] See mycommunity.org.uk/programme/neighbourhood-planning/.

[173] Above n 168.

[174] See locality.org.uk/projects/community-organisers/.

[175] Above n 168. Note also the link here to the 'Just Act' register, www.justact.org.uk/register/, where you can sign up 'to make things happen and improve your community'.

[176] Department for Communities and Local Government, 'PM praises Troubled Families Programme Success', Press Release, 22 June 2015, available at www.gov.uk/government/news/pm-praises-troubled-families-programme-success.

[177] Straw, 'Human Rights and Personal Responsibility', above n 4. Jack Straw was Home Secretary at the time.

A welfare system that encourages work—*families are the best welfare system there is*.[178] In the interests of securing strong families, extending opportunity and an ethic of togetherness, the Troubled Families Programme was launched in 2012 with a three-year budget of £448 million.[179] It aimed to target 120,000 families with an average of nine different problems, and by June 2015, the government estimated that 116,654 families have been 'turned around' so far.[180] These are families who 'are in chaos and can't see a way out'; the Programme deals with 'the strain they put on services' and allows for management of 'the unit as a whole'.[181] The language of 'troubled' versus 'turned around' families is interesting for how it reveals a policing of family behaviour and a conditioning of this core component of society into responsible private systems that will feed into a wider, responsibilised public welfare system.

To be targeted for help under the Programme, families must meet three of the following four criteria: they are involved in youth crime or anti-social behaviour; their children are regularly truanting or not in school; an adult in the family is on unemployment benefits; they cause high costs to the taxpayer.[182] Monitoring data qualifies troubled families as those having on average nine problems related to employment, education, crime, housing, child protection, parenting or health.[183] Statistics collated by December 2013 on a sample of troubled families (a random selection of at least 10 per cent of the families that the 152 upper tier local authorities had started working with) show, for instance, that 49 per cent are lone parent households compared with 16 per cent nationally; 82 per cent have a problem related to education, such as unauthorised absence; and 42 per cent have had police called out to their addresses in the past six months.[184] These indicators of monitoring and measurement, such as measuring whether a family is troubled enough to merit expert intervention (the family must tick three out of four boxes) and monitoring police call outs, are explained as a necessary intervention for 'managing families proactively'[185] so that they will be turned around. That they are 'turned around' is defined as all children being back in school for a year when previously truanting or excluded; youth

---

[178] Cameron, 'Opportunity', above n 5 (emphasis added).
[179] DCLG Press Release, above n 176.
[180] Ibid.
[181] Department for Communities and Local Government, *Understanding Troubled Families* (July 2014) 7, available at www.gov.uk/government/uploads/system/uploads/attachment_data/file/336430/Understanding_Troubled_Families_web_format.pdf, Foreword by Louise Casey CB, Head of the Troubled Families Programme, 4–5.
[182] Ibid.
[183] Ibid 10. The data was collected by each of the 152 upper tier local authorities and evaluated by an independent partner, Ecorys, who 'collected, cleaned and analysed the data', ibid 8–9.
[184] Ibid 10–11.
[185] Ibid 16.

crime and anti-social behaviour significantly cut across the whole family; an adult in the home moved off benefits and into work for three consecutive months or more.[186] The turning around is done by local authorities, who receive £4,000 per family to work with them.[187] This means a dedicated worker or team to 'get to the underlying problems', 'developing a relationship with the family, being persistent and building trust with them in order to challenge them to make the changes they need' and drawing in specialist services where necessary.[188]

The management of the 'unit as a whole' is a representation of the new politics of expertise that infiltrates the ethic of responsibility. Whilst families are encouraged to find a way out, counsellors, mentors and specialist advisors exercise a not-so-subtle pastoral power that conducts, directs, leads and guides behaviour based on the core community and society values of opportunity, responsibility and duty. The Troubled Families Programme, whilst liberating and empowering families who are in a 'cycle of despair',[189] also conditions them into becoming 'turned around'; units that are more responsible, more cohesive, more engaged. The family is then a microcosm for community, where *active* citizens take responsibility for themselves, govern themselves into contributing towards their community—by attending school, by being engaged in employment and by not abusing services. The Troubled Families Programme constructs the family as autonomous and responsible, in charge of its own destiny and at the same time answerable for it. The family unit is the cornerstone of ethical citizenship, where the community-based ethic is instilled and nurtured, and where an inactive and useless despair can be turned into an active and useful way to behave in community.

We should all want to contribute to community in this way. Therefore even good, hardworking citizens are being encouraged to take time off to volunteer. Hence the ethic of responsibility is not just about helping those who are 'troubled' to 'turn around' but about rewarding 'those who work and do the right thing' also.[190] And so the Conservative Party Manifesto for 2015 outlines as one its three main commitments towards building the Big Society (alongside a guaranteed place on the NCS for all children, and promoting equality and opportunity for all) a new workplace entitlement to volunteering leave for three days a year.[191] The leave would be open to those who work in big companies or the public sector and will be given with full pay. Ideas for what to do with the leave include: volunteering for a local

---

[186] DCLG Press Release, above n 176.
[187] Ibid 7.
[188] Ibid 8.
[189] Ibid 6.
[190] *Conservative Party Manifesto 2015*, above n 8, 81.
[191] Ibid 45.

charity, serving as a school governor and generally being part of a voluntary group, church or faith group who play an important role in the country's 'social fabric'.[192] The general message is 'we will help you volunteer'.[193] The initiative has been criticised as a 'tax on business', an 'unnecessary employment regulation' that resembles 'compulsion' more than incentivisation towards volunteering.[194] Yet this is the striking thing about the government's initiatives on Community and Society: compulsion in the name of opportunity; obligation in the name of right. Neighbourhood planning is, as we saw above, 'not an obligation but a right' and yet the rhetoric on opportunity, responsibility and duty all point to an obligation to your community—a right to community and a right way to be in community, rather than an emancipatory juridical right to planning. The Troubled Families Programme 'turns around' struggling families whilst at the same time monitoring them, measuring how they live and behave to create citizens who help themselves. And the new volunteering in the workplace law imposes a similar 'right way to be' ethic: *be responsible*. Volunteering maintains, therefore, the ethopolitical double relation of autonomisation and responsibilisation we saw in planning and family policy; you are free to volunteer but if you do not, you are not the right kind of responsible, active citizen.

IV. CONCLUSION: ACTIVE CITIZENSHIP

I have argued in this chapter for the recognition of an emergent ethic of responsibility within modern British society that replaces rights discourse and that allows for processes of governing (through) community. These can be witnessed in the case studies of the NCS and the government's Community and Society policy area, in particular the development of 'community rights'. Governing through community happens, as we saw in these case studies, through processes of pastoral power and ethopower, wherein guided reflection and adherence to community values such as responsibility, duty and opportunity create a new kind of governmentable subject: the active citizen. Governing community is then a self-referential process, since the active citizen takes care of herself—or governs herself—to exist better according to the moral codes of the emotional community to which she becomes attached. Moreover, aspiration towards an ever-better community is part of the ethic of responsibility, hence it represents an 'ethics of lifestyle maximisation'.[195]

---

[192] Ibid 46.
[193] Ibid 46.
[194] G Parker and E Rigby, 'Cameron harks back to Big Society with voluntary work proposal', *Financial Times*, 9 April 2015, available at www.ft.com/cms/s/0/32a12c84-decf-11e4-852b-00144feab7de.html#axzz3jMMISkvW.
[195] Miller and Rose, *Governing the Present*, above n 12, 100.

The active citizen is, you might argue, a desirable effect of the governmentality of society through a politics of community. Why not promote policies and initiatives that encourage cohesion, social action and engagement to foster responsibility? By way of conclusion, I would point to three 'dangerous', or problematic, effects of the ethic of responsibility as a *reaction against rights discourse*. First, the language of opportunity and empowerment through which the ethic of responsibility is communicated conceals the regulation and control of behaviour that accompanies it. The 'double movement of autonomization and responsibilization'[196] is hidden under the gloss of active citizenship, where being active is instilled as a way of being and behaviour that *you* chose and that has the positive connotations of *doing* something for your community that will better both you and your community. As I have shown, 'just saying yes' to the NCS, for example, is the beginnings of creating emotional ties and mentor relations that instruct and govern choice; for example, it is your choice once you graduate from the programme whether you continue to volunteer in your community but if you want to remain 'awesome' and become a 'champion' and 'a completely different person' then you should want to volunteer and aspire to change your community for the better. But what if you say 'no', or simply do not say 'yes'? The 'choice' to take up opportunities, like NCS or neighbourhood planning, is not so much an elective as an imperative decision since if you do not say 'yes' you will not fit in with the community *ethos*. You are not then the active citizen, you do not belong and are not welcome or even considered for betterment. Similarly, the Troubled Families Programme in the first place decides which units are troubled enough to address (families must tick three of four boxes to qualify for attention) and then determines how the turning around will happen. What if you do not want to be turned around *in that way*? There is no room to choose your own destiny or be responsible in your own way in the government's Community and Society initiatives, which thereby resemble ethopolitical relations of governing through an ethical code of conduct instilled by expert, pastoral technologies. So, second, the ethos instilled by responsibility is dangerous in that it creates new categories of 'affiliated' and 'marginalised' individuals, groups and families.[197] The affiliated is now the 'active citizen' and family, who exist in moral communities. The imperative placed on opportunity ignores those individuals who do not, or do not want to, for instance, fit in with their communities. Neighbourhood planning, for example, requires a majority community vote to succeed; if you are not the right kind of volunteering, responsible and involved individual you become marginalised. Moreover,

---

[196] Rose, 'Community, Citizenship, and the Third Way', above n 10, 1400.

[197] The 'affiliated' and 'marginalised' are referred to by Rose as new specifications of the subjects of government in Miller and Rose, *Governing the Present*, above n 12, 98.

the wider dangerous implication for rights is that the marginalised becomes that which 'activity' is a direct resistance to—entitlement, individual freedom, *rights*. The marginalised is then by implication the ordinary rights-bearing citizen whose existence is, by contrast to the active citizen, selfish and unethical. Not only this, but *rights* discourse itself becomes marginalised; it is no longer a, let alone *the*, empowering discourse, rather the ethic of responsibility and community is. Rights are made weak and undesireable, whilst community is strengthened and to be desired.

There is, third, something insidious in this construction. It is insidious because there has been a deliberate move on the part of the Conservative Government to step away from liberal values of individual freedom and right in the name of a supposed concern with opportunity. In the context of rhetoric that threatens abolition of the Human Rights Act 1998 and withdrawal from the EU and its free movement guarantees, 'community rights' as a replacement to liberal rights are a poor substitute since they are, as I have shown, less about juridical rights and more about a right *to community*. The nature of this right takes a tributary and obligatory form; not only do you have a right to community but an *obligation* to community. The effect of this is dangerous and disempowering. Rights, unlike the rhetoric of responsibility, is a language of empowerment that is not conditional on taking the opportunity to act. The ethic of responsibility claims to empower but only within very strictly proscribed limits. You are empowered to be a good, better young person, citizen and family *as defined by your government and by your community*. You are in fact disempowered from choosing your own destiny or your own understanding of what is a good, and better, way to live. Hence, the recalcitrant family has no recourse to empowerment through law and rights as they have refused their 'community rights' and thus the opportunity to become a proper family.

The reaction against rights that the ethic of responsibility manifests is therefore problematic. Whilst I do not argue anywhere in this book that we ought to rescue or redeem rights—in fact I have so far pointed to the dangers inherent within rights discourse itself—rights offer a powerful recourse against the state, its *ethos* and its rebranding of ethics as, say, 'community' or 'responsibility' that the 'active citizen' is left without. There is something in rights that we want to retain; rights rhetoric is not based in an opporuntity that will only be seized by those willing and able to take it but signifies entitlement regardless of behaviour within a prescribed ethical code based in the right way to be in community. Rights demand responsibility—but this is dependent on individual behaviour and not on recognition by a community standard of correct behaviour. Do rights offer a recourse to the marginalised of community? I come now, in the final substantive chapter, to looking at how and whether there is a way to reconceptualise how the rights-bearing subject can counter governments beyond the human rights architecture and beyond community-based resistance.

5

Counter-Conduct as Right and as Ethics

After all, we are all members of the community of the governed, and thereby
obliged to show mutual solidarity ... It is the duty of this international citizenship
to always bring the testimony of people's suffering to the eyes and ears of
governments, sufferings for which it's untrue that they are not responsible.
The suffering of men must never be a silent residue of policy. It grounds
an *absolute right to stand up and speak* to those who hold power.

Michel Foucault[1]

The enigma of revolts.

Michel Foucault[2]

I RECENTLY RETURNED home from a meeting of scholars committed
to recruiting students to study human rights in Europe. On the return
journey, I found myself thinking about the enigma of revolt. I was
stranded at the airport after bad weather had made me miss my connecting
flight by minutes and, frustrated, tired and unenthused at the prospect of
being carted off to the airport hotel I realised I *had no choice* but to do as
I was told. I could not go home; and I could not make a fuss about not going
home because who knows what negative consequences a bad-tempered
reaction would have on the flight attendant who was booking my hotel and
held my passport in his hands. I was lucky to be put up in a hotel; I would
accept the long wait for the crowded bus and use the food voucher I'd been
given because it was the right way to behave in my 'crisis'. In my in-between
state of not belonging and not being able to return home, I could not revolt.
Not without negative consequences; because if I did revolt—if I shouted
at the attendant, or refused to clear immigration again, or stripped naked
in protest, what if they didn't book me my flight home? What if they took
my passport? What if they arrested me? This perhaps facetious example is

[1] M Foucault, 'Confronting Governments: Human Rights' in *Power*, vol 3, *Essential Works
of Foucault 1954–1984* (J Faubion (ed), R Hurley (trans), London, Penguin, 2002) 474.
[2] M Foucault, 'Useless to Revolt' in *Power*, vol 3, *Essential Works of Foucault 1954–1984*
(J Faubion (ed), London, Penguin, 2002) 449, 450.

meant to point to a genuine, important and interesting issue: the possibility of revolt, or resistance, in rights.

If rights are, as I have argued in this book, about power or about a type of power we can call governmentality, then they must also be about resistance. Or rather, *resistance is* where there is rights discourse.[3] We know that there is in principle a right to resistance through free speech, freedom of expression and freedom of assembly. But there is also a *right way* to resist— and this is where we encounter the limitations of rights. Rights language does not and cannot recognise the subject who refuses the right way to resist and says, quite simply, I do not want to be conducted *like that*. Rights does not recognise the 'revolting subject',[4] who is characterised by enacting revolt and by thus being undesirable. Had I, in my example of being a disgruntled passenger, shouted at the attendant or removed clothing in protest, I would have become this 'revolting subject'—performing a stance that I do not want this form of regulation but as a result becoming unpalatable in the context of the right way to behave towards the immigration authorities. The 'revolting subject' is my focus in this chapter and I look at a specific form of countering governmentality through rights in my example of the rioting subject.

The rights-bearing subject is given the right channels through which to resist. The expert architecture that has been my focus in the previous chapters allows for the individual to express dissatisfaction through the correct channels of seeking advice from the Fundamental Rights Agency of the EU on the correct local channels for individual complaints,[5] or appealing to a non-governmental organisation to highlight victim-status. If your plight is of sufficient priority and en masse, you might even attract the concern of an international human rights actor like Human Rights Watch. If nurtured within the Big Society, you are encouraged to appeal to community rights— to take the opportunity to live in community, to solve your own problems through being responsible, dutiful citizens. You do not need to riot. You are not encouraged to riot. You are not recognised as enacting a right to resist if you riot. The rioters in the case studies of London and Ferguson that I examine here counter these ways of being told how to behave; they perform their struggle by saying we are going to resist by acting *otherwise*.

The enigma of their revolt is that we do not know how to label it, nor how to understand the *ethos* of the rioter. 'Resistance' is not the right label, for it only recognises the right way to resist; the rioter is not seen as a resisting subject, she is seen as behaving *only* in a criminal way and must be

---

[3] Note the comment '[w]here there is power, there is resistance': M Foucault, *The History of Sexuality*, vol 1, *The Will to Knowledge* (R Hurley (trans), London, Penguin, 1998) 95.

[4] Taken from I Tyler, *Revolting Subjects* (London, Zed Books, 2013).

[5] The FRA does not have the capacity to deal with individual complaints but can advise on 'Where to turn for help', see http://fra.europa.eu/en/about-fundamental-rights/where-to-turn.

punished for doing so. I suggest that we need the label of *counter-conduct* to recognise the struggle of the rioting subject, and to acknowledge her behaviour as a political reaction and not one that is only criminal. Counter-conduct also enables us to recognise the *ethos* of the rioter as behaviour that is *ethical*, fearless and improvised, and that exposes government through rights. The rioter enacts *parrhēsia*: a courageous truth-telling of her narrative of struggle that ought to be acknowledged by the liberal, democratic state. My objective in this chapter is then to show that the language of rights is inadequate to recognise the revolting subject. This subject challenges the language of rights, she refuses governance (through) rights by refusing the right channels for resistance and by rejecting the ethic of responsibility of the Big Society. The implications of this reading are significant for rights as 'the energy of our societies, the fulfillment of the Enlightenment promise of emancipation and self-realisation'[6] because rights has then failed as a discourse of emancipation and self-realisation for those who are not good behaving, active and so ideal rights-bearing citizens.

I begin by outlining 'counter-conduct' as a process and as a framework of analysis that allows us to see the political agency of the revolting subject. I go on to explore the 'enigma' of the riot through re-reading the riots in London in 2011 and in Ferguson, Missouri in 2014, suggesting that the enigma can be defined as counter-conduct and its *ethos* is one of improvisation allowing us to read the rioter's behaviour as ethical (or as *parrhēsia*). The chapter is not, in doing this, a call to see rights as insidious or a call for an alternative discourse; it is rather a challenge to interrogate and to remain continually dissatisfied with their promise—which, as I come to explain in the next and concluding chapter of the book, is how, as rights-bearing subjects and/or experts, we ought to remain.[7]

I. COUNTER-CONDUCT

The problem of government (through) rights reflects the general concerns of 'how to govern oneself, how to be governed, by whom should we accept to be governed, how to be the best possible governor?'[8] I have been concerned so far in this book with *how* government (through) rights happens and examined the role of rights experts in governing (through) rights and how rights are being resisted through a rhetoric based on responsibility

---

[6] C Douzinas, *The End of Human Rights* (Oxford, Hart, 2002) 1.

[7] Some of the arguments in this chapter also appear in B Sokhi-Bulley, 'Performing Struggle: *Parrhēsia* in Ferguson' (2015) 26(1) *Law and Critique* 7 and B Sokhi-Bulley, 'Re-Reading the Riots: Counter-Conduct in London 2011' (forthcoming 2016) *Global Society*.

[8] M Foucault, *Security, Territory, Population* (M Senellart (ed), G Burchell (trans), Basingstoke, Palgrave Macmillan, 2007) 88.

and community rights in the Big Society ethic. I want to expand now on the resistance to rights; or, rather, to how government (through) rights is *countered* by the subject of rights discourse/government (eg within the Big Society). So I want to explore the correlation between government (through) rights as *conduct* and *counter*-conduct in rights:

> *Conduct* is the activity of conducting (*conduire*), of conduction (*la conduction*) if you like, but it is equally the way in which one conducts oneself (*se conduit*), lets oneself be conducted (*se laisse conduire*), is conducted (*est conduit*), and finally, in which one behaves (*se comporter*) as an effect of a form of conduct (*une conduit*) as the action of conducting or of conduction (*conduction*).[9]

The 'badly constructed word'[10] *counter-conduct* represents a refusal of the form of being conducted; here, in this chapter, it represents a refusal of rights and of the type of governmentable subjectivity that rights creates. It refers to a form of behaviour that demonstrates "We do not want this salvation, we do not wish to be saved by these people and by these means ... We do not wish to obey these people ... We do not want this truth"'.[11] Counter-conduct is also then about a '*struggle* against the processes implemented for conducting others'.[12]

When faced with the problem of vocabulary in 1978, when 'resistance' was no longer adequate to designate this kind of refusal, Foucault focused on the *specificity* of refusal and struggle—on specific counter-conducts, the nature of *counter*-attacks or *counter*-movements.[13] So he rejected 'resistance' and the terms 'revolts of conduct', 'disobedience', 'dissent' and 'misconduct' as descriptors.[14] 'Revolt' is too strong a term, too precise to designate more diffuse and subdued forms of resistance. 'Disobedience' is purely negative and ignores the extent to which resistance is productive, consistent and based in solidarity. 'Dissidence' is perhaps the worst word, since it risks a type of presupposition or judgment that glorifies the dissident. Counter-conduct by contrast allows us to see the specifics of 'the way in which someone *actually acts*'[15] within the field of power relations (ie within the 'social') without the need to judge the behaviour as proper, or 'sacred'.[16] And this makes it possible to see the behaviour of 'delinquents, mad people, and patients',[17]

[9] Ibid 193 (emphasis added).
[10] Ibid 201. Note how Foucault reverts back to 'revolt' and talk of 'revolution', however, where he addresses the 'Iranian movement' or Iranian Revolution of 1979, in 'Useless to Revolt', above n 2.
[11] Ibid 201.
[12] Ibid.
[13] Ibid 194–6.
[14] Ibid 200–1.
[15] Ibid (emphasis added).
[16] Ibid 202.
[17] Ibid 202.

or of the revolting subject, for what it is: a *specific form of refusal or strug-gle that is a reaction* against government (through) rights.

Foucault's interest in counter-conducts is situated in revolts against the pastorate. The (Catholic and Christian) pastorate is discussed by Foucault at such length because it represents the interplay of government in modern Western societies, today manifested as pastoral power (discussed in previous chapters). The essential relationship is thus *not* between church and state but between the pastorate and government. The pastorate contains its own 'set of techniques and procedures' which lead to an 'economy of souls, where 'economy' refers to a 'government' or 'regimen' that ensures obedience.[18] Specific to the pastorate, he talks of asceticism as one of five main forms of counter-conduct that challenge and discredit pastoral power. As an active refusal of pastoral power, asceticism is a 'sort of exasperated and reversed obedience that has become egoistic self-mastery. Let us say that in asceti-cism there is a specific excess that denies access to an external power';[19] that is, it is an anti-pastoral movement which seeks to master oneself and the world without obedience to or without glorifying Christ. The develop-ment of these counter-conducts is a reactive response that both *happens* but is also sometimes an active refusal or movement (asceticism, for example, did not just 'happen'). Foucault also gives examples of counter-conducts to political institutions; for instance, desertion of the army. Once being a sol-dier becomes a form of political and moral conduct that is part of a general societal ethic that every good citizen should want to wage war, then refusing to be a soldier becomes a refusal of society's values, of civic education and of a certain obligation to the state that we can call 'counter-conduct'.[20] He talks also about the development of secret societies as an alternative to gov-ernmental direction—'a sort of different pastorate, a different governmen-tality with its chiefs, its rules, and its principles of obedience' to the extent that it 'possesses ... a considerable capacity both to appear as a different society, a different form of conduct, and to channel revolts of conduct'.[21] He refers too to medical dissent, highlighting the refusal of a kind of medi-cal rationality, techniques, and medications. I look at rioting as a specific form of counter-conduct to the form of government (through) rights. This is government managed by strong policing methods and by government poli-cies based in an ethic of responsibility that dictates the duty of the rights-bearing citizen to behave responsibly.

Counter-conduct is thus the process of refusal—what is actually happen-ing in the demonstration of that refusal. But it is also and at the same time a

---

[18] On pastoral power, see further B Golder, 'Foucault and the Genealogy of Pastoral Power' (2007) 10(2) *Radical Philosophy Review* 157.
[19] Foucault, *Security, Territory, Population*, above n 8, 208.
[20] Ibid 198.
[21] Ibid 199.

way of thinking about the process of refusal. It is thus a framework or methodology for examining and understanding the 'impulse not to obey'. It is
then another of Foucault's theory fragments, another tool of analysis much
like its counterpart governmentality (which is concerned with the mentality of government, a way of thinking about the problem of government).
As such, it allows for extended possibilities for understanding refusal. The
focus is *not* on whether the behaviour (eg rioting) is the *right way* for the
rights-bearing subject to resist, but on the struggle, on how the individual
actually acts, on the nature of the reaction and the specificity of the event.
Counter-conduct thus allows for creativity of response to refusing to obey
(rights); it means we can *see* the rioter and the components of her behaviour
as political and not dismiss it as *only* criminal. It means we can try to understand the *ethos* of improvisation and appreciate alternative forms of revolt
as ethical and not only criminal behaviour.

II. PERFORMING STRUGGLE AS RIGHT AND AS ETHICS

A. The Riots: London and Ferguson

The riots that took place in London in 2011 began as a peaceful protest of
about 200 people outside Tottenham police station following the fatal police
shooting of 29-year-old Mark Duggan, a member of the black community
of north London. Duggan was shot and killed on 4 August 2011, when the
minicab he was in was stopped in Ferry Lane, Tottenham, by officers of
the Metropolitan Police. Duggan had apparently been under surveillance
as part of Operation Trident, established by the Metropolitan Police as an
effort to control gun crime in black communities. The inquest, which considered the proportionality of the force used in the circumstances that led
to Duggan's death in relation to protecting persons against violence, found
the police shooting to be a 'lawful killing' in January 2014.[22] The first night
of rioting in London was followed by the pattern of violence, looting and
arson being repeated in several London boroughs (including Tottenham and
Hackney) and spread north to the major cities of Birmingham, Liverpool
and Manchester, replicating a 'disorder' that was reminiscent of the Brixton
Riots of 1981.[23] The everyday space of the commercial high street was

---

[22] *Inquest Touching upon the Death of Mark Duggan* (2014), Mark Duggan Inquest,
dugganinquest.independent.gov.uk/index.htm.
[23] *Guardian* in partnership with the London School of Economics and Political Science,
Reading the Riots: Investigating England's Summer of Disorder, available at eprints.lse.
ac.uk/46297/1/Reading%20the%20riots(published).pdf. See also www.theguardian.com/uk/
series/reading-the-riots; B Trott, 'Rebellious Subjects: The Politics of England's 2011 Riots'
(2013) 112(1) *South Atlantic Quarterly* 538.

spoiled, with over half (51 per cent) of all crimes committed against commercial premises.[24] Over just five days (6–10 August), 'all hell broke loose';[25] upwards of 15,000 people are thought to have taken part and 2,500 shops and businesses experienced looting. Statistics show that:

> [o]n just one night in the capital, an unprecedented sixteen thousand police officers were deployed to quash the riots and according to the Metropolitan Police, 4,714 riots-related arrests were made during the uprisings and their aftermath—with 2,905 formally charged or summoned to court so far, and 1,103 of these receiving prison sentences.[26]

The actions of the 'rioters' were described by politicians, councils, the courts, the media and academics as not simply criminal but *only* criminal. The courts dealt out excessively punitive sentences for the main crimes of burglary (50 per cent), violent disorder (22 per cent) and theft (15 per cent); the example of *Blackshaw* is particularly shocking, since two young men were sentenced to four years in prison for attempting, albeit unsuccessfully, to incite a riot via Facebook.[27] Politicians launched new legal penalties such as granting 'mandatory power of possession' to landlords, allowing them to evict tenants for antisocial behaviour and criminal convictions.[28] Prime Minister Cameron labelled the events as 'just *pure criminality*'.[29] He called for amendment to the Riot Damages Act 1986 so that any homeowner or business person whose property was damaged was able to seek compensation under the Act, even if they were uninsured.[30] Local councils supported the aim to evict rioters, claiming they had made themselves 'intentionally homeless' and asserting 'we do not want you in

---

[24] Ibid.

[25] P Lewis, 'Tottenham riots: a peaceful protest, then suddenly all hell broke loose', *Guardian*, 7 August 2011, available at www.theguardian.com/uk/2011/aug/07/tottenham-riots-peaceful-protest.

[26] Trott, 'Rebellious Subjects', above n 23, 538–39.

[27] *R v Blackshaw* [2011] EWCA Crim 2312. See S Lamble, 'The Quiet Dangers of Civilized Rage: Surveying the Punitive Aftermath of England's August 2011 Riots' (2013) 112 *South Atlantic* Quarterly 577 for further examples, including a six months prison sentence for a 23-year-old with no previous convictions for stealing a bottle of water worth £3.50.

[28] Ibid. See also UK Department for Communities and Local Government, *Strengthening the Powers Possession for Anti-Social Behaviour: Summary of Responses to Consultation and Next Steps* (May 2012), available at www.gov.uk/government/uploads/system/uploads/attachment_data/file/8462/2148929.pdf.

[29] D Cameron, 'The Fightback After the Riots', speech made on 15 August 2011, available at www.number10.gov.uk/news/pms-speech-on-the-fightback-after-the-riots/. See also D Cameron, 'PM Statement on Restoring Order to Cities', 9 August 2011, available at www.gov.uk/government/news/we-will-do-everything-necessary-to-restore-order-pm; and D Cameron, 'PM Statement on Violence in England', 10 August 2011, available at www.gov.uk/government/speeches/pm-statement-on-violence-in-england.

[30] For comment see Lamble, 'The Quiet Dangers of Civilized Rage', above n 27. By March 2012, of the almost 4,000 claims received by the Metropolitan Police Authority, only 181 uninsured claims had been dealt with; for comment see C Bloom, *Riot City: Protest and Rebellion in the Capital* (Basingstoke, Palgrave MacMillan, 2012) 100.

our community'.[31] The media engaged in a huge 'snitching' campaign, enticing the public to name and report suspected rioters.

Public intellectuals took to highlighting the 'abstract negativity'[32] of the events—Hegel's phrase, which Zizek used to call the rioters a 'rabble' and lament that:

> it tells us a great deal about our ideological-political predicament and about the kind of society we inhabit, a society which celebrates choice but in which the only available alternative to enforced democratic consensus is a *blind acting out*. Opposition to the system can no longer articulate itself in the form of a realistic alternative, or even as a utopian project, but can only take the shape of a *meaningless outburst*.[33]

Badiou dismisses the London events (which he compares to the Paris uprisings in 2005) as 'violent, anarchic, and ultimately without enduring truth'.[34] Those involved 'were nothing but gangs, hooligans, thieves, brigands—in short "dangerous classes" contrasted ... with ... good citizens'.[35] He makes a distinction between the 'immediate' riot and the more effective, lasting 'historical riot'; the latter stirs up historical possibilities and is motivated by a powerful Idea,[36] like the Egyptian historical riot of early 2011 which he cites as the most important and consistent example. The 'immediate riot', by contrast, has no such possibility for change. Badiou outlines three key features of the immediate riot: first, 'tumultous' youth participation; second, its territorial location—an immediate riot is localised to the territory of those who take part; and third, the subjective type—where the subjectivity is 'composed solely of rebellion and dominated by negation and destruction', making it impossible to distinguish between 'a partially universalizable intention and what remains confined to a rage with no purpose other than the satisfaction of being able to crystallize and find hateful objects to destroy and consume'.[37] MacDonald also surmises that 'exalting [the London rioter's] base consciousness as a revolutionary awareness is a mere flattery of the riotous looters'.[38] Furthermore, the immediate riot

---

[31] Lamble, 'The Quiet Dangers of Civilized Rage', above n 27, 581. See also UK Department for Communities and Local Government, *Ending Gang and Youth Violence: A Cross-Government Report including Further Evidence and Good Practice Case Studies*, Cm 8211 (Norwich, Stationery Office, 2011), available at www.gov.uk/government/uploads/system/uploads/attachment_data/file/97861/gang-violence-summary.pdf; and R Leese, 'The Only Place to Be', *Leader's Blog* (Manchester City Council, August 2011), www.manchester.gov.uk/blog/leadersblog/post/477.

[32] S Zizek, 'Shoplifters of the World Unite', *London Review of Books*, 19 August 2011, available at www.lrb.co.uk/2011/08/19/slavoj-zizek-shoplifters-of-the-world-unite.

[33] Ibid (emphasis added).

[34] A Badiou, *The Rebirth of History: Times of Riots and Uprisings* (London, Verso, 2012) 21.

[35] Ibid 16.

[36] Ibid 38–42.

[37] Ibid 23–25.

[38] A MacDonald, 'Nocturnal Games in the Streets' (2012) 23(3) *Law and Critique* 185–97, 196.

cannot 'purify itself', that is, the immediate riot lacks truth and intention; it can therefore not be victorious. It is thus not a properly political event.

The rhetoric around the riots also recognised a consensus around the outrage at the impetus, that is, Duggan's tragic death, which appears to have stemmed from two things: first, that he was *black* and, second, that it was an act of *police* violence that killed him. We witnessed a similar cause of outrage three years later in August 2014 in Ferguson, Missouri. 'Hands up, don't shoot', or simply 'Hands up' has become a powerful slogan in the United States to convey resistance to the unacceptable abuse of police power, which stemmed from the shooting of an unarmed teenager not linked to any crime.[39] Michael Brown was shot six times by police officer Darren Wilson in Ferguson, Missouri, on 9 August 2014. He was 18 years old and had no previous criminal record. In the days after, people marched to chants of 'hands up don't shoot', protests that later turned into 'violent clashes' between the protestors and police, the spectacle of which resembled that of Tottenham High Road—people throwing Molotov cocktails, looting businesses, burning down the QuickTrip gas station and vandalising vehicles. The state response escalated from police blockades in riot gear using tear gas, to Missouri Governor Jay Nixon declaring a state of emergency and imposing midnight curfews by 18 August when the riots showed no sign of abating. When these failed to control the violence, the escalation peaked with Nixon activating the Missouri National Guard to support police operations. This was the first time that the military has been deployed to quell civil unrest since the 1992 race riots in Los Angeles. Over 30 arrests, on charges of assault, burglary and theft, were made on the first night in Ferguson, increasing to 78 by 20 August when a new wave of rioting was sparked by the apparently unrelated shooting of another young black man, 23-year-old Kajieme Powell. Amongst the arrested were journalists.[40] President Obama distanced himself from the Governor's decision to militarise the local law enforcement response. But he did reprimand the protestors for 'stirring chaos' and chided them for '*giving in* to anger', which he argued only served to raise tension.[41] According to Obama the reaction in Ferguson was not 'resistance'; it was disorganised, irresponsible behaviour, characterised by what Ronald Johnson, the Missouri highway patrol captain, called 'premeditated criminal attacks'.[42]

[39] See www.handsupunited.org.

[40] On 13 August 2014, while police were clearing a McDonald's restaurant, *Washington Post* reporter Wesley Lowery and *Huffington Post* reporter Ryan Reilley were arrested.

[41] D Roberts, 'Ferguson crisis: Obama sends Attorney General as Governor lifts curfew', *Guardian*, 19 August 2014, available at www.theguardian.com/world/2014/aug/18/obama-attorney-general-eric-holder-ferguson?CMP=EMCNEWEML6619I2.

[42] G Young, 'In Ferguson the violence of the state created the violence of the street', *Guardian, Comment is Free*, 18 August 2014, available at www.theguardian.com/commentisfree/2014/aug/18/ferguson-violence-martin-luther-king-michael-brown?CMP=EMCNEWEML6619I2.

B. How to Label the Enigma: Counter-Conduct

'What do the [people] want?'[43] is the typical, somewhat frightened and certainly troubled question that is asked in the aftermath to these sorts of unruly, 'mindless' events. If the event cannot be classed as proper 'resistance' or 'revolution', we cannot find a way to see it as anything but criminal. I am not saying that the riots were *not* criminal. But reducing them to 'pure criminality' (Cameron) or 'stirring chaos' (Obama) dismisses the extent to which they are political events and removes the political agency of the actors. The rioter becomes criminal and *only* criminal. Yet, '[t]he protestors in Ferguson aren't irrational or apolitical. They are calling attention to their basic, unmet needs ... Far from a mindless, violent mob, the people of Ferguson were engaged in concerted political consciousness-raising leading up to the insurrection'.[44] Of course, the unrest was political because it was about politics. But 'politics' is of course distinct from 'the political'. The former refers to 'the institutional organisation of society'.[45] And although each and every participant was not consciously 'doing politics' through rioting, the riots are still political.[46] Labelling the riot 'counter-conduct' and observing the behaviour of the rioters through a counter-conduct framework highlights the political in that we see the power relations that construct the rioter as criminal. This is made possible because we are looking within this framework at, on the one hand, *what is being countered* and, on the other, at how the rioter *actually acts*, that is *the specifics* of her behaviour 'within the very general field of politics or in the very general field of power relations'.[47] But not only this; a counter-conduct framework also exposes *crisis*—a crisis in the Big Society ethic of responsibility, a crisis in policing, and most importantly a crisis *in rights*, which is shown to be a failing discourse. Not only is the rioter criminalised, she is no longer recognised in democratic society as a rights-bearing subject because she is not behaving in the right way in her community—she is not a responsible, active citizen deserving of and taking the opportunity of her (community) rights.

(i) What is Being Countered

In terms of what is being countered, the riots I argue are a counter-conduct against first, the ethic of responsibility and second, against policing.[48]

---

[43] C Douzinas, *Philosophy and Resistance in the Crisis* (London, Polity Press, 2013) 140.

[44] R Stephens, 'In Defense of the Ferguson Riots', *Jacobin*, 14 August 2014, available at www.jacobinmag.com/2014/08/in-defense-of-the-ferguson-riots/.

[45] F Kaulingfreks, *Making Trouble: Disruptive Interventions of Urban Youth as Unruly Politics* (Ridderkerk, Rifferprint BV, 2013) 14.

[46] R Nunes, 'Building on Destruction' (2013) 112(3) *South Atlantic Quarterly* 568, 572.

[47] Foucault, *Security, Territory, Population*, above n 8, 202.

[48] I am of course being reductive here; there are *other things* that the riot counters, such as a culture of consumerism, reduced mobility, increased isolation, for example. For my purposes

The previous chapter examined the political utility of the active citizen to the re-branded 'Community and Society', previously the Big Society. The active citizen is the ideal citizen of the Big Society: docile, obedient and a full volunteer. The example of the National Citizen Service (NCS) in Chapter 4 showed this to be a strategy of government in that it represents a programme of activity that employs tactics that regulate individual behaviour and nurture an attitude of collective action and responsibility. NCS was chosen as the flagship policy of the Big Society for its promising ability to shape behaviour through (re)education on the values of responsibility, duty and opportunity.[49] NCS is thus the solution to spontaneous, unpredictable ruptures such as the England Riots. These riots, as the Prime Minister stated, were not about poverty; '[n]o, this was about *behaviour*'—the unpleasant behaviour of unsavoury 'thugs' and 'gangs'.[50] So, the solution is to change behaviour through initiatives that educate as to what values we ought to respect. These in turn govern us 'at a distance'[51] to be more savoury citizens: responsible, dutiful and volunteers in our communities and *not thugs*. Countering these values and refusing a taming of the expression of struggle in the name of a right way to behave is what the riots represented. The rioter refuses active citizenship through a deliberate (intentional) or an indifferent (out of boredom) acting out.

Also, the government's focus on behaviour ignores the extent to which the riots *were* about poverty and about a dissatisfaction of the way in which the 'urban poor' is classified and then dismissed as 'marginal', even 'abnormal'. The pun in Tyler's subjectivity of the 'revolting subject'[52] is the subject who revolts but who is also and then necessarily unsavoury; it is the figure of 'the chav' as represented by the working and non-working (under)class of Britain. Recognising a work/workless dichotomy as Tyler does constructs the 'workless' chav as a 'figure of sloth, ignorance and welfare dependence stuck in time and place'.[53] It is this 'uneducated, unemployed sub-class' that Community Secretary Eric Pickles blamed for the riots, echoing a general public sentiment. The 'Riot Data' collected by the *Reading The Riots* Study used Home Office research to show that those summoned to court tended to be from poor and deprived backgrounds (as compared with the population as a whole).[54] Thus, 35 per cent of the adults who took part in the riots were claiming unemployment benefits (compared to

and in relation to *rights* I have identified responsibilisation and policing as the two dominant narratives that the riot counters.

[49] D Cameron, 'Big Society', speech made on 14 February 2011, available at www.number10.gov.uk/news/speeches-and-transcripts/2011/02/pms-speech-on-big-society-60563.

[50] Cameron, 'The Fightback After the Riots', above n 29.

[51] N Rose, 'Government and Control' (2000) 40 *British Journal of Criminology* 321, 324.

[52] Tyler, *Revolting Subjects*, above n 4.

[53] Ibid.

[54] *Guardian* and LSE, *Reading the Riots*, above n 23.

12 per cent of the working age population); 42 per cent of the young people who came before a judge were on free school meals, which are only available to 16 per cent of secondary school pupils from the poorest backgrounds.[55] Moreover, 58 per cent of rioters asked to appear in court lived within the 20 per cent most deprived areas in England. The city of Manchester in particular showed a correlation between suspects and poorer residence areas.[56] The point here is that demonising the rioting 'chav' shows a chronic misunderstanding of poverty and of the social hierarchy inherent within the Big Society's notion of community. A counter-conduct perspective on the riots does not demonise the rioter. But it does not glorify her either. The alternative narrative that the perspective tells has no villains and no heroes either. Rather, the counter-conduct perspective reorients our gaze towards *how* the rioter *actually acts* to behave *otherwise* than how the ethic of responsibility and rights demands. Second, the rioter's behaviour counters policing. The politics of policing is increasingly characterised by violence, which has become 'the hallmark of policing across the world'.[57] In arguing that the typical modality for those in power is to depoliticise the policing of radical protest by labelling it a crime (for instance, creating the offence of 'violent disorder' as happened through the 1986 Public Order Act), El-Enany lists examples of violent practices such as 'kettling', the use of batons and techniques to disperse the crowd such as horse charges.[58] This has the effect of politicising social conflict to the extent that protesters become not only criminal but an external threat, a terrorist threat to the very existence of the state which, in the case of Ferguson, it took the army (National Guard) to extinguish.[59]

There are of course stark contrasts between the militarisation of the police response in Ferguson and the police presence in England during the four days of rioting in 2011.[60] London, Birmingham, Liverpool and Manchester were not, for instance, characterised by '[t]ear gas, stun grenades, rubber bullets, camouflage uniforms, armoured cars, assault rifles, shotguns and automatic weapons have been an almost daily presence on the streets of St Louis'.[61] The situation in London was described by Adrian Roberts, Metropolitan Police Silver Commander (July-August 2011) as 'vast': 'in twenty eight years of policing I've never experienced it, I don't think the country has. It just

---

[55] S Rogers, 'England riots: was poverty a factor?', *Guardian*, 6 December 2011, available at www.theguardian.com/news/datablog/2011/aug/16/riots-poverty-map-suspects.
[56] Ibid.
[57] N El-Enany, 'Ferguson and the Politics of Policing Radical Protest' (2015) 16 *Law and Critique* 3.
[58] Ibid 4.
[59] Ibid.
[60] T Newburn, 'The Ferguson riots may seem similar to those in UK in 2011, but there are stark contrasts', *Guardian*, 20 August 2014, available at www.theguardian.com/commentisfree/2014/aug/20/ferguson-missouri-not-so-far-from-tottenham-toxteth.
[61] Ibid.

was completely vast'.[62] And yet the *Guardian* police interviews reveal regret that there were not enough police in London at the time of the most intense rioting and that the right radio channels were not used to deploy additional officers.[63] Nevertheless, of the 270 people interviewed by the *Reading The Riots* Study, 85 per cent commented that policing was an 'important' or 'very important' stimulus for the riots happening.[64] The study reports versions of the same stock antagonist sentiment, 'The police is the biggest gang out there'.[65] The police presence was characterised by police in riot gear and the Mayor of London, three years on from the events in the city, advocated a more violent response to 'protests' in the form of water cannon.[66] The *Reading the Riots* Study reported on a sense of revenge against the police:

> Rioters recounted how they sought revenge by wanting to hurt, intimidate, target and indiscriminately attack officers. Others described how they threw stones and bottles; rammed police with wheelie bins and shouted 'Fuck the police'.[67]

It is not only policing that the riots counter but *racialised* police tactics. The *Reading the Riots* study reports that the 'most acute sense of a longstanding mistrust was among black interviewees.'[68] Yet race, and a black versus (white) police rhetoric, was not the key factor; instead, as Newman observes, '[m]any of the English riots were defined at least as much by *poverty* and disadvantage as they were about ethnicity.'[69] By comparison, the reaction in Ferguson has been a remarkable and widespread call to 'expose the ongoing crisis of police-on-black crime'.[70] There is an overwhelming recognition of the *fact* that, '*The police* were the problem, and they had to be stopped.'[71] Ferguson is largely an African-American community—about two thirds of the city's 21,100 residents are black. The police force has 53 members and, strikingly, only three of the officers are black. Quoting a local resident, the *Washington Post* reports that relations between residents have been 'very hostile' for years—everybody, for instance, has been a victim of

---

[62] P Lewis and L Topham, 'Policing England's riots: "the scale was vast"—video', *Guardian*, 2 July 2012, available at www.theguardian.com/uk/video/2012/jul/02/policing-england-riots-scale-video.

[63] P Lewis and L Topham, 'Policing England's riots: "The Met had lost the streets" —video', *Guardian*, 2 July 2012, available at www.theguardian.com/uk/video/2012/jul/02/policing-england-riots-met-video.

[64] *Guardian* and LSE, *Reading the Riots*, above n 23, 18.

[65] Ibid.

[66] R Seymour, 'The real reason water cannon are coming to Boris Johnson's London', *Guardian*, 11 June 2014, available at www.theguardian.com/commentisfree/2014/jun/11/boris-johnson-water-cannon-blast-theresa-may.

[67] *Guardian* and LSE, *Reading the Riots*, above n 23, 19.

[68] Ibid.

[69] Newburn, 'The Ferguson riots', above n 60.

[70] See www.handsupunited.org.

[71] Stephens, 'In Defense of the Ferguson Riots', above n 44.

DWB ['driving while black'].[72] Having come to represent a 'microcosm—of all of the narratives about race and America that we fear and suppress',[73] Ferguson has brought to light how *only* (unarmed) black men are victims of police 'accidents'. Writing about his own (white) brother who shot a black man, Stafford says: 'Accident seemed like an odd word to use for me in this situation. When I hear the word "accident", I usually think about spilled milk or a dog urinating on the carpet ... Accidents were things you respond to with, "Whoops, sorry!" But with this accident I wondered: to whom can we even say "sorry" now that a man lay dead?'[74]

We are of course not talking about *a* man. The 'demands' of Ferguson Action, a growing national coalition of activist groups from 'affected communities',[75] are made on the basis that every 28 hours a black person is killed by someone employed or protected by the US government.[76] Michael Brown's death highlighted and made high profile other police killings, including 43-year old Eric Garner who had died on 17 July 2014 as a result of being placed in a chokehold by New York Police Department officer Daniel Pantaleo, who ignored his repeated cries of 'I can't breathe' and his initial insistence that 'I did nothing ... I'm minding my own business, officer'.[77] And 12-year old Tamir Rice, who was shot dead by police officer Timothy Leohmann in Cleveland, Ohio on 22 November 2014 when the fake gun he was carrying was mistaken for a firearm.[78] The 911 call is recorded as reporting 'a guy' in the park pointing a 'probably fake' gun at people, with the operator asking three times 'is he black or white'.[79] Neither Pantaleo, Leohmann or Wilson (the Ferguson officer who shot Brown) were criminally charged following the Grand Jury indictments that took place to

[72] W Lowery, C Leonnig and M Berman, 'Even before Michael Brown's slaying in Ferguson, racial questions hung over police', *Washington Post*, 13 August 2014, available at www.washingtonpost.com/politics/even-before-teen-michael-browns-slaying-in-mo-racial-questions-have-hung-over-police/2014/08/13/78b3c5c6-2307-11e4-86ca-6f03cbd15c1a_story.html.

[73] S McFadden, 'Ferguson goddamn: no indictment for Darren Wilson is no surprise. This is why we protest', *Guardian*, 25 November 2014, available at www.theguardian.com/commentisfree/2014/nov/24/ferguson-no-indictment-darren-wilson-protest.

[74] Z Stafford, 'I'm black, my brother's white ... and he's a cop who shot a black man on duty', *Guardian*, 25 August 2014, available at www.theguardian.com/commentisfree/2014/aug/25/white-brother-police-shot-black-man.

[75] See fergusonaction.com.

[76] See fergusonaction.com/demands/.

[77] See footage recovered by the *Guardian*, 'Eric Garner put in chokehold by NYPD officer—video', available at www.theguardian.com/us-news/video/2014/dec/04/i-cant-breathe-eric-garner-chokehold-death-video.

[78] Note the recent decision of a grand jury not to indict Leohmann: O Laughland, J Swain and D McGraw, 'Cleveland officer who fatally shot Tamir Rice will not face criminal charges', *Guardian*, 28 December 2015, available at www.theguardian.com/us-news/2015/dec/28/tamir-rice-shooting-no-charges-cleveland-officer-timothy-loehmann.

[79] P Lewis, 'Obama under pressure over response to police killings after Eric Garner decision', *Guardian*, 4 December 2014, available at www.theguardian.com/us-news/2014/dec/04/obama-police-killings-eric-garner-decision.

review their actions.[80] This placated response to police violence prompted a nationwide reaction that called for justice. As Maria Fudge, chair of the Congressional Black Caucus comments, 'it appears justice will not be served for Mr Garner and his family ... there is no accountability for taking black lives.'[81] And the question, highlighted by the counter-conduct of the *black rioter*, has become, 'What the fuck is policing that insists on using deadly force for the most minor of offences?'[82]

The rioter thus counters the way in which her behaviour is regulated by police tactics and policing through rights, which dictates that there is a *right way* to revolt by going through the *proper* channels to claim your rights and redress of their violation. Setting buildings and cars on fire or looting from shops is not the right way to be heard; in fact, you will be not be recognized as a political, ethical rights-bearing subject if you revolt in this way. There is no place for the rights-bearing citizen who creates a spectacle and refuses the police via such means and tactics in a democratic society.

(ii) The Specificity of the Riot

The specificity of the riot is defined then by spectacle and by an impulsive reaction to the conducting power of the state through its responsibilisation ethic, its use of extreme policing measures *and* its determination of a *right* way to resist through claiming rights. The riot produces a *spectacle* without being spectacular;[83] that is, it is a visual performance of refusal that is something to behold given the scenes of arson, looting and vandalism but it does not (or need not) have spectacular, or revolutionary, effect. The London and Ferguson riots are not the kind of spectacular protest of the Ukrainian Maidan (labelled the Hrushevskoho Street Riots of January 2014) or of the central business district in Hong Kong (labelled the 'Umbrella Movement/ Revolution' of 2014). Nor was the spectacle one of 'peaceful' protests as in New York following the death of Garner, where crowds gathered in Times Square, Grand Central Terminal and near Rockefeller Center holding slogans such as 'Black Lives Matter',[84] and others staged mass 'die-ins', where demonstrators lay in silence a block away from the Christmas Tree lighting ceremony at Rockefeller Center and around the country.[85] In this sense then,

---

[80] Ibid; Laughland, Swain and McGraw, 'Cleveland officer who fatally shot' Tamir Rice, above n 78; McFadden, 'Ferguson goddamn', above n 73.

[81] Quoted in Lewis, 'Obama under pressure', above n 79.

[82] Mcfadden, 'Ferguson goddamn', above n 73.

[83] Douzinas, *Philosophy and Resistance in the Crisis*, above n 43, 139–40.

[84] See #BlackLivesMatter, blacklivesmatter.com.

[85] Lewis, 'Obama under pressure', above n 79; P Lewis, 'Eric Garner: protests erupt in New York after officer is spared prosecution', *Guardian*, 4 December 2014, available at www.theguardian.com/us-news/2014/dec/03/justice-department-eric-holder-eric-garner-investigation; students staged a die-in at Emory University, Georgia, Atlanta.

the riots are a rather mundane and impulsive *reaction*. They are mundane because they are not particularly creative or innovative; they are rather an expected response. However, impulse betrays the extent to which the riots were a coordinated response by marginalised communities, individuals and youths; and not everything about them was expected.

Whilst impulsive and arguably lacking innovation (staging a die-in, for instance, is far more novel than setting fire to buildings), the riots were an *acting out*. This 'impulse not to obey' is important to recognise because it highlights refusal and suffering. Impulse also negates the need for intention: the rioters do not need to be innovative, organised or deliberately seeking to expose the violence of the Big Society ethic, its form of policing and the poverty of rights-claiming in the face of such tactics; their acting out, their behaviour, how they *actually act* shows this. Moreover, the rioters had means of coordinating activity that was improvised, for instance through the use of social media. Facebook and Twitter maintained a 'buzz' and continuously updated individuals on where the rioting was taking place. The instant messenger service on Blackberry, known as BBM, was used to advertise future riot locations, arrange times to meet, share updates, warn people of police locations and to sell looted goods.[86] In Ferguson, the burned down QuickTrip gas station on West Florissant Avenue close to where Michael Brown was shot became a focal meeting point for protestors. It became, as Wesley Lowrey (one of the arrested journalists for *Washington Post*) comments, their Tahrir Square, their Tiannamen Square.[87] 'This is our place. This is what we've got', commented Maria Chappelle-Nadal, a State senator who had herself been central in staging many of the daytime protests.[88] And they had an organising principle, or agenda: justice. This improvised coordination is a counter-narrative to how marginalised, poor and workless communities are told to behave; it is saying, consciously or unconsciously, 'We do not want this salvation, we do not wish to be saved by these people and by these means ... We do not wish to obey these people ... We do not want this truth'.[89] I come on to the value of this improvised ethic in the next section.

[86] B Trott, 'Reading the 2011 Riots: England's Urban Uprising, an Interview with Paul Lewis' (2013) 11(3) *South Atlantic Quarterly* 541, 547. In terms of coordinating movements, the riots were not 'new' in terms of their 'ferocity' and (loosely) coordinated 'mode of operation'; they resembled not only the riots of the 1980s but of the seventeenth and eighteenth centuries, which show a similar and 'peculiar pastiche of consuming and shopping driven by the very mechanisms of the consumer industries the looters abused' (note the anti-Catholic protests in London that led to the Gordon Riots of 1780, which involved the ruinous attack on Newgate Prison), see Bloom, *Riot* City, above n 30, 121–22.
[87] W Lowrey, 'The QuickTrip gas station, Ferguson protesters' staging ground, is now silent', *Washington Post*, 19 August 2014, available at www.washingtonpost.com/politics/ferguson-protesters-staging-ground-the-quiktrip-gas-station-is-now-silent/2014/08/19/a8e4382e-27db-11e4-958c-268a320a60ce_story.html.
[88] Ibid.
[89] Foucault, *Security, Territory, Population*, above n 8, 201.

Whilst the riot itself is not novel or unexpected then, what was perhaps unexpected was the extent of the destruction caused, the spread of violence and the extent of the violent state response. But what I think is even more interesting and unexpected is how the riots have forged *counter-communities* that are enacting improvised forms of struggle and refusal.

(iii) Crisis

Far from being disparate actions of rival or competing 'gangs', the riots in both England and Ferguson have instead united communities against a common enemy, the police, and have thus been a 'unifying experience'.[90] The dismissive and punitive response of the media, the judiciary and the government in London to the riots stigmatised and criminalised whole communities and not only the individuals who took part in rioting. The production of communities, defined by 'anger, desperation and disaffection'[91] is therefore reinforced. These individuals resemble Foucault's delinquents, madmen and sexual deviants. They are the 'abnormals' who must be regulated through managing their housing (eg eviction) and movement (eg through imprisonment). This regulatory relation of governmentality and sovereign power creates a 'politics of discomfort', where anxiety stems from an unsavoury relation to the 'other' (the rioter); it is an 'affective positioning of [the urban poor] as those forever at the border, those produced as the other'.[92] We are uncomfortable with placing 'suspicious subjects'[93] (here, suspicious because of their non-conformist, irresponsible behaviour) within mainstream society, by, for instance, offering them (added) welfare benefits, access to the job market and to affordable education. The communities are thus managed to the extent that we identify them as (only) outcasts: punishable as the state dictates through its policing methods and not rights-claiming or responsible citizens of the liberal, democratic (Big) Society.

'Community' is thus the unexpected result and *form* of counter-conduct; individuals seeking to counter being policed *like that* have forged groups with actual or virtual presence and are placing demands on the federal and local systems of government. The *Reading the Riots* study covers 'community conversations' across, for example, Tottenham, Croyden, Birmingham and Liverpool, exposing stories of community that bind individuals into a collective response to poverty and injustice. In one video, a local resident visits three organisations that are attempting 'rebuilding' of

---

[90] Trott, 'Reading the 2011 Riots', above n 86, 544.

[91] Lamble, 'The Quiet Dangers of Civilized Rage', above n 27.

[92] J Darling, 'Domopolitics, Governmentality and the Regulation of Asylum Accommodation' (2011) 30 *Political Geography* 263, 264. I have replaced Darling's 'asylum seekers' with 'urban poor'.

[93] Ibid.

their community in the aftermath of the riots and concludes that youth and leaders are 'uniting to tell a new narrative in Tottenham'—one that highlights not only the changed landscape following the riots but also the effects of the spending cuts which the community is struggling to overcome.[94] Put together by a producer who was arrested as a bystander during the riots, the documentary *Riots Reframed* tells the story of the England riots through 'voices of resistance' in a 'fierce challenge to the system we live under and the suffering it produces'.[95] These are voices of an oppressed community seeking justice. In Ferguson, movements such as Ferguson Action urge people to 'Take Action' and to 'find an action near you' in an attempt to make #BlackLivesMatter a dinner table conversation.[96] The homepage of the website proclaims that 'The Movement is Growing' and contains clips from Ferguson activists to discuss why it is Time to Act, where Brittany Ferrel, a member of Millenial Activists United, comments 'We're all *community*'.[97] The site lists both demands for a 'new America' and national level demands. The former are based in wanting 'justice for Michael Brown' and 'freedom for our *communities*'—these are 'brown, black and oppressed people'.[98] The latter asks for demilitarisation of local law enforcement—this is a reaction to Obama's call to invest a package of US$263 million to transfer military equipment to local police forces;[99] we are seeing, in other words, a reaction to the 'militarisation of local law enforcement',[100] which is contributing to the politicisation of social conflict and turning the protestors from the 'thugs' we saw in London to 'terrorists' that threaten the state.[101] Local police are being asked, as Attorney General Eric Holder comments, to assist in 'counterterrorism'—a response that can be 'counter-productive'.[102] Popular Resistance encourages people to Resist! Create! Organize! Strategize![103] People are constantly updated through movements such as #ShutItDown (where 'it' is 'the machine' of policing), another reaction to Ferguson. Communities are asked to post solutions using #FergusonNext on Twitter, Facebook, Instagram and Tumblr, a solution-based collaboration between various media outlets to 'work together to find *justice*' with the slogan 'No Justice. No Peace. What Next?'[104] Unexpected, creative events

---

[94] N Payne-Frank and S Brown, 'Tottenham riots—residents unite to rebuild community—video', *Reading the Riots: Community Conversations*, 3 July 2012, www.theguardian.com/news/video/2012/jul/03/tottenham-riots-video.

[95] See riotsreframed.com (*Riots Reframed*, documentary produced by Fahim Alam).

[96] See fergusonaction.com

[97] Ibid.

[98] Ibid.

[99] Lewis, 'Obama under pressure', above n 79.

[100] Ibid.

[101] El-Enany, 'Ferguson and the Politics of Policing Radical Protest', above n 57.

[102] Lewis, 'Obama under pressure', above n 79, 4.

[103] See www.popularresistance.org/across-the-us-people-shutitdown-over-fergson/.

[104] See #FergusonNext.

organised in these communities such as book clubs are scripting their own counter-narratives to the dominant narrative of the state, which is one of marginalisation and excessive policing. For instance, 'Books and Breakfast', an initiative of 'Hands Up United' aims to encourage dialogue, as well as local engagement with social justice issues, political theory and educational development of the community of Ferguson.[105]

The forging of these counter-communities as a result of the riots is significant in that it highlights a crisis in the Big Society ethic of responsibilisation as well as the rights-claiming response to repressive forms of policing.[106] In terms of the Big Society, the message that to be a 'good citizen' you are not automatically entitled to rights, including a right to struggle, but must be the right kind of active, communal and participatory individual in modern liberal democracy, has been rejected, or met with indifference. Hence, the attitude of 'we do not want to be governed *like that*' manifests itself as the spectacle of looting and arson and has the lasting effect of creating counter-communities: communities that have refused or are indifferent to the availability of community rights, for they are already the marginalised who cannot avail of a right to build, who have families who do not want to be 'turned around' in that way and whose youth have refused or do not want to choose between being active citizens or the marginalised and ignored underclass.[107] These counter-communities have also refused or are indifferent to liberal rights-claiming through NGOs, regional agencies and 'community' when confronted with policing that responds to their refusal and struggle with excessive force, with arrests and disproportionate penalties, and is something to be feared rather than protect them. These counter-communities refuse rights and thereby highlight a crisis in rights. Rights has failed them, for they are the marginalised—the 'delinquents' most in need of protection and yet they have not chosen the right way to be, or the right way to resist and so are not welcome in community (which is where rights in the Big Society now lie). Rights do not recognise counter-conduct, nor the *ethos* of the counter-conducting subject.

C. The *Ethos* of the Enigma: *Parrhēsia*

Having lectured on the meaning of '*ethos*' in ancient Greek culture, Foucault answers his own question of 'what about the modern epoch?' with

---

[105] See www.handsupunited.org. By March 2015, it reported having served 150 residents.

[106] For another take on 'crisis', namely, an increasingly noisy 'quiet crisis' in the 'ability of human beings to reproduce themselves and their livelihoods' (559), see D Harvie and K Milburn, 'The Moral Economy of the English Crowd in the Twenty-First Century' (2013) 112(3) *South Atlantic Quarterly* 559.

[107] See Chapter 4 on community rights, and the Community and Society policies of Neighbourhood Planning and the Troubled Families Programme.

'I don't really know'.[108] He has been accused, rightly I think, of 'a troubling political quietism in the idea of ethics of the self',[109] or in the relationship between counter-conduct–rights–ethics. I am arguing here that the response to the London and Ferguson events shows that the language of rights is not sufficient to recognise the political nature of what happened. Nor does it recognise the subject as *having rights*. We cannot talk about a 'right to counter-conduct'—or even what Foucault somewhat bizarrely called the 'new right' to 'intervene effectively' in governments[110]—because there is a *right way* to resist, which is *through rights*, and the sorts of unruly, spontaneous ruptures that the Ferguson and London riots represent do not fit the label of proper resistance. They are, rather, non-spectacular, improvised forms of counter-conduct that go unrecognised as anything except criminal. Perhaps we need then to move away from the useful but limited language of rights to a notion of *counter-conduct as ethics*; to the subjects of the riots as animal-like actors who improvise a form of truth-telling, which is an *ethos* that preserves creativity and allows for the possibility of social transformation.

The immediate challenge then is to conceive of the rioters in London and in Ferguson as *parrhesiasts*: they are drawing attention to the lies and constraints of the rhetorician as represented by the state, specifically the police, as well as the regional and international human rights architecture. They are refusing the legalism of liberal rights-claiming. And they are refusing the ethic of responsibility (or are indifferent towards it) and its emphasis on duty and opportunity and community rights. These values are integral to how responsible, active citizens ought to live, in the right kind of affiliated communities. The police, moreover, are there to protect us, to ensure equal rights for all, to not harm us—shooting an innocent citizen of an oppressed, marginalised community and leaving him in the street is not fulfilling these duties. Calling attention to this and the resultant pain and fear of an entire marginalised community that it highlights is telling the truth, it is *parrhēsia*.

A problem in Foucault's analysis comes when he explains (his context is ancient Greece and his city is Athens) that in a city it is the 'decent people' ('*khrēstoi*')[111] who deliberate and take decisions—so, the mad, the insane are not even given the right to speak. Are the people of Ferguson who took to the streets the 'decent people'? Are the teenagers who rioted in the streets of Hackney, Birmingham and Manchester? Well, no, in that they are

---

[108] M Foucault, *The Courage of Truth: The Government of the Self and Others II* (F Gros (ed), G Burchell (trans), Basingstoke, Palgrave Macmillan, 2011) 29.

[109] L McNay, 'Self as Enterprise: Dilemmas of Control and Resistance in Foucault's The Birth of Biopolitics' (2009) 26 *Theory Culture and Society* 55, 68.

[110] Foucault, 'Confronting Governments', above n 1, 474.

[111] Foucault, *The Courage of Truth*, above n 108, 41.

the 'abnormal', not ideal (active) citizens whose plight is ignored by the state, the police and the human rights architecture. But in Ferguson, for instance, these 'madmen' were supplemented by activists and leaders from the New Black Panthers, the Nation of Islam, Christian Groups such as Disciples of Justice, known civil rights campaigners such as Jesse Jackson and Al Sharpton. Can *they* speak the truth? Are they *decent* people? And should *parrhēsia* not extend to all—just as Foucault's 'new right' to intervene should extend to (all) private individuals?

This is an awkward position to argue. First, because true discourse, by which I mean telling the truth about your situation by *just acting* without concern for whether your actions are legal or palatable to the democratic state, is powerless in democracy. *Parrhēsia* as a courageous attitude is, as Socrates realised when he took the decision not to tell the truth when in prison, dangerous for the city and so has no place in democracy, Foucault says.[112] So the truth-teller must be courageous and take a risk: she will not be listened to, she will be punished maybe even with death. The arrests in the aftermath of London and Ferguson show the extreme punitive response to *parrhēsia*. And this response shows why the language of rights—even 'new right' and 'absolute right'—is not adequate: it fails. You do not have a right to perform the truth and not be arrested. Second, seeing the rioter as *parrhesiast* is awkward because we are not linking truth-telling with *speech*, certainly not with only speech. I suggest we can stretch the concept of fearless speech and truth-telling to truth-*being*. The riot, like the silent protest, is a performance; it a creative and improvised response, a *being* fearless and in doing so expressing the truth about the communities to which the actors belong. The elements of creativity and improvisation further explain truth-*being*.

That is, the value of this ethics lies in its creativity. The individual who exercises *parrhēsia* is an improvising individual. Critical Studies in Improvisation take the concept beyond its musical origins (for example, improvisation in jazz) and use it to understand forms of 'creative decision-making, risk-taking and collaboration'.[113] Improvisation is thus associated with creativity and innovation.[114] Ramshaw uses the concept to understand judicial decision-making, and I argue we can use it here to understand a political, rights-bearing subject who is exercising counter-conduct. Most importantly, the utility of the concept of improvisation is that it does not

[112] Ibid 38.

[113] A Heble and W Siemerling, 'Voicing the Unforeseeable: Improvisation, Social Practise, Collaborative Research', quoted in S Ramshaw, *Justice as Improvisation: The Law of the Extempore* (Abingdon, Routledge, 2014) 2.

[114] This is not to say that all improvisation is ethical and good; see Ramshaw, ibid, who alludes to the 'dark sides' of improvisation.

occur in isolation. It is 'less about original acts of self-creation than an ongoing process of community-building'.[115] Improvisation in theatre, specifically non-scripted theatre (NST), provides further insight. Fox describes that in Playback Theatre (one type of contemporary NST) the 'teller' plays back the stories of the audience. The theatre context provides a space 'for anyone and everyone to be heard'.[116] In their performances, the tellers provide a 'creative response to a liminal condition';[117] they must be quick and ready to adapt and to choose a mode of action that best tells the story. The looters, protestors, bystanders in London and Ferguson are the tellers—they take on a raw, 'animal-like' persona to tell the truth, the stories of their community. They need not *speak*, I am saying, but perform *acts* that are their *expressions* of truth-telling. Rather than '*acts* of citizenship',[118] which claim a right to which you do not have a right, the rioter is '*just acting*' in a non-claiming of rights. Much like the actors of NST, the rioters/protestors are not acting alone—they must be able to be good group members,[119] or else the whole performance will not work. And the riot is a performance. It is enacted according to certain rules (where to meet, what posters to hold, how to communicate, through the Blackberry messenger service, for instance, as was the case in the London) and as a performance it is 'setting out to do something and calling attention to the fact'. The fact being that policing in Missouri and in London uses excessive force against rights-bearing citizens and that we will not stand for this. And the fact being that some 'youth' do not want to choose between being active citizens, rights-bearing liberal subjects or a marginalised and ignored underclass.

Thus, the rioting 'thug' can and ought to be conceived of as a political actor, engaging in counter-conduct in reaction to an oppressive form of conducting power (the discourses of responsibilisation and the right way to resist repressive policing) and to express and highlight suffering. She is courageous and risks her identity as a rights-bearing citizen. We may disagree with the way that she chooses to do this or consider it counter-productive. But we cannot dismiss it as apolitical, mindless and merely criminal. Counter-conduct is thus an absolute, *new* right as an *ethics*.

---

[115] Ibid 85.

[116] J Fox, *Acts of Service: Spontaneity, Commitment, Tradition in the Nonscripted Theatre* (New York, Tusitala Publishing, 2003). On 'improvisation', see further K Johnstone, *Improvisation and the Theatre* (London, Methuen Publishing Ltd, 1989).

[117] Fox, *Acts of Service*, above n 116, 99.

[118] J Darling, 'Asylum and the Post-Political: Domopolitics, Depoliticisation and Acts of Citizenship' (2014) 46(1) *Antipode* 72, 80. See also E Isin, 'Citizenship in Flux: The Figure of the Activist Citizen' (2009) 29 *Subjectivity* 367 and P Nyers, 'Abject Cosmopolitanism: The Politics of Protection in the Anti-Deportation Movement' (2003) 24 *Third World Quarterly* 1069 (emphasis added).

[119] Fox, *Acts of Service*, above n 116, 105.

III. CONCLUSION

When I teach Legal Theory to my students and the 'alternative methodology'[120] of governmentality, the theme they connect with most is 'counter-conduct' as the other side of governmentality. Perhaps this is because they are attracted to the idea of rebellion, which is exciting and spectacular. But counter-conduct need not be any of these things; the riots show it to be unattractive behaviour, a form of actually acting rather than conscious and planned rebellion, mundane (or expected) and a spectacle but not spectacular in its failure to instil change. Moreover, the riot remains an enigma, yet one which the counter-conduct label helps us to recognise and within which we can see an *ethos* of improvisation.

Counter-conduct in rights is, I have tried to show in this chapter, not recognised. My objective has been to show that the language of rights is inadequate to recognise the revolting subject that refuses the right(s) way to counter governments, that behaves otherwise out of either conscious decision, or to follow an unruly mob, or out of indifference. This subject challenges the language of rights, she refuses government (through) rights by rebuffing the right channels for resistance and by rejecting the counter-ethic of responsibility of the Big Society. My conclusion is then that we ought to remain open to the *counter-narratives* in rights. That is, we need to be aware of the extent to which the language of rights creates resilient or counter-communities that have found *other ways to behave* such as through rioting to counter rights, the ethic of responsibility and repressive policing, to say 'we do not want to be governed like that'. These communities cannot be ignored as only criminal for they highlight political crises—a crisis on the one hand in the Big Society, wherein the ethic of responsibility, couched in duty and opportunity, is failing because it is either rejected or met with indifference by the 'revolting subject'. On the other hand, there is a failure in how the state, through violent policing, disregards its own ethic of responsibilisation through behaving irresponsibly in how it treats (punitively) the rioter. Most importantly, in terms of the concerns of this book, it also highlights a *crisis in rights*, which is failing because it does not recognise the behaviour of the revolting subject as anything other than criminal, and because the revolting subject rejects claiming rights as a way to resist; rights is thus not proving effective when confronted with institutionalised racism and militarised policing.

The idea of counter-conduct as right and as ethics offers, perhaps, hope. A hope vaguely and unsatisfying left open by Foucault, of an 'other world'

---

[120] See B Sokhi-Bulley, 'Alternative Methodologies' (2013) 2 *Law and Method (Rechte en Methode)* 6; contrast the 'properly legal' perspective of legal positivism.

when we examine counter-conducts in rights. Perhaps, as he says in conclusion in 1984, 'the world will be able to get back to its truth, will be able to transfigure itself and become other'.[121] What can this mean? Perhaps it means questioning whether there can be a world in which individuals speak truth by rioting and we listen. How will this manifest itself? Will governments initiate special inquires and grand jury investigations for every black man who is shot? Will they enact a right to riot? The methodology of counter-conduct gives us the space to question the political and ethical possibilities of the subject who refuses rights from a position of dissatisfaction with the way she is told to behave within a society that privileges an ethic of responsibility and heightened police power.

Or, perhaps the objective of an 'other world' needs a complete re-imagining of how we are governed; perhaps the struggling, ethical subject can only be recognised *outside rights discourse*. The 'other world' must, after all, come 'at the price of a change, a complete alteration, the complete change and alteration in the relation one has to self'.[122] The government of revolting citizens constrains behaviour in the name of rights. What *else* can we draw on then to not be 'governed quite so much'?[123] A counter-narrative of counter-conduct that reclaims a *new, ethical* right to act otherwise has been my suggestion here. My final chapter further tackles the problem of transformation.

---

[121] Foucault, *The Courage of Truth*, above n 108, 315.
[122] Ibid.
[123] M Foucault, 'What is Critique?' in M Foucault, *The Politics of Truth* (S Lotringer and L Hochroth (eds), Los Angeles, CA, Semiotext(e), 1997) 29.

6

Conclusion: A Permanent State of Dissatisfaction

> I would therefore propose, as a very first definition of critique, this general characterization: the art of *not being governed quite so much.*
>
> Michel Foucault[1]

> And then, above all, I believe that an opposition can be made between critique and transformation, 'ideal' critique and 'real' transformation. A critique is not a matter of saying that things are not right as they are. It is a matter of pointing out on what kinds of assumptions, what kinds of familiar, unchallenged, unconsidered modes of thought the practices that we accept rest ... In these circumstances, criticism (and radical criticism) is absolutely indispensible for any *transformation* ... It is not therefore a question of there being a time for criticism and a time for transformation ... In fact I think the work of deep transformation can only be carried out in a free atmosphere, one constantly agitated by permanent critique.
>
> Michel Foucault[2]

THIS BOOK HAS been written in a spirit of *dissatisfaction* with and *refusal* of rights as I have sought to expose rights as technologies of governmentality. And that dissatisfaction may now extend to my reader, who is perhaps looking, in these final pages, for an answer to the 'so what' question that leaves *them* satisfied. But what I am going to conclude is that dissatisfaction is and should be a permanent state for anyone looking to counter the regulatory potential of rights and so not be 'governed quite so much'. It is my hope to leave the reader thinking it is: 'Impossible, as one turns these pages not to think of ... the essential philosophical task: never to consent to being completely comfortable with one's own presuppositions'.[3] That an 'ethic of discomfort',[4] where we are 'constantly

---

[1] M Foucault, 'What is Critique?' in M Foucault, *The Politics of Truth* (S Lotringer and L Hochroth (eds) Los Angeles, CA, Semiotext(e), 1997) 29 (emphasis added).

[2] M Foucault, 'Practicing Criticism' in LD Kritzman (ed), *Michel Foucault, Politics Philosophy and Culture: Interviews and Other Writings 1977–1984* (A Sheridan (trans), New York and London, Routledge, 1988) 154–55 (emphasis added).

[3] M Foucault, 'For an Ethic of Discomfort' in *Power*, vol 3, *Essential Works of Foucault 1954–1984* (J Faubion (ed), London, Penguin, 2002) 443, 448.

[4] Ibid.

agitated by permanent critique' such that we explore the possibilities of transformation, and make the discourse of rights groan and protest, is the only 'conclusion' to the 'problem' of a governmentality of rights. This transformation, I suggest, can happen on two levels: where we, first, make the diagnosis of governmentality endemic and, second, we acknowledge the counter-narratives to rights.

I. RIGHTS AS/AND GOVERNMENTALITY

A. Intervening in the Discourse—Something 'Unfamiliar'?

The idea of re-thinking rights, that 'uneasy, (self-)critical stance of complicity, entanglement, ambivalence, of working within a discourse to attempt to leverage political possibilities from it, should by now feel quite familiar'.[5] Golder, who makes this statement, points to 'critical thinkers of rights' like Brown and Zivi, and himself proposes a Foucauldian reading of rights that concludes in a 'critical counter-conduct of rights'.[6] My intervention in these efforts to understand rights differently is to use the governmentality and counter-conducts lenses to expose sites at which a governing (through) rights happens by examining the minor tactics through which rights operate at this sites. So I undertook a critical but also empirical examination of the (lack of a) human rights architecture at the national (Britain's Big Society), regional (the European Union, with a focus on its Fundamental Rights Agency (FRA)) and international (through an examination of the role of international non-governmental organisations (INGOs), namely, Human Rights Watch (HRW)) levels to explore the articulation of forms of governing by rights. But I have also explored struggles against and cracks within this architecture. So I have also been interested in how rights are being resisted through alternative narratives (namely, the narrative of the Big Society that is couched in a ethic of responsibility) and struggles by those whom the rights narrative does not see (namely, the rioter). These forms of resistance to government (through) rights pose dangers and challenges of their own.

My position on critique, as a 'critical attitude'[7] based in 'curiosity'[8] and hence interrogation so as to understand a thing *differently*, was made clear

---

[5] See B Golder, *Foucault and the Politics of Rights* (Stanford, CA, Stanford University Press, 2015) 159.

[6] Ibid 159 and 153. See further W Brown, *States of Injury: Power and Freedom in Late Modernity* (Princeton, Princeton University Press, 1995) and K Zivi, *Making Rights Claims* (Oxford University Press, Oxford and New York, 2012).

[7] Foucault, 'What is Critique?', above n 1, 24. See also P Minkkinen, 'Critical Legal "Method" as Attitude' in D Watkins and M Burton (eds), *Research Methods in Law* (Abingdon, Routledge, 2013) 119 and B Sokhi-Bulley, 'Alternative Methodologies' (2013) 2 *Law and Method (Rechte en Methode)* 6.

[8] On 'curiosity' as 'a certain determination to throw off familiar ways of thought and to look at the same things in a different way', see M Foucault, 'The Masked Philosopher' in

in Chapter 1. Being curious about what *else* rights do keeps us open to the ways in which they might be dangerous. So, in Chapter 2, we saw how the EU's FRA governs (through) rights using the tactics of expertise, rights indicators and a rights-based approach. Rights are made technical by the complexity of the expert assemblage, which 'does rights' through a rights-based approach and rights indicators to measure progress, good practice and good governance in rights. Rights become a discourse of conducting power that empowers expertise and leaves certain rights holders (eg the migrant) unable to claim the rights they want, and unable to use rights as a means of resisting their illegitimate status. Chapter 3 looked at the role of HRW, as an INGO, in governing (through) rights. Through the governmental tactics of expertise, narration and (self-)scrutiny, and operating within an ethic of crisis, HRW exercises a humanitarian government (through) rights and so illustrates the significance of international non-governmental actors as 'rulers' within a wider human rights architecture. The 'dangers' that the FRA and HRW pose, then, are to do with the extent to which they construct dominant narratives on how best to do rights and what rights are, which risks silencing alternative techniques and alternative stories. The dangers concern the extent to which these rights actors construct dominant identities, for themselves, for the EU and the UN, as *virtuous* rights actors. None of this is necessarily bad—but engaging in a critique of who these experts are, how they collect and disseminate data and statistics, how they develop measurement indicators, how they tell 'victim' stories and the methodologies that they use to 'do' rights, are all vital if we are not to be governed quite so much through rights.

Yet 'resistance' to rights poses dangers of its own. The ethic of responsibility that is built in to the new Community and Society framework of British society (previously labelled 'Big Society') replaces 'rights' with 'responsibility', 'duty' and 'opportunity'. Pastoral schemes like NCS that work to create a responsibilised mass of youth, and schemes sold under the guise of 'community rights' represent governmental tactics that seek to replace the rights-bearing citizen with the active citizen. The active citizen has no need for rights, for she is responsible for herself and for the community that she (should have) taken the opportunity to be part of. The insidious nature of community rights is that they form a *right to* community, rather than recognise an independent, autonomous subject of juridical rights. Moreover, the ethic of responsibility creates 'community' as the right way to be in society, marginalising those who do not or cannot be productive volunteers, who do not (want to) fit within their communities or whom the community does not recognise. It also stifles the kind of improvised struggle that I discussed in Chapter 5 as being essential to political and

M Foucault, *Ethics*, vol 1, *Subjectivity and Truth: Essential Works of Foucault 1954–1984* (P Rabinow (ed), R Hurley (trans), London, Penguin, 2000) 321, 325.

ethical agency—riotous behaviour. Against the counter-narrative of responsibility, the language of rights is inadequate to recognise the revolting subject. So counter-conduct is a useful analytics for construing the 'revolting subject' as a political, ethical actor (or *parrhesiast*).

Where does this leave us? If rights are not *bad*, and we are not calling for their abandonment, so *what* if they are dangerous? The 'end of human rights'[9] can only come when we stop questioning their utopian potential and the extent to which they have yet 'to come'.[10] I want to take this concluding point made by Douzinas further and say that acknowledging the dangers of rights leaves us in a necessary condition of permanent dissatisfaction *and* offers hope of transformation. I will attempt to elaborate—but first I must acknowledge the limits of my own methodology in saying so.

B. Acknowledging the Limits of Governmentality

Walters makes an important observation when he says that governmentality as a 'new cartography of power' is not an innocent or neutral practice.[11] Just as maps are not innocent or neutral, so the critical practice of governmentality imposes a 'well-institutionalised paradigm' on my analysis here. Perhaps my curious, critical attitude is part of an already established framework in the social sciences and so not as challenging, novel or 'refusing' of rights as I have suggested. Adopting a methodology, as I have in this book, of exploring the minor tactics of the wider technology of rights, is itself claiming a correct way to look at rights, to better understand what (else) they do and so risks imposing its own kind of machinery in place of that of (positivist) rights. Walters suggest we 'encounter' governmentality (rather than 'map' it), so become 'political amplifiers' by inventing new concepts and making interventions in politics today, and become 'political genealogists' by tracking and resurrecting historically tested but forgotten practices. I cannot disagree, but neither can I claim to be the kind of amplifier or genealogist he calls for. Having written a book based entirely on the methodology of governmentality, I also agree we should not 'forget governmentality'. I suggest something perhaps more mundane: that we concern ourselves less with whether we are doing governmentality but with *how* we are doing it and with the *other side* of governmentality. That we look not for how to replace or re-invent the grand narratives (such as rights) but look at the minor, tedious and sometimes forgotten ways in which they operate. So, we look at actors, statistics, legislation, policies, reports, stories,

---

[9] C Douzinas, *The End of Human Rights*, (Oxford, Hart, 2000) 380.

[10] J Derrida and B Stiegler, *Echographies of Television: Filmed Interviews* (J Bajorek (trans), Oxford, Polity, 2002) 13.

[11] W Walters, *Governmentality: Critical Encounters* (Abingdon, Routledge, 2012) 141.

speeches. And that we consider, importantly, the other side of governmentality as counter-conduct—those sites of struggle, those cracks where it fails
as a governing technology. This is not only mundane, it will also leave us
dissatisfied. But it also promises transformation; at least, that is the hope
that sustains the critique.

II. TRANSFORMATION: TOWARDS AN ETHIC OF DISCOMFORT

I ended the previous chapter by asking what an 'other world' would look
like; whether we need a complete re-imagining of how we are governed that
happens *outside of rights discourse*. Perhaps this is the only way in which
the dangerous nature of rights can be refused and the only way in which to
recognise the ('revolting') subject who struggles against it. But, of course,
I am not going to suggest that. I am not *refusing rights* in themselves but
their regulatory potential and instrumentalisation. This book has been
about saying 'I do not want to be governed *like that*', rather than about
undertaking the impossible task of refusing government by rights altogether.
The transformation then is about two things: first, about making the diagnosis of rights as governmentality endemic and, second, about recognising
counter-narratives to rights.

A. Diagnosis Becomes Endemic

Diagnosis is an important critical position and as such can be an end in
itself.[12] By this I mean that critique is both the diagnosis and the treatment.
The critique is identifying rights as technologies of governmentality. The
treatment is an agitated state of 'permanent critique'. The critique diag-
noses the inherent 'paradox' within rights—and treats it through constant
negotiation.[13] Of course, as Brown points out, paradox is 'very difficult to
negotiate … [it is] a predicament of discourse',[14] hence the permanent state
of dissatisfaction that I predict and encourage. Even critiques of rights that
re-claim rights, perhaps as an 'optics of rightlessness' that will highlight
and challenge a modern governmental rationality that treats the rightlessness as 'disposability',[15] question the paradigm of rights they are working

---

[12] P Miller and N Rose, *Governing the Present* (Cambridge, Polity Press, 2008) 89, 112 on
the value of critical analysis as the ability to 'diagnose'.

[13] On critique and negotiation, see D Bulley, *Ethics as Foreign Policy: Britain, the EU and
the Other* (Abingdon, Routledge, 2009) ch 5.

[14] W Brown, 'Suffering the Paradoxes of Rights' in W Brown and J Halley (eds), *Left
Legalism/Left Critique* (Durham, NC, Duke University Press, 2002) 420, 432.

[15] L Odysseos, 'The Question Concerning Human Rights and Human Rightlessness: Disposability and Struggle in the Bhopal Gas Disaster' (2015) 36(6) *Third World Quarterly* 1041.

within as colonising suffering. But it is in the negotiation (eg of what options rightlessness can (re-)claim) that the possibility of transformation resides. And I do not propose a radical, revolutionary transformation that replaces rights with something else. I have proposed a very specific form of critique of rights: a governmentality framework that looks at rights as governing practices and at how these practices are countered. And this specific critique aims to understand the *how* of rights, not to suggest what might come next. 'Governmentality doesn't tell us what to struggle for or against';[16] nor does/ can it then provide solutions. Rather, it identifies what the struggle is and, importantly, what subjugated struggles, patterns, practices and tactics have been hidden to produce dominant narratives of which rights has been my focus.

Making governmentality endemic means making this focus on *how* just as important as the focus on *what next*. It means a focus on diagnosis. In the first instance, I think legal education has a large responsibility to change the view that 'legal positivism' is 'the "properly" legal perspective'.[17] There is an inherent lack of curiosity that is perpetuated within legal education, which means that both law academics and the students we teach are disengaged from alternative methodologies.[18] It means these students go on to become lawyers, experts and even educators who are unaccustomed to asking the *how* question. We ought to be teaching courses on human rights practice that promote the practice of critique as integral to how to do rights; where we, and our students, ask questions to do with how rights are measured, who practices rights and *how* they have become the dominant emancipatory discourse of the twentieth and early twenty-first centuries. Making governmentality endemic would also necessitate expert-level education. So, the FRA and HRW experts that I looked at in Chapters 2 and 3 should receive training on the attitude to have towards rights; how to *think* rights differently, creatively and perhaps improvisationally in their processes of self-scrutiny.

Moreover, in Foucault's brief engagement with rights in the mid to late-1970s, he identifies a 'new interventionist politics of rights'[19] exercised by a group of private individuals he names as 'Amnesty International, Terre des Hommes, and Médicins du monde'.[20] These private individuals are 'members of the community of the governed' and have created a 'new right'

---

[16] Walters, *Governmentality*, above n 11, 150.

[17] Minkkinen, 'Critical Legal "Method" as Attitude', above n 7, 119. Minkkinen takes this from HLA Hart, *The Concept of Law* (Oxford, Oxford University Press, 2012).

[18] Sokhi-Bulley, 'Alternative Methodologies', above n 7.

[19] J Whyte, 'Is Revolution Desirable? Michel Foucault on Revolution, Neoliberalism and Rights' in B Golder (ed), *Re-Reading Foucault: On Law, Power and Rights* (Abingdon, Routledge, 2012) 207, 210.

[20] M Foucault, 'Confronting Governments: Human Rights' in *Power*, vol 3, *Essential Works of Foucault 1954–1984* (J Faubion (ed), R Hurley (trans), London, Penguin, 2002) 474, 475.

to 'stand up and speak to those in power'.[21] I agree they are 'the governed'; I have shown in Chapters 2 and 3 how government through rights happens to produce the FRA and HRW as 'suitable participants' within the EUropean/global human rights architecture who must modify their behaviour to maintain standing. And of course it is the role of FRA and HRW as rights experts of their specific kinds to be independent from and resist governments; to speak to those in power using the language of rights. Yet I have shown that the FRA and HRW also *govern* rights. The FRA, as a regional rights agency representing the virtuous international human rights actor identity of the EU, exercises regulation and control of rights through the tactic of expertise and through numerical technologies (including indicators). HRW acts as an expert and a narrator to define how to do rights (through its methodology), what rights are (through its reports), and enters into extractive relationships determining how to tell victims' stories. At the same time as being 'members of the community of the governed' and drawing attention to suffering, the argument I have presented in this book is precisely to question what *else* they do: they govern (through) rights. So it is then more interesting, and pertinent, to ask: How can they, and why would they, refuse the way they are governed through rights? These inadvertent *governors* have, I suggest, a *duty* to expose where rights fails; a duty to interrogate how rights shape an understanding of progress, good practice and good governance in ways that might be problematic.

Rights experts like FRA and HRW can both perform more of a spectacle in their countering of the governmentality of rights and also improvise more unexpected forms of behaviour. This could be seen as both their ethical right *and duty* to perform. Those with political authority have a duty towards 'candid, truthful and trustworthy speech'.[22] This is the other, less typical, function of *parrhēsia*, 'that those in power might speak truthfully to citizens about what must be done, how, why, etc'.[23] So the regional agency and the INGO could speak to the governing potential of rights by refusing the 'suitable participant' status demanded by the human rights architecture.[24] An INGO like HRW, or *even* like HRW given its unique watchdog status, must show 'special status', make 'sustained and substantial contributions' and be 'representative';[25] but what if it chose not to be? What if it countered the code of conduct, selection procedures and strategic framework for action that rights imposes and decided instead to set its own agenda and focused exclusively on priority regions and priority rights in a refusal of the government of rights? Their status must be maintained and is monitored through

---

[21] Ibid 474–75.

[22] TB Dyrberg, 'Foucault on *Parrhesia*: The Autonomy of Politics and Democracy' (2015) *Political Theory* 1, 3.

[23] Ibid 4.

[24] ECOSOC Resolution 1996/31 of 25 July 1996. See also Chapter 3.

[25] Ibid Parts I and III.

periodic review (HRW) and evaluation of performance (FRA).[26] The INGO and Agency could refuse being monitored in this way in a resistance to the way in which rights manages how they behave—how they narrate and do rights—and instead improvise its own forms of scrutiny; a public vote of confidence, perhaps, or an annual public broadcast of its activities via (social) media.

Likewise, conditional to engagement with the FRA's architecture, HRW must contribute to 'exchange of information and pooling of knowledge';[27] could it refuse this requirement to cooperate and instead label the information as its own biased narrative on rights and not conflate knowledge into a grand narrative on rights? Rights demand independence—from governments and *also* from the experts who work in rights. What if HRW started accepting funding from governments in a refusal of this narrative and in a decision to further its reach, or to acquire funding to pay their interns? Human rights jobs currently go to those wealthy enough to sustain unpaid internships; is this an injustice that INGOs can seek to correct by refusing the right way to do rights as independent from government funding? Perhaps they can remove funding from some of their areas of work to fund a new generation of expert, even the lay-expert. HRW, and FRA, currently specify the type of expert you have to be to work within the organisations. The 'lay person' is not welcome within this architecture. But what if rights agencies and organisations refused this *right/s* code of conduct and hired lay people in a bid to make themselves truly representative? Or perhaps they might specify that experts should only be lawyers, or only be anthropologists in a reaction against how rights have previously been construed? FRA requires 'independence' as a defining feature of all its experts.[28] What if its experts openly declared biases in all its dissemination of data and information, rather than denying or removing it? This undermining or redefining of 'expertise' as a key feature of the governmentality of rights would be a counter-conduct to the acknowledged framework. All the suggestions here are meant merely as indicative of how organisations which are both governed and govern through rights could become more *riotous*, counter-conducting rights subjects.

The significance of the *duty* to counter-conduct on the part of rights experts is that it satisfies what Kennedy called that search for 'grace in governance',[29] whereby non-state human rights experts enact a responsible

---

[26] Ibid Part VIII and Council Regulation 168/2007/EC of 15 February 2007 establishing a European Union Agency for Fundamental Rights [2007] OJ L53/1, art 30 ('FRA Regulation').

[27] Ibid art 10(2).

[28] Ibid especially recital 20, arts 12(3), 14(3) (which allow for revocation of membership of the FRA's Management Board for lack of independence) and art 16.

[29] D Kennedy, *The Dark Sides of Virtue: Reassessing International Humanitarianism* (Princeton, NJ, Princeton University Press, 2004) xxvi and 343.

human rights that is not blind to its own government (through) rights. This is not a call for one or two whistleblowers in the agency or the INGO; this is a call for a change in *ethos*, so that we make visible the governing potential of rights and instil counter-conduct in rights as an absolute right, an ethics and a *duty* for the human rights actor. And, of course, it is an impossible call—one that maintains the state of dissatisfaction with how rights are taught and how experts continue to be governed through them.

B. Counter-Narratives

Transformation thus necessitates a focus on counter-narratives. That is, we need a critical perspective on rights that encounters not just governmentality (the conduct of conducts) but also its other side: counter-conduct. This poses a challenge to those who *govern through rights*, the human rights experts, to refuse government through rights and to interrogate the governing potential of rights. It also redirects our focus towards examining the mundane, minor and spontaneous processes and practices that those who *are governed through* rights perform in a refusal of rights. So, we acknowledge, as I spoke about in Chapter 5, the unruly 'revolting' subject of the riot as a political, ethical actor struggling against non-existence (and 'rightlessness'). It also means that we will see that those resistances to rights are actually threatening and dangerous *to* rights, like the discourse based on the ethic of responsibility coming out of the Big Society that I focused on in Chapter 4. This removal of rights in favour of responsibility and opportunity creates the rights-bearing citizen as a marginalised, selfish and outdated class that has no place in 'community'. How might the active citizen of responsibilised community act to struggle against an ethics of responsibility (which by its nature stifles struggle/the enactment of an ethical right of refusal)? Is this only possible outside of reclaiming rights discourse? In my state of dissatisfaction, these are further questions which I feel need asking. And so my work, or the work of a governmentality critique, is not 'done'.

What then is the 'other world'? It is not a world in which we have stopped being governed (through) rights. It is, for me, an uncomfortable, agitated and struggling world. As I write this, the front page of the French newspaper *Libération*, in which Foucault published, is inked in black and features three stark red roses to mark the recent 'Paris attacks' in which at least 129 people have been killed following attacks by gunmen and suicide bombers outside the Stade de France stadium and other sites within the tenth and eleventh arondissements.[30] France has declared a state of emergency. As tributes pour

---

[30] See www.liberation.fr.

in on social media, we are faced again with the security/rights dilemma and how to perform struggle in #solidarite.[31] Will we find the answer in rights? In heightened military response? Perhaps we will find it in an 'ethic of discomfort' where the rights holder, the discourses that govern her behaviour (be they responsibility, opportunity or *solidarité*), the actors that narrate her story and that formulate what her rights are, are constantly interrogated, displaced and we are never satisfied.

---

[31] Responses on social media flooded in, amongst the hashtags used on Twitter were #paris, #parisattacks and #solidarite, twitter.com/hashtag/solidarité?lang=en-gb.

Bibliography

Akrap, D, 'Germany's welcome for refugees has to survive the Cologne attacks', *Guardian*, 10 January 2016, available at www.theguardian.com/commentisfree/2016/jan/10/ensure-germany-welcome-refugees-cologne-attacks

Alston, P, 'Does the Past Matter?: On the Origins of Human Rights' (2013) 126(7) *Harvard Law Review* 2043

Amnesty International, *Human Rights for Human Dignity: A Primer on Economic, Social and Cultural Rights*, 2nd edn (28 July 2014), available at www.amnesty.org/en/documents/POL34/001/2014/en/

Badiou, A, *The Rebirth of History: Times of Riots and Uprisings* (London, Verso, 2012)

Barron, A, 'Foucault and Law' in J Penner *et al* (eds), *Jurisprudence and Legal Theory: Commentary and Materials* (Oxford, Oxford University Press, 2005) 955

BBC News, 'Election 2015: Cameron pledges "paid voluntary leave"', 10 April 2015, available at www.bbc.co.uk/news/election-2015-32243680

Bell, DA, 'Introduction: Reflections on Dialogues between Practitioners and Theorists of Human Rights' in DA Bell and J-M Coicaud (eds), *Ethics in Action: The Ethical Challenges of International Human Rights Non-Governmental Organisations* (Cambridge, Cambridge University Press, 2007) 1

Bialasiewicz, L (ed), *Europe and the World: EU Geopolitics and the Transformation of European Space* (Aldershot, Ashgate, 2011)

Bigo, D, 'Security and Immigration: Toward a Critique of the Governmentality of Unease' (2002) 27 *Alternatives* 63

Blair, T, *New Britain: My Vision of a Young Country* (London, New Statesman, 1996)

—— *The Third Way* (London, Fabian Society, 1998)

Bloom, C, *Riot City: Protest and Rebellion in the Capital* (Basingstoke, Palgrave MacMillan, 2012)

Brown, W, *States of Injury: Power and Freedom in Late Modernity* (Princeton, NJ, Princeton University Press, 1995)

—— 'Suffering the Paradoxes of Rights' in W Brown and J Halley (eds), *Left Legalism/Left Critique* (Durham, NC, Duke University Press, 2002) 420

—— *Edgework: Critical Essays on Knowledge and Politics* (Princeton, NJ, Princeton University Press, 2005)

—— *Regulating Aversion: Tolerance in the Age of Identity and Empire* (Princeton, NJ, Princeton University Press, 2006)

Brown, W and Halley, J, 'Introduction' in W Brown and J Halley (eds), *Left Legalism/Left Critique* (Durham, NC, Duke University Press, 2002) 1

Bulley, D, *Ethics as Foreign Policy: Britain, the EU and the Other* (Abingdon, Routledge, 2009)

Bulley, D and Lisle, D, 'Rethinking Hospitality: How London Welcomed the World at the 2012 Olympic and Paralympic Games' in V Girginov (ed), *Handbook of the London 2012 Olympic and Paralympic Games*, vol 2, *Celebrating the Games* (Abingdon, Routledge, 2014)

Bulley, D and Sokhi-Bulley, B, 'Big Society as Big Government: Cameron's Governmentality Agenda' (2014) 16(3) *British Journal of Politics and International Relations* 452

Burke, J and Traynor, I, 'Brussels "very dangerous" as several terrorist suspects remain at large', *Guardian*, 2 November 2015, available at www.theguardian.com/world/2015/nov/22/brussels-lockdown-terror-threat-paris-attacks

Cameron, D, 'The Big Society', Hugo Young Lecture, 10 November 2009, available at www.conservatives.com/News/Speeches/2009/11/David_Cameron_The_Big_Society.aspx

—— 'Let's Mend our Broken Society', speech made on 27 April 2010, available at conservative-speeches.sayit.mysociety.org/speech/601479

—— 'Big Society', speech made in Liverpool, 19 July 2010, available at www.gov.uk/government/speeches/big-society-speech

—— Speech at Conservative Party Conference 2010, 6 October 2010, available at www.theguardian.com/politics/2010/oct/06/david-cameron-speech-tory-conference

—— 'Big Society', speech made on 14 February 2011, available at www.number10.gov.uk/news/speeches-and-transcripts/2011/02/pms-speech-on-big-society-60563

—— 'Big Society', speech made on 23 May 2011, available at www.gov.uk/government/speeches/speech-on-the-big-society

—— 'PM Statement on Restoring Order to Cities', 9 August 2011, available at www.gov.uk/government/news/we-will-do-everything-necessary-to-restore-order-pm

—— 'PM Statement on Violence in England', 10 August 2011, available at www.gov.uk/government/speeches/pm-statement-on-violence-in-england

—— 'The Fightback After the Riots', speech made on 15 August 2011, available at www.gov.uk/government/speeches/pms-speech-on-the-fightback-after-the-riots

—— 'Big Society Awards Address', 6 December 2011, available at www.gov.uk/government/speeches/big-society-awards-address

—— 'PM/s Christmas Message 2013', 24 December 2013, available at www.gov.uk/government/news/pms-christmas-message-2013

—— 'Opportunity', speech made on 22 June 2015, available at www.gov.uk/government/speeches/pm-speech-on-opportunity

Cameron, D and Clegg, N, 'PM and Deputy PM's Speeches at Big Society Launch', 18 May 2010, available at www.gov.uk/government/speeches/pm-and-deputy-pms-speeches-at-big-society-launch

Carens, JH, 'The Problem of Doing Good in a World that Isn't: Reflections on the Ethical Challenges Facing INGOs' in DA Bell and J-M Coicaud (eds), *Ethics in Action: The Ethical Challenges of International Human Rights Non-Governmental Organisations* (Cambridge, Cambridge University Press, 2007) 257

Chandler, D, 'The Road to Military Humanitarianism: How the Human Rights NGOs Shaped a New Humanitarian Agenda' (2001) 23(3) *Human Rights Quarterly* 678

Charlesworth, H, 'International Law: A Discipline of Crisis' (2002) 65(3) *Modern Law Review* 377

Civil Exchange, *Whose Society? The Final Big Society Audit* (January 2015), available at www.civilexchange.org.uk/wp-content/uploads/2015/01/Whose-Society_The-Final-Big-Society-Audit_final.pdf

Coicaud, J-M, 'INGOs as Collective Mobilisation of Transnational Solidarity: Implications for Human Rights Work at the United Nations' in DA Bell and J-M Coicaud (eds), *Ethics in Action: The Ethical Challenges of International Human Rights Non-Governmental Organisations* (Cambridge, Cambridge University Press, 2007) 279

Conservative Party, *The Conservative Party Manifesto 2015: Strong Leadership, A Clear Economic Plan, A Brighter, More Secure Future* (2015)

Conservatives, *Big Society Not Big Government: Building a Big Society* (2010), available at www.conservatives.com/~/media/Files/Downloadable%20Files/Building-a-Big-Society.ashx

Crampton JW and Elden, S, *Space, Knowledge and Power: Foucault and Geography* (Aldershot, Ashgate, 2007)

Crépeau, F, *Report of the Special Rapporteur on the Human Rights of Migrants, Regional Study: Management of the External Borders of the European Union and Its Impact on the Human Rights of Migrants* (24 April 2013), available at www.ohchr.org/Documents/HRBodies/HRCouncil/RegularSession/Session23/A.HRC.23.46_en.pdf

Crépeau, F, *Report of the Special Rapporteur on the Human Rights of Migrants: Labour Exploitation of Migrants* (3 April 2014), available at www.ohchr.org/Documents/Issues/SRMigrants/A.HRC.26.35.pdf

Crépeau, F, 'EU must develop innovative mobility solutions now to stop deaths at sea', *UN OHCHR News*, 20 April 2015, available at www.ohchr.org/EN/NewsEvents/Pages/DisplayNews.aspx?NewsID=15865&LangID=E

Cryer, R, Hervey, T and Sokhi-Bulley, B, *Research Methodologies in EU and International Law* (Oxford, Hart, 2011)

Cubie, D, 'Clarifying the Acquis Humanitaire: A Transnational Legal Perspective on the Internationalization of Humanitarian Law' in

DD Caren, MJ Kelly and A Telesetsky (eds), *The International Law of Disaster Relief* (Cambridge, Cambridge University Press, 2014)

Dahrendorf, R, 'Whatever Happened to Liberty?', *New Statesman*, 6 September 1999

Darling, J, 'Domopolitics, Governmentality and the Regulation of Asylum Accommodation' (2011) 30 *Political Geography* 263

—— 'Asylum and the Post-Political: Domopolitics, Depoliticisation and Acts of Citizenship' (2014) 46(1) *Antipode* 72

de Búrca, G, 'New Modes of Governance and the Protection of Human Rights' in P Alston and O de Schutter (eds), *Monitoring Fundamental Rights in the EU: The Contribution of the Fundamental Rights Agency* (Oxford, Hart, 2005) 36

—— 'The European Court of Justice and the International Legal Order after *Kadi*' (2010) 51(1) *Harvard International Law Journal* 1

Dean, M, *Governmentality: Power and Rule in Modern Society* (London, Sage, 1999)

Department for Communities and Local Government, White Paper, *Communities in Control: Real People, Real Power* (July 2008)

—— *Ending Gang and Youth Violence: A Cross-Government Report including Further Evidence and Good Practice Case Studies*, Cm 8211 (Norwich, Stationery Office, 2011), available at www.gov.uk/government/uploads/system/uploads/attachment_data/file/97861/gang-violence-summary.pdf

—— *Strengthening the Powers of Possession for Anti-Social Behaviour: Summary of Responses to Consultation and Next Steps* (May 2012), available at www.gov.uk/government/uploads/system/uploads/attachment_data/file/8462/2148929.pdf

—— *Neighbourhood Planning* (November 2012), available at www.gov.uk/government/uploads/system/uploads/attachment_data/file/229749/Neighbourhood_planning.pdf

—— *Supporting Communities in Neighbourhood Planning 2013–15* (March 2013), available at www.gov.uk/government/uploads/system/uploads/attachment_data/file/141999/Supporting_Communities_in_Neighbourhood_Planning_2013-15_FINAL.pdf

—— *Understanding Troubled Families* (July 2014), available at www.gov.uk/government/uploads/system/uploads/attachment_data/file/336430/Understanding_Troubled_Families_web_format.pdf

—— 'PM praises Troubled Families Programme Success', Press Release, 22 June 2015, available at www.gov.uk/government/news/pm-praises-troubled-families-programme-success

—— 'Your Guide to Organising a Street Party', www.gov.uk/government/publications/your-guide-to-organising-a-street-party

Derrida, J and Stiegler, B, *Echographies of Television: Filmed Interviews* (J Bajorek (trans), Oxford, Polity, 2002)

Deutsche Welle, 'Amnesty International slams EU Migrant Policy in Fortress Europe Report', 9 July 2014, available at www.dw.com/en/amnesty-international-slams-eu-migrant-policy-in-fortress-europe-report/a-17769353

Douzinas, C, *The End of Human Rights* (Oxford, Hart, 2002)

—— *Human Rights and Empire: The Political Philosophy of Cosmopolitanism* (Abingdon, Routledge-Cavendish, 2007)

—— *Philosophy and Resistance in the Crisis* (London, Polity Press, 2013)

Dudai, R, '"Can You Describe This?" Human Rights Reports and What They Tell Us About the Human Rights Movement' in RA Wilson and RD Brown (eds), *Humanitarianism and Suffering: The Mobilization of Empathy* (Cambridge, Cambridge University Press, 2009) 245

Dyrberg, TB, 'Foucault on *Parrhesia*: The Autonomy of Politics and Democracy' (2015) *Political Theory* 1

Economist, 'Why, and how, Britain might leave the European Union', 29 April 2015, available at www.economist.com/blogs/economist-explains/2015/04/economist-explains-29

El-Enany, N, 'Ferguson and the Politics of Policing Radical Protest' (2015) 16 *Law and Critique* 3

Elden, S, *The Birth of Territory* (Chicago, IL, Chicago University Press, 2013)

Esposito, R, *Communitas: The Origin and Destiny of Community* (Stanford, CA, Stanford University Press, 2010)

European Commission, *European Governance: A White Paper*, COM (2001)428 final (25 July 200)

Evans, S '"Mother's Boy": David Cameron and Margaret Thatcher' (2010) 12(3) *British Journal of Politics and International Relations* 325

Fassin, D, *Humanitarian Reason: A Moral History of the Present* (Berkeley and Los Angeles, CA, University of California Press, 2012)

Foucault, M, 'Prison Talk' in *Power/Knowledge: Selected Interviews and Other Writings 1972–1977* (C Gordon (ed), C Gordon *et al* (trans), London, Longman, 1980) 37

—— 'On the Genealogy of Ethics: An Overview of Work in Progress' in P Rabinow (ed), *The Foucault Reader* (New York, Pantheon Books, 1984) 340

—— 'Practicing Criticism' in LD Kritzman (ed), *Michel Foucault, Politics Philosophy and Culture: Interviews and Other Writings 1977–1984* (A Sheridan (trans), New York and London, Routledge, 1988) 154

—— 'Technologies of the Self' in Luther H Martin, Huck Gutman and Patrick H Hutton (eds), *Technologies of the Self: A Seminar with Michel Foucault* (Amherst, University of Massachusetts Press, 1988) 16

—— 'The Concern for Truth' in LD Kritzman (ed), *Politics, Philosophy, Culture: Interviews and Other Writings 1977–1984* (A Sheridan (trans), London, Routledge, 1988) 255

—— *Discipline and Punish: The Birth of the Prison* (A Sheridan (trans), London, Penguin, 1991)

—— 'On the Genealogy of Ethics' in P Rabinow (ed), *Michel Foucault: Ethics—Essential Works of Foucault 1954–1984* (London, Penguin, 1997) 253

—— 'The Ethics of the Concern of the Self as a Practice of Freedom' in P Rabinow (ed), *Michel Foucault: Ethics—Essential Works of Foucault 1954–1984* (London, Penguin, 1997) 291

—— 'What is Critique?' in M Foucault, *The Politics of Truth* (S Lotringer and L Hochroth (eds), Los Angeles CA, Semiotext(e), 1997) 24

—— *The History of Sexuality*, vol 1, *The Will To Knowledge* (R Hurley (trans), London, Penguin, 1998)

—— 'The Masked Philosopher' in M Foucault, *Ethics*, vol 1, *Subjectivity and Truth: Essential Works of Foucault 1954–1984* (P Rabinow (ed), R Hurley (trans), London, Penguin, 2000) 321

—— 'Confronting Governments: Human Rights' in *Power*, vol 3, *Essential Works of Foucault 1954–1984* (J Faubion (ed), R Hurley (trans), London, Penguin, 2002) 474

—— '"*Omnes et Singulatem*": Toward a Critique of Political Reason' in M Foucault, *Power*, vol 3, *Essential Works of Foucault 1954–1984* (J Faubion (ed), R Hurley (trans), London, Penguin, 2002) 298

—— 'Governmentality' in *Power*, vol 3, *Essential Works of Foucault 1954–1984* (J Faubion (ed), R Hurley (trans), London, Penguin, 2002) 201

—— 'The Subject and Power' in *Power*, vol 3, *Essential Works of Foucault 1954–1984* (J Faubion (ed), R Hurley (trans), London, Penguin, 2002) 326

—— 'For an Ethic of Discomfort' in *Power*, vol 3, *Essential Works of Foucault 1954–1984* (J Faubion (ed), R Hurley (trans), London, Penguin, 2002) 443

—— 'Useless to Revolt' in *Power*, vol 3, *Essential Works of Foucault 1954–1984* (J Faubion (ed), R Hurley (trans), London, Penguin, 2002) 449

—— *The Hermeneutics of the Subject: Lectures at the Collège de France 1981–1982* (F Gros (ed), G Burchell (trans), New York, Picador, 2005)

—— *Security, Territory, Population: Lectures at the Collège de France 1977–1978* (M Senellart (ed), G Burchell (trans), Basingstoke, Palgrave Macmillan, 2007)

—— *The Birth of Biopolitics, Lectures at the Collège de France 1978–1979* (M Senellart (ed), G Burchell (trans), Basingstoke, Palgrave Macmillan, 2008)

—— *The Government of the Self and Others: Lectures at the Collège de France 1982–1983* (F Gros (ed), G Burchell (trans), Basingstoke, Palgrave Macmillan, 2010)

—— *The Courage of Truth: The Government of the Self and Others II* (F Gros (ed), G Burchell (trans), Basingstoke, Palgrave Macmillan, 2011)

Fox, J, *Acts of Service: Spontaneity, Commitment, Tradition in the Nonscripted Theatre* (New York, Tusitala Publishing, 2003)

FRA (European Union Agency for Fundamental Rights), *Homophobia and Discrimination on the Grounds of Sexual Orientation in the EU Member States: Part I: Legal Analysis* (30 June 2008), available at fra.europa.eu/sites/default/files/fra_uploads/192FRA_hdgso_report_Part%201_en.pdf

—— *Fundamental Rights Platform Consultation: Suggestions for the FRA Work Programme 2010, Report on the Fundamental Rights Platform Consultation* (February 2009), available at fra.europa.eu/sites/default/files/fra_uploads/425-CS-FRP-Consultation-report-WP2010.pdf

—— *Homophobia and Discrimination on the Grounds of Sexual Orientation in the EU Member States: Part II: The Social Situation* (31 March 2009), available at fra.europa.eu/sites/default/files/fra_uploads/397-FRA_hdgso_report_part2_en.pdf

—— *Developing Indicators for the Protection, Respect and Promotion of Rights of the Child in the European Union, Summary Report* (2009), available at fra.europa.eu/sites/default/files/fra_uploads/358-RightsofChild_summary-report_en.pdf

—— *Developing Indicators for the Protection, Respect and Promotion of the Rights of the Child in the European Union* (Conference edn, November 2010), available at fra.europa.eu/sites/default/files/fra_uploads/1308-FRA-report-rights-child-conference2010_EN.pdf

—— *Using Indicators to Measure Fundamental Rights in the EU: Challenges and Solutions, FRA Symposium Report*, 2nd Annual FRA Symposium, Vienna, 12–13 May 2011, available at fra.europa.eu/sites/default/files/fra_uploads/1697-FRAsymp2011-outcome-report.pdf

—— *Fundamental Rights of Migrants in an Irregular Situation, Comparative Report* (2011), available at fra.europa.eu/sites/default/files/fra_uploads/1827-FRA_2011_Migrants_in_an_irregular_situation_EN.pdf

—— *FRA Booklet: Who We Are, What We Do, How We Do It* (February 2012), available at fra.europa.eu/sites/default/files/fra-2014-booklet_en_0.pdf

—— 'Code of Conduct for the Participants of the Fundamental Rights Platform', Decision of the Director, 22 June 2012, CAR/002/2012, available at fra.europa.eu/sites/default/files/fra_uploads/2270-FRP-code-of-conduct-2012.pdf

—— 'FRP Selection: Internal Procedures', Decision of the Director, 22 June 2012, CAE/001/2012, available atfra.europa.eu/sites/default/files/fra_uploads/2279-FRP-selection-internal-procedures.pdf

—— *EU Solidarity and FRONTEX: Fundamental Rights Challenges* (14 September 2013), available at fra.europa.eu/sites/default/files/tk3113808enc.pdf

—— *Criminalisation of Migrants in an Irregular Situation and of Persons Engaging with Them* (March 2014), available at fra.europa.eu/en/publication/2014/criminalisation-migrants-irregular-situation-and-persons-engaging-them

—— *The Right to Political Participation for Persons with Disabilities: Human Rights Indicators* (May 2014), available at fra.europa.eu/sites/default/files/fra-2014-right-political-participation-persons-disabilities_en.pdf

—— *Strategic Framework for the FRA: Civil Society Cooperation* (December 2014), available at http://fra.europa.eu/sites/default/files/fra-cso_strategy_framework_2014.pdf

—— *Legal Entry Channels to the EU for Persons in Need of International Protection: A Toolbox* (February 2015), available at fra.europa.eu/sites/default/files/fra-focus_02-2015_legal-entry-to-the-eu.pdf

—— 'FRA Re-iterates Call for Rights-based EU Migration Policy Following Latest Deaths in Mediterranean' (24 April 2015), available at http://fra.europa.eu/en/news/2015/fra-reiterates-call-rights-based-eu-migration-policy-following-latest-deaths-mediterranean

—— 'Weekly Data Collection on the Situation of Persons in Need of International Protection, Update #1' (28 September–2 October 2015), available at fra.europa.eu/sites/default/files/fra_uploads/fra-2015-weekly-compilation-1_en.pdf

—— 'Child Rights' Indicators in the Field of Family Justice', fra.europa.eu/sites/default/files/child-friendly-justice-indicators-v1-0.pdf

—— 'Introducing FRA: The EU Agency for Fundamental Rights', fra.europa.eu/sites/default/files/2014-fra-factsheet_en.pdf

Garland, D, 'Governmentality and the Problem of Crime' (1997) 1 *Theoretical Criminology* 172 Giddens, A, *The Third Way and its Critics* (Cambridge, Polity, 2000)

Goering, C, 'Amnesty International and Economic Social and Cultural Rights' in DA Bell and J-M Coicaud (eds), *Ethics in Action: The Ethical Challenges of International Human Rights Non-Governmental Organisations* (Cambridge, Cambridge University Press, 2007) 204

Golder, B, 'Foucault and the Genealogy of Pastoral Power' (2007) 10(2) *Radical Philosophy Review* 157

—— *Foucault and the Politics of Rights* (Stanford, CA, Stanford University Press, 2015)

Golder, B (ed), *Re-Reading Foucault: On Law, Power and Rights* (B Golder (ed), Abingdon, Routledge, 2013)

Gordon, C, 'Governmental Rationality: An Introduction' in G Burchell *et al*, *The Foucault Effect: Studies in Governmentality* (Chicago, IL, University of Chicago Press, 1991) 1

Gready, P, 'Introduction: "Responsibility to the Story"' (2010) 2(2) *Journal of Human Rights Practice* 177

Gready, P and Vandenhole, W, 'What are We Trying to Change? Theories of Change in Development and Human Rights' in P Gready and W Vandenhole (eds), *Human Rights and Development in the New Millenium: Towards a Theory of Change* (Abingdon, Routledge, 2013) 6

Guardian, 'Amnesty International's Protect the Human campaign', 21 September 2008, available at www.theguardian.com/world/gallery/2008/sep/21/amnesty.international

Guardian, 'Eric Garner put in chokehold by NYPD officer—video', 4 December 2014, available at www.theguardian.com/us-news/video/2014/dec/04/i-cant-breathe-eric-garner-chokehold-death-video

Guardian in partnership with London School of Economics and Political Science, *Reading the Riots: Investigating England's Summer of Disorder* (2011), available at eprints.lse.ac.uk/46297/1/Reading%20the%20riots(published).pdf

Harris, SA, 'Angela Merkel says she'll consider making it easier to deport migrants who commit crimes in the wake of Cologne attacks', *Huffington Post*, 9 January 2016, available at www.huffingtonpost.co.uk/2016/01/09/angela-merkel-deport-migrants-crimes-cologne-attacks_n_8943508.html

Hart, HLA, *The Concept of Law* (Oxford, Oxford University Press, 2012)

Harvie, D and Milburn, K, 'The Moral Economy of the English Crowd in the Twenty- First Century' (2013) 112(3) *South Atlantic Quarterly* 559

Herrmann, J, 'Sofyen Belamoudden murder: the inside story of a crime that horrified Britain', *Independent*, 25 April 2015, available at www.independent.co.uk/news/uk/crime/sofyen-belamouadden-murder-the-victims-mother-and-one-of-the-boys-involved-reveal-a-different-side-10197147.html

Hopgood, S, *Keepers of the Flame: Understanding Amnesty International* (Ithica, NY, Cornell University Press, 2006)

—— *The Endtimes of Human Rights* (Ithica, NY, Cornell University Press 2013)

Human Rights Watch (HRW), *The Mediterranean Migration Crisis: Why People Flee, What the EU Should Do* (25 June 2015), available at www.hrw.org/report/2015/06/19/mediterranean-migration-crisis/why-people-flee-what-eu-should-do

—— *World Report 2015: Events of 2014* (2015), available at www.hrw.org/sites/default/files/wr2015_web.pdf

Hunter, R, McGlynn, C and Rackley, E, *Feminist Judgments: From Theory to Practice* (Oxford, Hart, 2010)

Hutton, P, "Foucault, Freud and the Technologies of the Self' in LH Martin, H Gutman and PH Hutton (eds), *Technologies of the Self: A Seminar with Michel Foucault* (Amherst, MA, University of Massachusetts Press, 1988) 120

Inda, JX, *Targeting Immigrants: Government, Technology, and Ethics* (Oxford, Blackwell, 2006)

Ipsos MORI, Social Research Institute, *National Citizen Service 2013 Evaluation: Main Report* (August 2014), available at www.ncsyes.co.uk/sites/all/themes/ncs/pdf/ncs_2013_evaluation_report_final.pdf

Isin, E, 'Citizenship in Flux: The Figure of the Activist Citizen' (2009) 29 *Subjectivity* 367

Johnson, D, 'This migration crisis could test the European project to destruction', *Daily Telegraph*, 26 August 2015, available at www. telegraph.co.uk/news/worldnews/europe/germany/11826675/This-migration-crisis-could-test-the-European-project-to-destruction.html

Johnstone, K, *Improvisation and the Theatre* (London, Methuen Publishing Ltd, 1989)

Kaulingfreks, F, *Making Trouble: Disruptive Interventions of Urban Youth as Unruly Politics* (Ridderkerk, Rifferprint BV, 2013)

Kendall, G, 'Global Networks, International Networks, Actor Networks' in W Walters and W Larner (eds), *Global Governmentality: Governing International Spaces* (Abingdon, Routledge, 2004)

Kennedy, D, *The Dark Sides of Virtue: Reassessing International Humanitarianism* (Princeton, NJ, Princeton University Press, 2004)

—— 'Challenging the Expert Rule: The Politics of Global Governance' (2005) 27(1) *Sydney Law Review* 5

Kerr, P, Byrne, C and Foster, E, 'Theorising Cameronism' (2011) 9 *Political Studies Review* 193

Kingsley, P, Kitchgaessner, S and Bonomolo, A, 'EU ministers meet for crisis talks after hundreds of migrants drown in the Mediterranean', *Guardian*, 25 April 2015, available at www.theguardian.com/world/2015/apr/19/italian-prime-minister-matteo-renzi-emergency-summit-700-drown-mediterranean?CMP=EMCNEWEML6619I2

Kisby, B, 'The Big Society: Power to the People' (2010) 81(4) *Political Quarterly* 484

Kjærum, M, Director of the European Union Agency for Fundamental Rights, *Preparatory Study for Impact Assessment and Ex-Ante Evaluation of the Fundamental Rights Agency: Public Hearing Report* (European Policy Evaluation Consortium (EPEC), February 2005)

—— Speech at FRA Symposium, Vienna, 12–13 May 2011, available at fra.europa.eu/sites/default/files/fra_uploads/1598-MK-speech-fra-symposium2011.pdf

Klusonova, M, 'Communion in the Czech Judicial Argumentation', paper presented at Critical Legal Conference, Poland, 3–5 September 2015, available at www.muni.cz/people/210387/publications

Lakoff, A, 'Two Regimes of Global Health' (2010) 1(1) *Humanity: An International Journal of Human Rights, Humanitarianism, and Development* 59

Lamble, S, 'The Quiet Dangers of Civilized Rage: Surveying the Punitive Aftermath of England's August 2011 Riots' (2013) 112 *South Atlantic Quarterly* 577

Laqueur, TW, 'Mourning, Pity, and the Work of Narrative in the Making of "Humanity"' in RA Wilson and RD Brown (eds), *Humanitarianism and Suffering: The Mobilization of Empathy* (Cambridge, Cambridge University Press, 2009) 31

Latour, B, *Reassembling the Social: An Introduction to Actor-Network-Theory* (Oxford, Oxford University Press, 2007)

Laughland, O, Swain, J and McGraw, D, 'Cleveland officer who fatally shot Tamir Rice will not face criminal charges', *Guardian*, 28 December 2015, available at www.theguardian.com/us-news/2015/dec/28/tamir-rice-shooting-no-charges-cleveland-officer-timothy-loehmann

Leese, R, 'The Only Place to Be', *Leader's Blog* (Manchester City Council, August 2011), www.manchester.gov.uk/blog/leadersblog/post/477

Lewis, P, 'Tottenham riots: a peaceful protest, then suddenly all hell broke loose', *Guardian*, 7 August 2011, available at www.theguardian.com/uk/2011/aug/07/tottenham-riots-peaceful-protest locality.org.uk/projects/community-organisers/

—— 'Eric Garner: protests erupt in New York after officer is spared prosecution', *Guardian*, 4 December 2014, available at www.theguardian.com/us-news/2014/dec/03/justice-department-eric-holder-eric-garner-investigation

—— 'Obama under pressure over response to police killings after Eric Garner decision', *Guardian*, 4 December 2014, available at www.theguardian.com/us-news/2014/dec/04/obama-police-killings-eric-garner-decision

Lewis, P and Topham, L, 'Policing England's riots: "the Met had lost the streets"—video', *Guardian*, 2 July 2012, available at www.theguardian.com/uk/video/2012/jul/02/policing-england-riots-met-video

Lowrey, W, 'The QuickTrip gas station, Ferguson protestors' staging ground, is now silent', *Washington Post*, 19 August 2014, available at www.washingtonpost.com/politics/ferguson-protesters-staging-ground-the-quiktrip-gas-station-is-now-silent/2014/08/19/a8e4382e-27db-11e4-958c-268a320a60ce_story.html

Lowery, W, Leonnig, C and Berman, M, 'Even before Michael Brown's slaying in Ferguson, racial questions hung over police', *Washington Post*, 13 August 2014, available at www.washingtonpost.com/politics/even-before-teen-michael-browns-slaying-in-mo-racial-questions-have-hung-over-police/2014/08/13/78b3c5c6-2307-11e4-86ca-6f03cbd15c1a_story.html

MacDonald, A, 'Nocturnal Games in the Streets' (2012) 23(3) *Law and Critique* 185

Mander, H, '"Words from the Heart": Researching People's Stories' (2010) 2(2) *Journal of Human Rights Practice* 252

McFadden, S, 'Ferguson goddamn: no indictment for Darren Wilson is no surprise. This is why we protest', *Guardian*, 25 November 2014, available at www.theguardian.com/commentisfree/2014/nov/24/ferguson-no-indictment-darren-wilson-protest

McNay, L, 'Self as Enterprise: Dilemmas of Control and Resistance in Foucault's *The Birth of Biopolitics*' (2009) 26 *Theory Culture and Society* 55

Mepham, D, *Dispatches: Where is Britain's Compassion for Migrants in Crisis?* (12 May 2015), available at www.hrw.org/news/2015/05/12/dispatches-where-britains-compassion-migrants-crisis

Merrick, J, 'Teenage volunteers show true grit at the National Citizen Service', *Independent*, 1 September 2013, available at www.independent.co.uk/news/uk/politics/teenage-volunteers-show-true-grit-at-the-national-citizen-service-8793020.html

Merry, SE, 'Measuring the World: Indicators, Human Rights and Global Governance' (2011) 52(3) *Current Anthropology* 83

Miller, P and Rose, N, *Governing the Present* (Cambridge, Polity Press, 2008)

Minkkinen, P, 'Critical Legal "Method" as Attitude' in D Watkins and M Burton (eds), *Research Methods in Law* (Abingdon, Routledge, 2013) 119

Moyn, S, 'On the Genealogy of Morals', *Nation*, 16 April 2007, 25

—— *The Last Utopia: Human Rights in History* (Cambridge, MA, Belknap Press of Harvard University Press, 2010)

Murphy, T, 'Public Health *sans frontières*: Human Rights NGOs and "Stewardship on a Global Scale"' (2011) 62(5) *Northern Ireland Legal Quarterly* 659

Mutua, M, *Human Rights: A Political and Cultural Critique* (Philadelphia, PA, University of Pennsylvania Press, 2002)

NatCen Social Research, *Evaluation of the National Citizen Service: Findings from the Evaluations of the 2012 Summer and Autumn NCS Programmes* (July 2013), available at natcen.ac.uk/media/205475/ncs_evaluation_report_2012_combined.pdf

Neumann, IB and Sending, OJ, *Governing the Global Polity: Practice, Mentality, Rationality* (Ann Arbor, MI, University of Michigan Press, 2010)

Newburn, T, 'The Ferguson riots may seem similar to those in UK in 2011, but there are stark contrasts', *Guardian*, 20 August 2014, available at www.theguardian.com/commentisfree/2014/aug/20/ferguson-missouri-not-so-far-from-tottenham-toxteth

Nunes, R, 'Building on Destruction' (2013) 112(3) *South Atlantic Quarterly* 568

Nyers, P, 'Abject Cosmopolitanism: The Politics of Protection in the Anti-Deportation Movement' (2003) 24 *Third World Quarterly* 1069

Odysseos, L, 'The Question Concerning Human Rights and Human Rightlessness: Disposability and Struggle in the Bhopal Gas Disaster' (2015) 36(6) *Third World Quarterly* 1041

Orford, A, *Muscular Humanitarianism: Reading the Narratives of the New Interventionism* (London, Palgrave Macmillan, 2007)

Parker, G and Rigby, E, 'Cameron harks back to Big Society with voluntary work proposal', *Financial Times*, 9 April 2015, available at www.ft.com/cms/s/0/32a12c84-decf-11e4-852b-00144feab7de.html#axzz3jMMISkvW

Payne-Frank, N and Brown, S, 'Tottenham riots: residents unite to rebuild community—video', *Reading the Riots: Community Conversations*, 3 July 2012, available at www.theguardian.com/news/video/2012/jul/03/tottenham-riots-video

Pegram, T, 'Governing Relationships: The New Architecture in Global Human Rights Governance' (2015) 43(2) *Millenium: Journal of International Studies* 618

Pittaway, E, Bartolomei, L and Hugman, R, '"Stop Stealing our Stories: The Ethics of Research with Vulnerable Groups' (2010) 2(2) *Journal of Human Rights Practice* 229

Plewes, B and Stuart, R, 'The Pornography of Poverty: A Cautionary Fundraising Tale' in DA Bell and J-M Coicaud (eds), *Ethics in Action: The Ethical Challenges of International Human Rights Non-Governmental Organisations* (Cambridge, Cambridge University Press, 2007) 23

Pogge, T, 'Respect and Disagreement: A Response to Joseph Carens' in DA Bell and J-M Coicaud (eds), *Ethics in Action: The Ethical Challenges of International Human Rights Non-Governmental Organisations* (Cambridge, Cambridge University Press, 2007) 273

Ramshaw, S, *Justice as Improvisation: The Law of the Extempore* (Abingdon, Routledge, 2014)

Redfield, P, *Life in Crisis: The Ethical Journey of Doctors Without Borders* (Oakland, CA, University of California Press, 2013)

—— 'Conclusion: A Measured Good' in S Ambramowitz and C Panter-Brick (eds), *Medical Humanitarianism: Ehtnographies of Practice* (Philadelphia, PA, University of Philadelphia Press, 2015) 242

Rhodes, R, 'The New Governance: Governing Without Government' (1996) 44 *Political Studies* 652

Roberts, D, 'Ferguson crisis: Obama sends Attorney General as Governor lifts curfew', *Guardian* 19 August 2014, available at www.theguardian.com/world/2014/aug/18/obama-attorney-general-eric-holder-ferguson?CMP=EMCNEWEML6619I2

Rogers, S, 'England riots: was poverty a factor?', *Guardian*, 6 December 2011, available at www.theguardian.com/news/datablog/2011/aug/16/riots-poverty-map-suspects

Rose, N, 'Community, Citizenship, and the Third Way' (2000) 43(9) *American Behavioural Scientist* 1395

—— 'Government and Control' (2000) 40 *British Journal of Criminology* 321

—— 'The Politics of Life Itself' (2001) 18 *Theory, Culture and Society* 1

Rosenau, JN, 'Change, Complexity, and Governance in Globalizing Space' in J Pierre (ed), *Debating Governance: Authority, Steering and Democracy* (Oxford, Oxford University Press, 2000) 167

Rosga, A and Satterthwaite, ML, 'The Trust in Indicators: Measuring Human Rights' (2009) 27(2) *Berkeley Journal of International Law* 253

Roth, K, 'Defending Economic, Social and Cultural Rights: Practical Issues faced by an International Human Rights Organisation' in DA Bell and J-M Coicaud (eds), *Ethics in Action: The Ethical Challenges of International Human Rights Non-Governmental Organisations* (Cambridge, Cambridge University Press, 2007) 169

Sandvik, KB, 'Review Essay, Unpacking World Refugee Day: Humanitarian Governance and Human Rights Practice' (2010) 2(2) *Journal of Human Rights Practice* 287

—— 'Introduction to the Multiple Tracks of Human Rights and Humanitarianism' in B Derman, A Hellum and KB Sandvik, *Worlds of Human Rights: The Ambiguities of Rights-Claiming in Africa* (Leiden, Koninklijke Brill NV, 2013) 245

—— 'Rights-based Humanitarianism as Emancipation or Stratification? Rumours and Procedures of Verification in Urban Refugee Management in Kampala, Uganda' in B Derman, A Hellum and KB Sandvik, *Worlds of Human Rights: The Ambiguities of Rights-Claiming in Africa* (Leiden, Koninklijke Brill NV, 2013) 257

Satterthwaite, ML, 'Indicators in Crisis: Rights-based Humanitarian Indicators in Post-Earthquake Haiti' (2011) 43 *International Law and Politics* 865

Seymour, R, 'The real reason water cannon are coming to Boris Johnson's London', *Guardian*, 11 June 2014, available at www.theguardian.com/commentisfree/2014/jun/11/boris-johnson-water-cannon-blast-theresa-may

Slocock, C, 'What happened to David Cameron's "Big Society"', *Huffington Post*, 20 January 2015, available at www.huffingtonpost.co.uk/caroline-slocock/big-society_b_6505902.html

Smith, MJ, 'From Big Government to Big Society: Changing the State-Society Balance' (2010) 63(4) *Parliamentary Affairs* 818

Sokhi-Bulley, B, 'Governing (Through) Rights: Statistics as Technologies of Governmentality' (2011) 20(2) *Social and Legal Studies* 139

—— 'Government(ality) by Experts: Human Rights as Governance' (2011) 22(3) *Law and Critique* 251

—— 'The Fundamental Rights Agency of the EU: A New Panopticism' (2011) 11(4) *Human Rights Law Review* 683

—— 'Alternative Methodologies' (2013) 2 *Law and Method (Rechte en Methode)* 6

—— 'The EU as a "Virtuous International Actor": Human Rights Indicators and Global Governmentality' in D Schiek (ed), *The EU Economic and Social Model after the Global Crisis: Interdisciplinary Perspectives* (Aldershot, Ashgate, 2013) 187

—— 'Performing Struggle: *Parrhēsia* in Ferguson' (2015) 26(1) *Law and Critique* 7

—— 'Re-Reading the Riots: Counter-Conduct in London 2011' (2016) *Global Society* (forthcoming) DOI: 10.1080/13600826.2016.1143348. Available online: http: //dx.doi.org/10.1080/13600826.2016.1143348

—— 'Learning Law Differently: The Importance of Theory and Methodology' in B van Klink and B de Vries (eds), *Academic Learning in Law: Theoretical Positions, Teaching Experiments and Learning Experiences* (Cheltenham, Edward Elgar Publishing, forthcoming 2016)

Stafford, Z, 'I'm black, my brother's white … and he's a cop who shot a black man on duty', *Guardian*, 25 August 2014, available at www.theguardian.com/commentisfree/2014/aug/25/white-brother-police-shot-black-man

Stephens, R, 'In Defense of the Ferguson Riots', *Jacobin*, 14 August 2014, available at www.jacobinmag.com/2014/08/in-defense-of-the-ferguson-riots/

Stone, J, 'Human Rights Act: What is it and why does Michael Gove want to scrap the policy?', *Independent*, 11 May 2015, available at www.independent.co.uk/news/uk/politics/what-is-the-human-rights-act-and-why-does-michael-gove-want-to-scrap-it-10240527.html

Straw, J, 'Human Rights and Personal Responsibility: New Citizenship for a New Millenium', speech made at St Paul's Cathedral, London, 2 October 2000, available at www.britishpensions.org.au/straw_speech.htm

Trilling, D, 'Europe could solve the migrant crisis—if it wanted', *Guardian*, 31 July 2015, available at www.theguardian.com/commentisfree/2015/jul/31/europe-migrant-crisis-political-choice-toxic-waste-sanctuary

Trott, B, 'Rebellious Subjects: The Politics of England's 2011 Riots' (2013) 112(1) *South Atlantic Quarterly* 538

—— 'Reading the 2011 Riots: England's Urban Uprising, An Interview with Paul Lewis' (2013) 11(3) *South Atlantic Quarterly* 541

Tyler, I, *Revolting Subjects* (London, Zed Books, 2013)

United Nations Development Programme (UNDP), *Governance Indicators: A User's Guide* (New York, UNDP Oslo Governance Centre, 2004)

United Nations High Commissioner for Refugees (UNHCR), 'Saving migrant lives is imperative but what next? UN human rights experts ask EU leaders', Press Release, 24 April 2015, available at www.ohchr.org/EN/NewsEvents/Pages/DisplayNews.aspx?NewsID=15889&LangID=E

United Nations Office of the High Commissioner for Human Rights (UNHCR), *Transforming our World: Human Rights in the 2030 Agenda for Sustainable Development* (2015), available at www.ohchr.org/Documents/Issues/MDGs/Post2015/HRAndPost2015.pdf

Vaughan, B, 'The Government of Youth: Disorder and Dependence?' (2000) 9(3) *Social and Legal Studies* 347

Vaughan-Williams, N, 'We are Not Animals!' Humanitarian Border Security and Zoopolitical Spaces in EUrope' (2015) 45 *Political Geography* 1

Vulliamy, E, 'Paris attacks: security and surveillance cast a dark shadow over France's love of "liberté" and "fraternité"', *Guardian*, 22 November 2015, available at www.theguardian.com/world/2015/nov/22/paris-attacks-security-liberte-fraternite

Walters, W, 'Secure Borders, Safe Haven, Domopolitics' (2004) 8(3) *Citizenship Studies* 237

—— *Governmentality: Critical Encounters* (Abingdon, Routledge, 2012)

Walters, W and Larner, W (eds), *Global Governmentality: Governing International Spaces* (Abingdon, Routledge, 2006)

Whyte, J, 'Is Revolution Desirable? Michel Foucault on Revolution, Neoliberalism and Rights' in B Golder (ed), *Re-Reading Foucault: On Law, Power and Rights* (Abingdon, Routledge, 2012) 207

Williams, P, *The Alchemy of Race and Rights* (Cambridge, MA, Harvard University Press, 1991)

Wilson, RA and Brown, RD, 'Introduction' in RA Wilson and RD Brown (eds), *Humanitarianism and Suffering: The Mobilization of Empathy* (Cambridge, Cambridge University Press, 2009) 1

Young, G, 'In Ferguson the violence of the state created the violence of the street', *Guardian, Comment is Free*, 18 August 2014, available at www.theguardian.com/commentisfree/2014/aug/18/ferguson-violence-martin-luther-king-michael-brown?CMP=EMCNEWEML6619I2

Zivi, K, *Making Rights Claims* (Oxford University Press, Oxford and New York, 2012)

Zizek, S, 'Shoplifters of the World Unite', *London Review of Books*, 19 August 2011, available at www.lrb.co.uk/2011/08/19/slavoj-zizek/shoplifters-of-the-world-unite

CASES AND LEGISLATIVE INSTRUMENTS

C-357/09 [2009] ECR I-11189, *Kadzoev*, 30 November 2009

R v *Blackshaw* [2011] EWCA Crim 2312

Communication from the Commission, *Towards a Strategy on the Rights of the Child*, COM(2006) 367 final (4 July 2006)

Communication from the Commission, *A European Agenda on Migration*, COM(2015) 240 final (13 May 2015)

Communication from the Commission, Managing the Refugee Crisis: State of Play of the Implementation of the Priority Actions under the European Agenda on Migration, COM(2015) 510 final (14 October 2015)

Council Directive 2002/90/EC of 28 November 2002 defining the facilitation of unauthorised entry, transit and residence ('Facilitation Directive') [2002] OJ L328/17

Council Directive 2008/115/EC of 16 December 2008 on common standards and procedures in Member States for returning illegally staying third-country nationals ('Return Directive') [2008] OJ 2008 L348

Council Regulation (EC) 2201/2003 of 27 November 2003 on jurisdiction and the recognition and enforcement of judgments in matrimonial matters and in matters of parental responsibility [2003] OJ L338

Council Regulation (EC) 2007/2004 of 26 October 2004 establishing a European Agency for the Management of Operational Cooperation at the External Borders of the Member States of the European Union [2004] OJ L349/1

Council Regulation 168/2007/EC of 15 February 2007 establishing a European Union Agency for Fundamental Rights [2007] OJ L53/1 ('FRA Regulation')

Council Regulation (EC) 4/2009 of 18 December 2009 on jurisdiction, applicable law and enforcement of decisions and cooperation in matters relating to maintenance obligations [2009] OJ L7

Council Regulation (EU) 1168/2011 of 25 October 2011 amending Council Regulation (EC) 2007/2004 establishing a European Agency for the Management of Operational Cooperation at the External Borders of the Member States of the European Union [2011] OJ L304/1 ('Frontex Regulation')

Council Regulation (EU) 1052/2013 of 22 October 2013 establishing the European Border Surveillance System (Eurosur) [2013] OJ L295/11

ECOSOC Resolution 288 X (B), 1950

ECOSOC Resolution 1996/31, 25 July 1996

European Parliament Resolution, 'Migratory flows in the Mediterranean, with particular attention to the tragic events off Lampedusa', 2013/2827 (23 October 2013)

European Parliament Resolution, 'The situation in the Mediterranean and the need for a holistic EU approach to migration', 2014/2907 (11 December 2014)

Index

www.ingramcontent.com/pod-product-compliance
Lightning Source LLC
Chambersburg PA
CBHW050515280326
41932CB00014B/2335